Intellectual Disability and the Right to a Sexual Life

One of the perennial political/philosophical questions concerns whether it is ever justifiable for a third party to paternalistically restrict an adult's freedom to ensure their own, or society's, best interests are protected. Wherever one stands on this debate, it remains the case that, unlike their non-impaired contemporaries, many intellectually disabled adults are subjected to a paternalistic regime of care. This is particularly true regarding members of this population exercising more control of their sexuality.

Utilizing rare empirical data, Foucault's theory of power and Kristeva's concept of abjection, this work shows that many non-disabled people— including family members—hold ambivalent attitudes towards people with visible disabilities expressing their sexuality. Through a careful examination of the autonomy/paternalism debate, this is the first book to provide an original, provocative, and philosophically compelling analysis to argue that where necessary, facilitated sex with prostitutes should be included as part of a new regime of care to ensure that sexual needs are met.

Intellectual Disability and the Right to a Sexual Life is essential reading for scholars, students and policy-makers with an interest in philosophy, sociology, political theory, social work, disability studies, and sex studies. It will also be of interest to anybody who is a parent or a sibling of an adult with an intellectual disability and those with an interest in human rights and disability more generally.

Simon Foley of QUB Belfast has taught Sociology in various universities throughout the United Kingdom and the Republic of Ireland for the past 10 years. He has published widely on issues of sexuality, social theory, and social change, and is an acknowledged international expert on the sociology of disability.

Routledge Advances in Disability Studies

www.routledge.com/Routledge-Advances-in-Disability-Studies/book-series/
RADS

Changing Social Attitudes Toward Disability
Perspectives from Historical, Cultural, and Educational Studies
Edited by David Bolt

Disability, Avoidance and the Academy
Challenging Resistance
Edited by David Bolt and Claire Penketh

Autism in a De-centered World
Alice Wexler

Disabled Childhoods
Monitoring Differences and Emerging Identities
Janice McLaughlin, Edmund Coleman-Fountain and Emma Clavering

Intellectual Disability and Being Human
A Care Ethics Model
Chrissie Rogers

The Changing Disability Policy System
Active Citizenship and Disability in Europe Volume 1
*Edited by Rune Halvorsen, Bjørn Hvinden, Jerome Bickenbach, Delia Ferri
and Ana Marta Guillén Rodriguez*

Intellectual Disability and the Right to a Sexual Life
A Continuation of the Autonomy/Paternalism Debate
Simon Foley

The Changing Disability Policy System
Active Citizenship and Disability in Europe Volume 2
*Edited by Rune Halvorsen, Bjørn Hvinden, Jerome Bickenbach, Delia Ferri
and Ana Marta Guillén Rodriguez*

Intellectual Disability and the Right to a Sexual Life

A Continuation of the Autonomy/Paternalism Debate

Simon Foley

Routledge
Taylor & Francis Group

LONDON AND NEW YORK

First published 2018
by Routledge
2 Park Square, Milton Park, Abingdon, Oxon OX14 4RN

and by Routledge
711 Third Avenue, New York, NY 10017

Routledge is an imprint of the Taylor & Francis Group, an informa business

British Library Cataloguing-in-Publication Data
A catalogue record for this book is available from the British Library

Library of Congress Cataloging-in-Publication Data
Names: Foley, Simon, author.
Title: Intellectual disability and the right to a sexual life: a continuation of the autonomy/paternalism debate / Simon Foley.
Description: Abingdon, Oxon; New York, NY: Routledge, 2017. | Series: Routledge advances in disability studies | Includes bibliographical references and index.
Identifiers: LCCN 2017013294
Subjects: LCSH: People with mental disabilities. | People with mental disabilities—Sexual behavior. | Sexual ethics. | Sociology of disability.
Classification: LCC HV3004 .F75 2017 | DDC 306.7087/4—dc23
LC record available at https://lccn.loc.gov/2017013294

ISBN: 978-1-138-62824-3 (hbk)
ISBN: 978-1-315-21073-5 (ebk)

Typeset in Times New Roman
by codeMantra

Contents

Acknowledgements

As with most nominally individual achievements, the writing of this book did not take place within a social vacuum. To this end, I would like to thank the following people for their contribution to its completion. First among equals in this regard is the vital emotional and intellectual succour provided by Dr Jen Goddard of QUB. I am also deeply grateful to the respondents who gave so generously of their time and insights and without which this book would have obviously not taken the form it does. Last but not least, I want to acknowledge the supportive role played by my family—both that which I was born into and that which I have since had a hand in creating. Regarding the former, the fact that I have a sister with Down syndrome and the fact that my mother has spent most of her adult life fighting to improve the quality of life led by people with Down syndrome remain constitutive factors in shaping my professional academic trajectory. Regarding the latter, I want to especially thank my very young, and very demanding, children for unwittingly providing me with the stimulus to meet the very rigid writing deadlines they, again unwittingly, effectively put in place.

Introduction

Why another academic book on the issue of intellectual disability and sexuality? Hopefully, the prospective reader will not be asking themselves this question. However, if they are, my response takes multiple forms. Firstly, I do not think one can have enough books on this vital, and still, from certain perspectives, underexplored subject matter. This is especially the case in observing the nature of the current sexual status quo for intellectually disabled adults. In contemporary western society, to be intellectually disabled is to be infantilised and to be infantilised is to be desexualised. Amongst all the populations subsumed under the intellectual disability umbrella term, one of the most common to be ascribed the 'Peter Pan' (or perennial child) subject position by third parties is adults with Down syndrome. The prevalence of this 'Peter Pan' meme has bestowed adults with Down syndrome with an essentialist identity that positions them as disembodied, desexualised legal subjects. Consequently, the need to challenge this state of affairs is, from a certain ideological perspective at least, a self-evident affair.

Secondly, there are in fact very few sociological/philosophical books that specifically focus on the autonomy/paternalism debate as it relates to the sexuality of intellectually disabled adults. Thirdly, there are in fact very few such books that care to collect the views of both the intellectually disabled adults and their parents regarding this matter. Fourthly, as far as can be established, there are no such books that argue for a normalisation of the facilitated sex mechanism to ameliorate some of the autonomy/paternalism dilemmas identified by the respondents I interviewed. Fifthly, there are in fact very few such books that are not explicitly written from a social model perspective. As will be explained in detail in the following chapters, the cash value of such scholarly work usually entails blaming, at some level, the third party—such as all the mothers I spoke to—who privileges paternalism over increased freedom for the individual with an intellectual disability. As an extension of the last point, there are in fact very few such books written by a professional sociologist who has a sibling with an intellectual disability. Such intimate, all-consuming, experiential knowledge of the dilemmas thrown up by the autonomy/paternalism debate provide, I would suggest, more realistic insights than some of those proffered by the 'usual subjects'.

The latter phrase is not meant pejoratively. Rather, it is being used descriptively to report the fact that of the very few such books in question, many of them are authored by an academic with both a social work background and a social model mantra to preach. Because of such ideological affinities and their irreducibly professional relationship with intellectually disabled people, a convincing argument can be made that such 'experts' are less than ideally equipped to grasp, either phenomenologically or conceptually, the complicated emotional entanglements that typically characterise the family dynamics this book is addressing.

What is an intellectual disability?

Since the inception of disability studies as a scholarly subject in its own right, the issue of definitions has become a matter of contention when dealing with issues of disability. For example, there is a predilection in much of this literature to use the term 'disabled people' when the author/s are really talking about physically disabled people. Similarly, in relation to issues of cognitive impairment, there is a tendency to conflate or use as synonyms the 'intellectual disability' and 'learning disability' umbrella terms (Foley, 2016). However, this is not the approach this book is adopting. Rather, to avoid any confusion in the reader's mind, and to highlight the issues of relevance in what is essentially a variation on the age-old autonomy/paternalism debate, it is solely concerned with the issue of intellectual disability.

How do these terms differ? The answer is that unlike an intellectual disability, a learning difficulty or learning disability, such as dyslexia or Attention Deficit Hyperactivity Disorder (ADHD), does not affect general intelligence (IQ), whereas an intellectual disability does. In other words, and as will be explained in detail throughout this book, it is the issue of general intelligence and not specific difficulties in reading, writing, etc., that raise autonomy/paternalism issues for disabled adults in the sexual realm.

To unpack the intellectual disability classification, and to aid the reader in evaluating the arguments made, both by myself and the respondents, this book will employ the following two definitions:

1 The American Association of Intellectual and Developmental Disabilities states an intellectual disability is a cognitive impairment (that originates before the age of 18) characterised by significant limitations in both intellectual functioning and in adaptive behaviour that covers many everyday social and practical skills. The term *intellectual functioning*—also called intelligence—refers to general mental capacity and involves the ability to reason, plan, solve problems, think abstractly, comprehend complex ideas, learn quickly, and learn from experience. The term *adaptive behaviour* refers to the collection of age-appropriate conceptual, social, and practical skills that are learned and performed by people in their everyday lives.

2   The World Health Organisation (WHO) states that the *intellectual disability* term refers to a significantly reduced ability—biological in origin—to understand new or complex information and to learn and apply new skills (impaired intelligence). This results in a reduced ability to cope independently (impaired social functioning), and begins before adulthood, with a lasting effect on development. As with the American Association of Intellectual and Developmental Disabilities, the WHO definition is a holistic one in that it also emphasises the role played by environmental factors in closing the potentiality/actuality gap regarding the full participation and inclusion in society of intellectually disabled people.

Apropos of my critiques of an exclusive social model approach this definitional clarification is also designed to alert the reader as to my own ideological affiliations regarding the very specific autonomy/paternalism issues under investigation. That is, I, in common with the noted disability studies scholar Tom Shakespeare (2004), and all the mothers I interviewed, adhere to a so-called realist understanding of intellectual impairments such as Down syndrome. This means we agree with the overwhelming medical consensus on the issue. This states that while people with intellectual impairments such as Down syndrome are "undoubtedly further disabled by society", they are also affected by "organic pathologies in brain anatomy or physiology which cannot be wished away by a social modellist redefinition" (Shakespeare, 2004:14). Thus, we subscribe to the belief propagated by, but not the copyright of, the so-called medical model of disability that Down syndrome is a congenital intellectual impairment caused by anomalous biological development. We also subscribe to the belief that this biological condition is intrinsically disabling in that it prevents people with Down syndrome from functioning in ways that are considered normal or desirable when applied to their non-intellectually disabled contemporaries. This, moreover, is a state of affairs that would exist regardless of how a given society is organized (Cunningham, 2006). This conclusion still stands even when it is taken into consideration that the impairment of Down syndrome, like most intellectual impairments, refers to a cognitive continuum. Hence, people with Down syndrome vary hugely in their intellectual abilities and other characteristics.

Of course, this does not mean, and in no way, is this book arguing, that biology should determine the social destiny of members of this population. However, a key premise underpinning the substantive claims made and conclusions drawn, is an acknowledgement that biology does mean that intellectually disabled people will never transcend a cognitive threshold (Newton, 2004; Pueschel, 2006). Consequently, it is the fact that intellectual disabilities such as Down syndrome are real biological pre-discursive impairments with very real consequences in the real world that informs the subject matter of this book. The only remaining question is what is to be done? In answering this, it is necessary to take a position on the autonomy/ paternalism debate to argue why in a certain situation more freedom for the individual with an intellectual disability to act on their choices is required or why third-party intervention—however this term is defined—is deemed necessary.

The focus on Down syndrome

My concentration on a specific sub group of the disparate populations subsumed under the intellectual disability catch-all umbrella term departs from conventional 'disability studies' practice that typically utilises such confusing terminology in an unpacked fashion. However, when trying to seriously deal with autonomy/paternalism issues, it is a necessary analytical move to make as different cognitive impairments locate those differently impaired in different positions in relation to the structure/agency debate and the concomitant distribution of social goods. Therefore, it is imperative when trying to coherently problematize current societal practices, to delineate in a precise fashion what intellectual impairments are being referred to and why X contingent social practice should, at the very least be questioned, if not overhauled outright to be replaced with contingent social practice Y.

In addition, this book's specific focus on adults with Down syndrome also ties in with two different but equally valuable conceptual perspectives that argue that forms of embodiment matter when informing the degrees of paternalism that third parties feel they are entitled to deploy when it comes to intervening in the lives of intellectually disabled adults. This is the proposition that because of their distinct facial appearance, adults with Down syndrome—unlike adults with other intellectual impairments—possess what Goffman (1990) calls a 'spoiled identity'. This means that at no point in time can they pass for being 'normal'; a state of affairs that may have implications for how third parties perceive and treat them. A similar point is made by Shildrick (2003, 2007, 2009), who argues that when intellectually disabled people are embodied non-normatively, the effect on third parties at the psychic level is greater and longer lasting than if one was talking about intellectually disabled adults who are not similarly 'marked'.

From both perspectives, the conjecture advanced is the fact that the inability of the third party, in the case of this book the mothers of the people with Down syndrome, to forget that their adult son or daughter has a cognitive impairment is a key factor informing how they consequently behave towards them. Equally important in terms of exploring the nature of the autonomy/paternalism debate is the fact that there seems to be a growing consensus in the relevant literature that adults with Down syndrome, due to a predisposition to 'please people', are liable to be more malleable than other intellectually disabled populations when it comes to changing their minds or having their minds changed for them in the face of third-party pressure (Newton, 2004; Selikowitz, 2008; Saaltink et al., 2012). However, this qualification regarding the specific focus on Down syndrome demands another. Namely, the issues addressed in this book, and indeed the arguments it presents, particularly in relation for a normalisation of facilitated sex, are also applicable to any form of intellectual disability that raise autonomy/paternalism issues for the respective individuals and their parents.

Finally, and as already alluded to there is the personal reason. I have a sister with Down syndrome and my mother has for most of her adult life been involved in the politics of disability. Because of this, I have long had an interest in the status and treatment of people with Down syndrome. The decision to focus on the area of the sexual autonomy of adults with Down syndrome was also precipitated by a personal event: namely, the fact that my adult sister has recently become 'engaged' to her 'boyfriend' (her first) of three years. This scenario in turn forced me to re-examine my attitude to this issue. The scare quotes are included to denote the ambivalence with which this announcement was received by me and the rest of my family, all of whom have either actively been involved in advocating for the rights of people with Down syndrome, or have tacitly supported the struggle for the same.

After a process of reflection, in combination with conversations with family members, the conclusion arrived at was that our bemused reaction was due to the fact we all held a very ambivalent attitude towards my adult sister with Down syndrome. Yes, she was an adult in her late thirties with the right to do what other adults of a similar age do, but her cognitive limitations meant that she was also a child, didn't it? And children do not have the right to act as adults do. Rather, their position is one in which they need to be protected from the adult world. But if my sister is also an adult, then surely to paternalistically deprive her of the experiences that constitute being an adult, would be to condemn her, and people with intellectual disability like her, to leading an impoverished, vicarious existence, when it comes to conventional markers of adulthood, such as those of entering a sexual relationship and getting married.

For these reasons, the decision to write a book focusing on the sexual or asexual lives lived by adults with Down syndrome still living in the parental home was effectively made for me. The hook to hang it on, so to speak, was in turn dictated by a theory I wanted to explore. This hypothesis, developed inductively, was borne out of my own observations of living at home with my sister. One consequence of which was that I spent most of my teenage and adult life socialising with people with Down syndrome. Based on these two on-going experiences, I observed what I considered to be an anomaly. The peculiarity in question, which is the sociological/philosophical puzzle or problem that this book sets out to investigate, was that although nearly all the people with Down syndrome that I knew wanted to have a boyfriend or a girlfriend, very few of them managed to find one. It was clear that my sister with Down syndrome was treated in a more paternalistic fashion than I or any of my other siblings were—a regime of care that continues to this very day. Based on my experience of talking to other people with Down syndrome, and their parents, this appears to be in no way unusual. Hence the need for a book which documents, and indeed respects the views of parents who deploy such regimes of care, as opposed to starting from the default social model position: namely, that any practice which curtails the freedom of people with disabilities, is 'wrong', and should be condemned accordingly.

Due to witnessing such regimes of care in action, I formed the thesis that one of the reasons that could explain the mismatch between the stated desires of people with Down syndrome to have a boyfriend or girlfriend and the fact that so many of them lived celibate lives was due to the paternalistic regime of care they were subject to. As words like 'care' carry an array of connotations that are irrelevant to the subject matter of this book, it is important to note at the outset that in using the phrase 'paternalistic regime of care' I am only looking for one condition to be met to claim such a regime exists. Namely, if adults with Down syndrome, or any other form of intellectual disability, either must ask permission and/or are prevented by their parents from taking control over their social/sexual lives (that is, if they are not allowed do what they want, and particularly at night time), they are being subjected to a paternalistic regime of care. Thus, a paternalistic regime of care can be quite involved and 'hands-on'. Equally, however, it can solely consist of the parent/s saying no to a request by their adult son or daughter with Down syndrome to do something they want to do, whether inside or outside the parental home.

Having provided the reader with an insight into the overarching aims of the study and the theoretical framework upon which my research endeavour is based, I now set out briefly the contents of the chapters that follow. The book is divided into six further chapters and draws extensively upon existing scholarship in the domains of disability studies, sociology, philosophy, and the original empirical research carried out for this project.

Chapter 1 addresses the 'what', the 'who', the 'how' and the 'whys' of the study. To this end, it sets out the nature of my research questions, explains why I chose the research methods I did, and how I accessed both research populations. In addition, this chapter includes an explanation of the conceptual frameworks I am using to analyse the empirical data I have collected and also outlines where I stand on the autonomy/paternalism issues under investigation.

Chapter 2, as well as providing a genealogy of the autonomy/paternalism debate as it pertains to contemporary western liberal democracies, explicates the essence of the autonomy/paternalism debate as it relates to the subject matter of this book. It will also provide the reader with an overview of three of the most dominant models used to conceptualise disability vis-à-vis their stance towards autonomy/paternalism issues. Finally, this chapter also includes a detailed outline and rationale of the conceptual approach I am adopting to analyse and contextualise the empirical data this project has collected.

Chapters 3 and 4 is given over to a thematic presentation and analysis of the research findings. In Chapter 3, the parent's and their adult sons and daughter's responses are subsumed under relevant themes and analysed by reference to the conceptual frameworks already outlined. Regarding the parental responses, the themes in question are:

1   Parental perception of what it means to be normal—the rationale behind the paternalistic regime of care
2   Parental refutation of the charge that their regime of care is to 'blame' for the celibate lives led by some of their adult children with Down syndrome
3   Parental view of their adult sons and daughters with Down syndrome as sexual beings—and the desire that they find a girlfriend/boyfriend
4   The privileging of 'loving' boyfriend/girlfriend relationships over sexual expression for its own sake: the gender bias in action

Regarding the responses provided by the adults with Down syndrome the themes in question are:

1   More autonomy please
2   The role played by the mother as reluctant jailor
3   The desire to have a boyfriend/girlfriend
4   The abject in action and the desire to be normal

Chapter 4, which I have titled 'Third-rail sexual politics under scrutiny: the question of facilitated sex', is given over to a presentation and analysis of the parental responses garnered via the focus group focusing specifically on the issue of whether they would consider availing of the facilitated sex mechanism to ensure the sexual needs of their adult children are met.

The purpose of these chapters is fourfold. Firstly, they provide detailed insight into the mind-set of the mothers I spoke to regarding whether they believe their paternalistic regime of care facilitates or presents obstacles to their intellectually disabled offspring from entering a sexual relationship. Secondly, they provide a detailed account of the parent's views regarding the issue of availing of the facilitated sex mechanism for their intellectually disabled adult sons and daughters. Thirdly, they will also provide a detailed account of the responses offered by the sample of adults with Down syndrome regarding whether they believe they are subjected to a paternalistic regime of care and whether they have and/or aspire to be in a sexual relationship. Finally, utilising insights from the Foucauldian and the psychoanalytical frameworks, these chapters provide a sociological/philosophical account regarding why the respondents' replies take the form they do.

Chapter 5, titled 'A modest proposal regarding the normalisation of facilitated sex', is where I present my own normative argument, based on the empirical data collected—but not beholden to it—that a recourse to facilitated sex on the part of the parents provides a solution to their expressed wishes that their adult sons and daughters experience what it is like to have sex while at the same time remaining safe from possible abuse and exploitation. It also argues that facilitated sex can offer a solution to the various *Catch-22*-type situations—which heretofore are preventing many intellectually disabled adults from having sex—this book has identified.

Chapter 6, as the concluding chapter, is where I provide the reader with an overview of the content thus far. This will entail a detailed précis of both the key themes that have emerged and the pros and cons of the theoretical frameworks that were utilised to explore the conjectures under consideration. Finally, I proffer a series of recommendations as to how to close the potentiality/actuality gap regarding how the sexual needs of adults with Down syndrome living in the parental home can be better met.

1 The who, the what and the why

Research methodology

I had several objectives behind the research I embarked on for this book. Firstly, and most importantly, it gives voice, via the use of semi-structured interviews and the focus group method, to members of two populations who remain woefully underrepresented in the 'relevant literature', namely, mothers of adults with Down syndrome living in the parental home and their respective sons and daughters. To this end, it

1 Garners insights into the mind-set of the mothers I spoke to regarding whether their behaviour facilitates or presents obstacles to their intellectually disabled offspring entering a sexual relationship.
2 It elicits their views regarding whether they would consider availing of the facilitated sex mechanism for their intellectually disabled sons and daughters. Facilitated sex in this context refers to paying a third party (prostitutes/sex workers) to engage in sexual activities with their sons and daughters.
3 It establishes whether the sample of adults with Down syndrome I spoke to believe they are subjected to a paternalistic regime of care that limits their freedom to do what they want when they want.
4 It establishes whether they are, have been, or aspire to be in a sexual relationship.

Secondly, because this book is an exercise in applied critical analysis, the data findings will be used to explore the explanatory reach of the conceptual frameworks—the Foucauldian and the psychoanalytical—being utilised to offer a sociological and philosophical *reading* as to why the respondent's replies take the form it does. Finally, this data will also be used as important premises to ground my argument that facilitated sex represents a rational secular liberal solution to the problems expressed by both sets of respondents regarding the difficulties that prevent many intellectually disabled adults from having sex.

The research populations

The research participants, referred to by pseudonyms, consist of two overlapping populations. These are made up of ten adults with Down syndrome living in the parental home, and their mothers. The average age of the adults with Down syndrome is thirty, whereas the ages of the mothers fall into the 55–65 age range. The mothers are self-selected as each replied to a leaflet I designed and only made available at a public meeting in Dublin convened to discuss the nature of the sex education classes provided by the major Irish disability services.

Due to the nature of this recruitment process, the fact that all the parents are mothers can be explained by reference to practical considerations. For example, some fathers, and indeed father and mother couples, did approach me expressing an interest in participating in the study. However, because of scheduling issues, I decided that such involvement was simply not feasible. This pragmatic decision not to include fathers in this study was also bolstered by prior research that suggests that Irish mothers play an important role in the socialisation of the next generation, especially regarding the emotional/affective domain (Inglis, 1997).

In socio-economic terms, the mothers and their families can be considered middle class—this was also the self-description they offered when asked—with all the mothers (in addition to their husbands) working in a professional capacity, or having worked in a professional capacity and now being retired. Regarding those mothers who are still in full-time employment, Sofia and Angela are both secondary school teachers, Claire is a medical doctor, Aileen is a psychiatrist employed by one of Ireland's biggest disability service providers, and both Mary and Katy work as lecturers in academia. Meanwhile, the other four mothers have all retired from jobs in the Irish civil service (Jennifer and Susan), accountancy (Eimer), and the advertising sector (Rebecca).

In addition to this shared socio-economic status, another common feature that unites all the mothers is that they are involved in campaigning for the rights of people with Down syndrome—and have been since their sons and daughters were very young. This phenomenon of political activism on the part of the mothers is one which reflects a common theme in the literature on mothering, care, and disability. Thus, although instances of mothers acting as advocates for their children is not an unusual one, regarding mothers of disabled children, research suggests that this role is typically more intensive, longer lasting, and different in kind from the form such care takes when the relationship concerns mothers and their non-disabled children (Ryan and Runswick-Cole, 2008). The nature of such sustained engagement with challenging the status quo can be explained by reference to several factors that are unique to parenting a disabled child, particularly one with an intellectual impairment. These include the nature of the impairment, society's response to the impairment, and the role played by the network of health and medical professionals who actively intervene in the lives of people with disability (Cuskelly et al., 2006). Consequently, as with the mothers I spoke to, mothers of disabled children often "become involved in interactions with other mothers of disabled children and this frequently happens through 'self-help' groups and support networks" (Ryan and Runswick-Cole, 2009:45). Such activism can be subsumed under what's known as the 'crusadership' model of parenting—a typology that overlaps closely with the normative agenda propagated by normalisation/Social Role Valorisation (Darling, 1979). The philosophies propagated by these frameworks will be fully explained in the following chapter.

In relation to the adults with Down syndrome I spoke to, all of them are working part-time in the service sector (for example, working in supported employment at relatively menial jobs in shops or cafes). When not at work, their time is either spent at home (mainly watching TV) or out socialising. Such socialising is typically spent in the company of family members or other intellectually disabled adults. When with the latter, the social interaction that ensues—which usually takes the form of bowling or a trip to the cinema—occurs in a supervised setting under the aegis of the disability service provider they are affiliated with.

My use of semi-structured interview was informed by Kvale's contention that: "if you want to know how people understand their world and their life, why not talk with them"? (1996:1). According to Flick (1998), such interviews are more flexible than alternative approaches in that they allow the researcher the freedom to react and to adapt the interview accordingly. For example, the use of semi-structured interviews allows participants to deviate from the script, so to speak, to follow up on an unexpected remark, to pursue a line of reasoning that emerges organically from the interaction between interviewer and interviewee—one which may otherwise have remained unexpressed and or unthought-of. These characteristics are clearly of crucial importance when talking to respondents about their attitudes towards their own sexuality or that of the sexuality of their adult children with Down syndrome. When such sensitive subjects are under investigation, the need to seek clarity on a given answer, to ask 'what do you mean' or 'why do you think that way' can essentially be predicted before embarking on the fieldwork in question.

Another advantage of using this research method is it allows the "respondents to answer in their own terms" (Bryman, 2008:145). Given both the subject matter and the nature of the populations taking part, this benefit is an important one to note. For example, while alternative approaches, such as the use of questionnaires, can help alleviate the embarrassment some people may experience while talking about issues of sexuality, they run the risk, especially when dealing with people with intellectual disabilities, of 'language working through them'. That is, respondents may give answers they do not truly understand to questions they do not fully comprehend. While in no way fool-proof—no research method is—semi-structured interviews do allow the researcher to interact with his interviewee on a more 'human', more natural level in the sense that the face-to-face conversation is the method of choice that adults with Down syndrome, in common with most of us, employ when conversing with family and friends.

This emphasis on treating adults with Down syndrome in as normal a fashion as possible also corresponds to my own ethical sensibilities regarding the nature of the research design one should employ when doing research seeking the views of intellectually disabled people. This is the belief that members of this population retain the right to bear witness to their own lives via the medium of a one-on-one conversation as opposed to being subject to the ever-increasing panoply of so called 'innovative research methods' that utilises picture and other visual aids to facilitate 'better communication' (Booth and Booth, 2003). As an addendum to this principled position, the reader might be interested to know that in my capacity as a professional academic, I have seen such innovative research methods in action, and whatever merits they may have for people with severe communication problems, for people with mild to moderate to levels of Down syndrome, they are from my experience typically a source of embarrassment for the people with Down syndrome who are subjected to their use.

Staying with the pragmatics of employing semi-structured interviews, another benefit of this approach is that it lends itself to both interviewer and interviewee building a relationship of mutual trust between the two of them which in turn facilitates "the free flow of information" (Spradley, 1979:78). Such rapport, built upon how the researcher and respondent initially connect with each other on their initial pre-interview meeting, can be facilitated by the researcher explaining his motivation for conducting the research in question and a willingness to act as an engaged interlocutor—someone who is open to answering questions from the respondents themselves. As already stated, this was the stance I adopted. In addition, and as I alluded to earlier, because I have a sibling with Down syndrome, such an affinity seemed to be present from the outset. Apropos of this claim, it should be noted that many of the mothers informed me in our pre-interview conversations that had I not had a sibling with Down syndrome, they would not have agreed to participate in the research to begin with. Hence, I believe that this sense of a shared connection limited the levels of suspicion as to why someone would want to talk to the interviewees about the sexuality of their sons and daughters with Down syndrome in the first place. In addition, from my reading of how the respondents interacted with me, and based on the quality of the data collected, this belief that everyone involved had something in common went some way in transforming me from the subject position of 'official inquisitor' to that of sympathetic listener.

The semi-structured interview has been used with much success in previous interviews with people with intellectual disabilities (Griffin and Balandin, 2004) and its advantages have been discussed in much depth by McCarthy (1999). This method has moreover been chosen by many people with intellectual disabilities as their preferred method when taking part in research projects. For example, during a series of interviews with people with a range of intellectual disabilities, Kitchin states:

> there was strong support for qualitative methods of research, particularly those of interviews because they allow respondents to express and contextualise their true feelings, rather than having them pigeonholed into boxes with no or little explanation for contextual explanation.
>
> (Kitchin, 2000:43)

A final benefit to note in using semi-structured interviews is the fact that they help to equalise the otherwise asymmetrical relationship that can sometimes exist between researcher and respondent. The semi-structured interview retains this facility because it allows respondents more room to direct discussion in that they retain the power to regulate the accounts they decide to proffer (Bryman, 2008).

My original intention was to interview each member of both populations twice. The rationale behind doing two interviews with each respondent was based on the belief that the relevant issues that arose in the first interview could then be addressed in more detail in the succeeding one. In relation to the population of adults with Down syndrome, the reasons for not carrying out a second interview, or indeed a focus group, were due to a combination of factors. Firstly, while this population of research respondents were willing to participate in another interview, they essentially said they would prefer to change the subject if it took place. Secondly, it was decided that the data collected during the first interviews was of sufficient quality to address both the research questions and for an applied theoretical analysis to be carried out. Finally, and as an extension of the last point, because of the nature of the questioning style I deliberately adopted, it was decided that neither a further interview nor a focus group made up of the adults with Down syndrome would yield relevant data over and above that already collected. My decision in this respect was based on the fact that while the sexuality of adults with Down syndrome is one of the key issues under investigation, I was adamant that in order to avoid any undue embarrassment, awkwardness, etc. that I would not ask sexually explicit questions of this population. Rather, the emphasis was on conducting those interviews in as sensitive a manner as possible to limit the possibility of any of the respondents getting in any way upset. Hence, questions took the form of 'do you have a boyfriend/girlfriend?' and 'would you like a boyfriend/girlfriend?' and so on rather than 'have you ever had sex?' and/or 'would you like to have sex?' and so on.

Interviewing people with intellectual disability

Because people with Down syndrome have a diminished capacity regarding comprehension and verbal expression (Cunningham, 2006) the task of interviewing members of this population raises many methodological issues over and above those that arise when embarking on semi-structured interviews with a non-intellectually disabled group. Thus, in line with Porter and Lacey's recommendations (2003), the specific simplified questioning style applied the following principles:

1   Use of short words and sentences
2   Use of single-clause sentences
3   Use of active verbs: that is, "Did you...?"
4   When possible, use of the present tense
5   Avoidance of jargon and abstract concepts
6   Avoidance of leading questions, keeping things as neutral as possible: for example, 'How does that feel?', 'Can you explain that?', or 'What do you mean? Can you say more about this?'

However, Porter and Lacey (2003) go on add that semi-structured interviews are by their very nature unpredictable and all eventualities cannot always be prepared for. For example, neither they nor any of the other relevant authors I reviewed could agree on how much time the interviewer should give the interviewee to respond to a given question before the former should rephrase the question or move on to another. McCarthy, meanwhile, claims that interviewing somebody with an intellectual disability "is not a fundamentally different process from interviewing anybody else" (1999:24). However, she qualifies this statement by going on to claim that while the literature around the mechanics of interviewing people with intellectual disabilities is small, there is widespread agreement that how questions are worded is of greater importance then when interviewing people without an intellectual disability. By this she means, that, factoring the impairment, it is generally the case that the likelihood of eliciting productive answers can be influenced by the kind of language used to formulate the questions and the order and frequency in which they are then put.

The focus group method

According to Morgan and Spanish, the purpose of using a focus group is to "bring together several participants to discuss a topic of mutual interest to themselves and the researcher" (1984:253). The rationale behind the use of a focus group for this book was a post facto one. As already stated, the original intention was to rely on the use of the semi-structured interviews to collect the required data. However, on reflection, I concluded that a few of the interviews with the sample of mothers were done too 'sensitively' in that their attitudes towards the sexuality of their adult children with Down syndrome were not pursued vigorously enough.

In addition, midway through the interviewing process, I came across a newspaper article featuring a story about a British mother of an adult son with Down syndrome who declared her intention to employ the services of a prostitute to ensure that her son's sexual needs were met. While the issue of facilitated sex has lost some of its taboo status concerning physically disabled adults, it retains its status as a Pandora's box where the sexuality of intellectually disabled people is concerned—see Chapter 2 for more detail. For this reason, I decided that the use of this newspaper article could act as a perfect jumping-off point to structure a more explicit group discussion dealing specifically with the mother's views on whether they would consider utilising the facilitated sex mechanism for their sons and daughters.

The initial decision to privilege semi-structured interviews over the use of the focus group was based on the contention that that the latter had a fatal flaw. Namely, that "if the subject matter is sensitive and the participants are expected to talk about intimate aspects of their experience, semi-structured interviews may be more appropriate" (Willig, 2008:31). I was also concerned that a group setting would inhibit some of the mothers expressing their views in a way they would if the scenario was a one-to-one conversation/interview. However, on reflection, I concluded that the reason I had put myself in the difficult situation in relation to the content of some of the interviews was because I found asking such questions on a one-to-one level a little embarrassing. Based on this epiphany, I made the decision to employ the focus group approach, rather than to complete a second tranche of interviews. In relation to my embarrassment, although it may sound slightly paradoxical, the rationale behind using a focus group was based on the belief that with a larger number of people present, I could pretend the focus group was a University tutorial and behave in kind: that is, assume a more confident, more detached persona.

One of the advantages—especially apposite given the issues under investigation—is that the focus group, in bringing together a group of people facing the same dilemmas, "can help in the discussion of taboo subjects since less inhibited members may break the ice or provide mutual support" (Robson, 2006:285). A related reason behind me using this method was that unlike the semi-structured interview, where the interviewer is ever mindful of the distinction between challenging and probing an interviewee's answer to a given question, the focus group has the potential to transform itself into a quasi-Socratic debate where the participants actively challenge their fellow respondents' views (Robson, 2006). This process of presenting one's own and refuting the arguments of others means "that the researcher may stand a chance of ending up with more realistic accounts of what people think, because they are forced to think about and possibly revise their views" (Bryman, 2008:348). As events unfolded, the decision to use the focus group was thoroughly vindicated. It proved to be lively and productive, with none of the respondents holding back on their opinions, while at the same time being mindful not to monopolise the conversation.

Ethical considerations

The principles guiding this research project are informed by the need to treat all research participants with the utmost respect and dignity. In this regard, Blaxter states that ethical research involves getting the informed consent of those you are going to interview, observe, or take materials from, a process which involves reaching agreement with the respondents about the use of the data, how its analysis will be reported and disseminated.

(2001:158)

Informed consent refers to the necessity of ensuring that the participants in a piece of research have given their full and informed consent to their participation. When adult respondents, who are not members of a vulnerable group, freely agree to give their informed consent to participate in the research process, the ethical obligations of the researcher essentially centre on the basic principle of not exploiting or harming the population in question, but rather respecting their needs and requirements (Blaxter, 2001).

For the population of adults with Down syndrome, informed consent was obtained both verbally and by means of a written consent form. Regarding verbal consent, it is my belief, which also has precedent in the literature (Walmsley, 1997; Rodgers, 1999; Porter and Lacey, 2003) that a brief discussion is the best medium to convey all the information the individual needs to make an informed decision as to whether they wish to participate. Throughout these 'chats', the strategy I adopted was to be ever mindful that the conversations never became any way uncomfortable for the interviewees. This involved checking with the respondent that they did indeed comprehend what was being said and giving them the opportunity to ask questions if clarification was needed. It was also made very clear from the beginning of this process that if the respondents changed their minds at any stage and decided that they do not want to continue the interview, that was their right, and no repercussions would follow. When it came to the parents, a similar process was employed.

In relation to the protection of data and information provided by the research respondents, the guidelines provided by the UK's Data Protection Act (1988,) have been adhered to. Consequently, participants were assured of complete confidentiality and anonymity in relation to their identities and the data they provided. However, it was made clear that an exception to this rule would be made regarding the population of intellectually disabled adults if information relating to what could reasonably be construed as a danger of any sort to the individual was disclosed.

Regarding where to carry out the interviews, in relation to interviewing the population of adults with Down syndrome, the location in question was either chosen by the respondent themselves, or in consultation with their key worker and/or parents. The only stipulation on my part was that the parents were not present at the agreed location. In relation to interviewing the parents themselves, they chose the location.

When doing research with vulnerable groups, there is a need to be ready for every eventuality no matter how unlikely any problems occurring really are (Porter and Lacey, 2003). To this end, I put several strategies in place to ensure, in as much as possible, that my ethical obligations to the adults with Down syndrome were met. For example, there was the possibility of some-body getting upset when talking about his/her likes and dislikes regarding living at home with parents and/or wanting to be in a boyfriend/girlfriend relationship. In such a situation, a recommended tactic is to take a break and ask the respondent whether he/she wants to stop the formal interview (Gilbert, 2004). If the answer to this question is no, then the interviewer can gently inquire as to what is wrong, or alternatively assure the interviewee that they do not have to continue with the interview and/or to talk about those issues which they find upsetting. In addition, an inquiry can be made at this stage as to whether the respondent would like to talk to their key worker and/or social worker and/or have same present while the interview continues.

As things currently stand, all adults with Down syndrome in the Repub-lic of Ireland, even those living at home with parents, are affiliated with a specialist disability organisation. The system in place is that everyone is assigned both a 'key worker' (whom they meet with on a regular basis to discuss issues relating to work, socialising, etc.) and a social worker, whom they meet less frequently. I proposed to have either one or both professionals present at the interview location but not actually present for the interview itself. Consequently, if one of the adults with Down syndrome gets upset or feels emotionally uncomfortable in any way, they would have someone they trusted on hand: professionals specifically trained to deal with such eventualities. In the end, the relevant key worker was present at each of the initial meetings that took place with the adults with Down syndrome. All of the key workers also agreed to accompany their 'charges' for the actual interviews. However, without exception, all the adults with Down syndrome insisted that they wanted to do their interviews on their own.

The contested politics of researching disability

As the reader may be aware, due to the power wielded by champions of the social model of disability, there is a current dogma within Disability Studies (particularly its United Kingdom incarnation) that stipulates that several conditions must be met when embarking on research with disabled people, or indeed into the issue of disability generally. This section is designed to explain why I did not adhere to this arbitrary set of prescriptions. To un-derstand my decision, one needs more information regarding the political origins of British Disability Studies and its commitment to the social model of disability.

According to Harpur, "the social model was formed as a radical Marxist model that identifies capitalism as a major cause of the oppression of persons with disabilities" (2012:326). To make explicit what such a characterisation entails, Harpur goes on to state that a key tenet of social model thinking is that people with disabilities "will never be free of their oppression until capitalism is replaced with a more humane system" (Ibid.). Hence, this discourse around who gets to research whom and the normative criteria dictating the methods that 'should' be used is not simply the effect of a new paradigm shift in relation to how to advance knowledge regarding the lives of people with disabilities. Rather, while the production of new insights into how contemporary society treats people with disabilities is indeed part of the rationale behind the social model of disability, its emergence is also borne out of a political anger with the wholesale exclusion and objectification of people with disabilities. This anger, moreover, is directed not just at society and its exclusionary practices, but also at the way "that the social sciences in general and medical sociology in particular constructed disability and disabled people" (Watson, 2012:93). The essence of this approach to disability research is captured by Oliver in his declaration that "disability research should not be seen as a set of technical objective procedures carried out by 'experts' but part of the struggle by disabled people to challenge the oppression they currently experience in their lives" (1992:102). Hence his contention that "disabled people have come to see research as a violation of their experiences, as irrelevant to their needs and as failing to improve their material circumstances and quality of life" (1992:106). As an antidote to such abuses, proponents of the social model conclude that one of the most important ways of guarding against such 'exploitation', 'objectification', and 'alienation' is the application of the principle that people with disability need to become 'full participants' in the research process via the use of 'emancipatory' research methods (Mercer, 2002; Oliver and Barnes, 2012).

Emancipatory research is an approach to disability research that advocates the use of so-called empowering and empathetic research methods. It collapses the positivist fact/value distinction (which has no relationship to the meta ethical fact/value distinction developed by Hume that my analysis is employing and which will be explained anon) in which the researcher is expected to adopt, in so far as possible, a neutral, objective stance towards their research subjects (Danieli and Woodhams, 2005). In this respect, the emancipatory research model "represents the overt 'politicization' of research in which the researcher struggles for transformative change" (Barnes, 2003:6). The optimal means of achieving such ends allegedly lies in researchers learning "how to put their knowledge and skills at the disposal of disabled people" (Barnes, 1992:122).

This stipulation that the experiential knowledge of disabled people should be privileged over the credentialed non-disabled social scientists has its roots in various kinds of standpoint research methodologies more commonly associated with certain branches of feminist thinking (Harding, 2009). In effect, this strand of disability studies has co-opted the assertion made by some feminist scholars that only women can 'adequately' research women, to conclude that, ergo, only disabled people can adequately embark on research with their disabled 'counterparts'. With claims of this sort acting as his premises, Barnes argues that,

logic dictates that if a researcher is to empathise with those being researched it follows that their life history must be as near as possible to
that of the people being studied; women researchers are better placed to
do research on women, and people with impairments are best equipped
to research disability.

(Barnes, 1992:116)

However, the problem with such reasoning is that it conflates experience
with understanding. In addition, there is the inconvenient fact that the
contention that people with disabilities share a 'culture' that is different
and inaccessible to others, is less a research finding than an *a priori*
essentialist assumption, one moreover that fails to recognize the heterogeneous nature of every social grouping. For example, one puzzles at what
the elective affinity binding somebody confined to a wheelchair due to a
physical disability and somebody with Down syndrome could possibly be.
In my experience, I have never encountered a friendship between these
two disparate disabled populations. The reality of the situation, as Barnes
himself notes, is that "having a designated impairment does not automatically give someone an affinity with people with similar conditions
or disabled people generally nor, indeed, an inclination to do disability
research" (2003:8). While there is some disagreement over the necessary
and sufficient conditions that must be met before a given piece of social research can be 'legitimately' deemed to be emancipatory, many influential
definitions have been formulated. For example, Stone and Priestley (1996)
enumerate the following key principles that need to be followed when conducting emancipatory research:

1   The adoption of the social model of disability as the ontological and
    epistemological basis for research production
2   The rejection of 'spurious' claims to objectivity by making an overt polit-
    ical commitment to the struggles of disabled people for self-emancipation
3   The willingness only to undertake research where it will be of some
    benefit to the self-empowerment of disabled people and/or the removal
    of disabling barriers
4   The devolution of control over research production to ensure full ac-
    countability to disabled people and their organisations (1996:706)

While in 2003, Barnes stipulated that the necessary conditions that must be
met for disability research to be deemed emancipatory are that it should:

1   Be accountable to disabled people and their organisations
2   Adhere to the social model of disability
3   Be politically committed to the emancipation of disabled people
4   Be relevant and produce research that has a meaningful outcome for
    disabled people

The problems with the emancipatory research programme

Whatever value emancipatory research has as a research manifesto involving physically disabled people, its normative noises, when applied to research into the area of intellectual disability—particularly the intellectual disability that is Down syndrome—are from my own perspective, of much less relevance. As we have seen, emancipatory research constitutes a political/ethical manifesto as to how one should go about doing so-called proper ethical disability research. However, most of the authors cited seem to be unaware of the wider meta-ethical debates within moral philosophy that are currently trying to determine whether any value judgement to the effect that 'one should do X' has any special properties that distinguish it from a self-interested claim, devoid of propositional content, along the lines of 'do X because I say so' (Mackie, 1977). For example, does the fact that the researcher benefits materially and/ or professionally from the research really taint the research itself? Is there an ethical difference between benefiting in those ways and benefiting materially and professionally from criticising mainstream approaches to disability? Is there an ethical difference between benefiting materially and professionally from conducting mainstream research and benefiting materially, professionally, and psychologically from adhering to the principles of emancipatory research? If yes, what criterion is employed to arrange such judgements? Answers to these and other relevant questions are conspicuous by their absence in the nominally relevant literature. A possible explanation as to why this should be the case is offered by Watson in his observation that:

> The social model is at its roots normative; it implies judgements of good and bad, of what ought and what ought not to be. This normative dimension is barely acknowledged and unless it is, linked as it can be to the Marxian idea of false consciousness, it has the potential to be seen as illiberal and paternalistic.
>
> (2012:99)

Due to the centrality played by the false consciousness concept—mentioned previously by Watson—throughout this book, it is wise at this stage to provide the reader with a definition of this much-disputed concept. Thus, Jost states that "a consciousness is 'false' when it serves to perpetuate inequality by leading members of a subordinate group to believe that they are inferior, deserving of their plight, or incapable of taking action against the causes of their subordination" (1995:400). Meanwhile, returning to the argument at hand, while I agree with some of the normative sentiments that have become associated with this approach to researching disability, emancipatory research has no monopoly on such ethical principles. Consequently, if one accepts my argument that there are no necessary connections between the urge to empower disabled people and following the tenets of emancipatory research, the numerous problems with this paradigm are much easier to discern.

First, there is the principled problem in researchers interested in the field of disability being forced or pressurised to adopt a certain methodology. Ethics, particularly the sub field of research ethics, is not a branch of physics. Hence, when making prescriptive noises as to what constitutes 'proper disability research practice', one needs to be ever mindful that such claims do not carry the propositional content as that enjoyed by the statement that $E = MC^2$. Consequently, it logically follows that there is something totalitarian in a 'vanguard' party of self-appointed 'experts' constructing, and worse still having the power to get other equally reflexive and equally concerned researchers to adhere to their wholly subjective blueprint as to what constitutes 'ethical' disability research. The danger of such a phenomenon is noted by Danieli and Woodhams in their contention that "the advocacy of emancipatory research is itself an exercise of power which can result in the silencing of some voices, thereby becoming a form of oppression itself" (2005:281).

A further problem with the emancipatory research program involves some of its main proponents collapsing the distinction between making a normative claim and making an empirical claim. For example, how does Oliver empirically support his empirical claim that "disabled people have come to see research as a violation of their experiences, as irrelevant to their needs and as failing to improve their material circumstances and quality of life" (1992:106)? The surprising answer is he does not. This moreover is a rhetorical strategy adopted by most of the authors cited. Such practices clearly raise the question as to why this technique, which it could be argued lacks scholarly rigour, has had no effect on the academic reputation of Oliver, Barnes, and their legion of acolytes. For an answer to the question as to how such intellectual sleights of hand have heretofore worked their magic, one can again turn to Foucault. A key insight of the Foucauldian framework is that when it comes to the 'truth claims' propagated by the human sciences, power plays a crucial role in determining who does and does not count as an intellectual authority on a given subject, and by extension determines whose voice is to be heard and respected and whose is to be ignored (O'Farrell, 2005).

A similar problem arises with the claim that any research undertaken must be accountable to disability organisations, which are, for some unexplained reason, deemed to 'represent' all disabled people. Why should this be the case? Again, coherent answers are in short supply. No explanation is offered as to who has given a disability group the mandate, moral or otherwise, to claim to represent all intellectually disabled people. The lacuna of explanations is also apparent regarding the distinction between being an 'active participant' rather than simply a 'passive subject'. One looks in vain for a systematic and coherent justification to ground such a hierarchy. The inference seems to be that it is self-evident that acting as a research respondent is a 'passive' inferior role when compared to those who have played a central role in the research process from start to finish. However, this is a wholly stipulative definition as to what constitutes empowering disabled people. The same 'logic' can be employed to invert this hierarchy. Hence, one can state that the ethical/political contention that acting as a research respondent is empowering enjoys an equal epistemic status to its opposite—that of being involved in the research process from beginning to end.

As will be explained further in the following chapter, there is also the problem that the social model of disability privileges the concerns of physically disabled people over those with an intellectual disability. Consequently, in its attempt to impose social model politics onto research methodology it seems to have forgotten the obvious point. This is the fact that because "the research process relies heavily on intellectual skills, it is less easily accessible to people with learning disabilities than to groups of people with disabilities who do not experience intellectual impairments" (Kiernan, 1999:46). This is especially the case when the research respondents are individuals with Down syndrome, which, let us remind ourselves, is an intellectual impairment characterised by a significantly reduced ability to understand new and complex information (Cunningham, 2006). This on-going mismatch between the principles expounded by advocates of emancipatory research and the empirical facts is well made by Watson when he states

> ...while participation by disabled people is held up as a cornerstone of disability studies, the obvious question is to what extent have disabled people been consulted in the priorities put forward in disability research? The answer is they have not and instead disability scholars and activists have assumed that role.
>
> (2012:98)

Participatory research

Regarding this lack of fit between a wholesale application of the principles that characterise emancipatory research and embarking on research with intellectually disabled people, Walmsley argues that it is "necessary to recognise that a direct translation of action developed for people with physical impairments is too crude a tool to deliver real and lasting changes for people with learning disabilities" (2005:74). In its attempt to take on board the fact that many intellectually disabled people may not be able to play the roles in the research process envisioned by the emancipatory model, the participatory approach has been mooted as a middle way between the two extremes of research being carried out on and with intellectually disabled people. Thus, although Stalker (1998) has argued that too often the terms are used as synonyms in the relevant literature, Gilbert states that "the designation 'participatory research', rather than 'emancipatory research', is used to distinguish between contexts where people with (learning) disabilities participate, but are not in control of the research process" (2004:300). A similar definition of the distinction between the two approaches is proffered by Walmsley and Johnson when they state that "a participatory approach to research raises the possibility of people with learning disabilities working alongside academics as advisors or co-researchers, whilst in emancipatory research, disabled people are expected to control all aspects of the research" (2003:146). Consequently, one chief difference between these two approaches is that in contradistinction to emancipatory research, which sees the researcher's skills being used as a resource to meeting an agenda set by people with disabilities, the participatory approach views this relationship as more of a partnership between the two parties; hence, for example there is no *a priori* stipulation that the research agenda itself must be dictated by disabled people (Walmsley and Johnson, 2003).

To add to this terminological confusion, the participatory approach is also subsumed under the umbrella term that is 'inclusive research'. To this end, Walmsley states that 'inclusive research' is "a term used to refer to a range of research approaches that have traditionally been termed 'participatory' or 'emancipatory'" (2001:187). Thus, both participatory and inclusive approaches frameworks are informed by the principle that when it comes to doing research with intellectually disabled people, there should be 'nothing about us without us'. What I find contentious, however, is what the 'without us' entails. For instance, Johnson states that

> inclusive research is based on values and ideas which strongly emphasise the importance of research arising from the expressed interests and issues of people with intellectual disabilities, and in which they are involved not as sources of information or data, but in a research capacity.
>
> (2009:252)

She goes on to insist that when inclusive research is undertaken, it must adhere to the following principles:

1   The research question, problem, or issue must be one that is owned (though not necessarily initiated) by people with intellectual disabilities.
2   It should further the interests of intellectually disabled people: non-disabled researchers should be on the side of people with intellectual disabilities.
3   It should be collaborative. People with intellectual disabilities should be involved in the process of doing the research.
4   People with intellectual disabilities should be able to exert some control over the process and outcomes.
5   The research question, process and reports must be accessible to people with intellectual disabilities (Johnson, 2009:255).

As this explication illustrates, while there are minor differences between the different characterisations of participatory and inclusive research, a basic precept common to them both is the stipulation that people with intellectual disabilities should be actively involved in the research process as more than just research respondents. Without rehashing arguments I advanced in my critique of the emancipatory approach to research, some of which also apply to the participatory/inclusive models, I will now explain why my book did not venture down either the participatory or inclusive road in terms of involving the adults with Down syndrome in the research process from the beginning to end—a process that includes embarking on quite abstract theoretical analysis. The first and very important obstacle refers to Walmsley and Johnson's insistence is the principle that "if people with learning disabilities are to become researchers then they should be paid for their work at 'normal' rates" (2003:155). However, as is the norm when writing academic books, I did not receive any funding to complete this project and hence did not have the resources to cover such expenses. In addition to this crucial question of paying people with intellectual disabilities, it is clear from the literature under scrutiny that many of the pertinent issues that both inclusive and participatory research are concerned with, such as liaising with disability organisations, training adults with intellectual disabilities in research skills or including them in the research process from start to finish, are only really applicable to professional research projects. Such endeavours can include the writing of a monograph, but only where the author is affiliated with an organisation that has commissioned and/or set the parameters for how the research is to proceed. For those authors who do not fall into such categories—such as myself—the ability to access such resources can be next to impossible to acquire.

In addition to these financial factors, there is also the more controversial (in some people's eyes) contention alluded to above that due to the nature of a given intellectual impairment many of those subsumed under the intellectual disability umbrella term would not possess the requisite intellectual skills to occupy the 'research capacity' role—in a non-tokenistic fashion— as envisioned by any of the authors cited. Hence, while I agree with the proposition that in some respects people with intellectual disabilities are experts in their own experience, because this book is an exercise in applied theoretical analysis, it does not follow that they would be either interested in, or capable of, being intimately involved in the research process from start to finish. For example, in my attempt to make the empirical component of this project as 'inclusive' as possible, the option was open to all the adults with Down syndrome to read a transcript of their interview or to have the views they recounted verbally explained back to them and to take part in a second interview if they thought they wanted to expand on any answers originally given. However, without fail, when contacted, none of the members of this population were interested in availing of these opportunities.

My conceptual framework

The conceptual toolbox that informs the research questions and the conceptual lens through which the empirical data will be analysed, are drawn from the work of Michel Foucault (1977, 1978, 1980), the psychoanalyst Julia

Kristeva's (1982) concept of abjection, and the cultural theorist Margrit Shildrick's (2003, 2007, 2009) use of this concept to posit an explanation as to why many non-disabled people—including parents and siblings—hold ambivalent attitudes towards people with visible disabilities expressing their sexuality.

In metaphorical terms, the all-seeing 'panopticon' that plays such a constitutive role in the 'regime of care' Foucault describes in *Discipline and Punish* (1977) had a resonance of sorts in how I saw my own and the parents I know treat their adult sons and daughters with Down syndrome. In *Discipline and Punish* (1977), Foucault appropriates Bentham's ideal-type prison to argue that contemporary societies have become surveillance societies. In the specific context of a prison, the panopticon is a central tower that allows an unseen prison guard to constantly monitor all the prisoners. The fact that the prisoners can always be observed means that whether they are or not is irrelevant to the effects produced. Namely, to further their own self-interests, the prisoners must act as if they are always subject to the guard's gaze. In Foucauldian terminology, this leads them to becoming 'docile bodies'—where for fear of external sanction, they police their own behaviour in accordance to the prisons norms (Clegg, 1989). Foucault in turn abstracted this notion of the omnipotent, omnipresent, omniscient unobservable observer and the practices of self-surveillance it produces to argue that the prison constructed along such lines constitutes a much wider apposite metaphor in that "the carceral archipelago transported this technique from the penal institution to the entire social body" (Foucault, 1977:298). This is the contention that the panoptic model of surveillance has diffused throughout society to such an extent that it now constitutes the primary mode of social organization. Consequently, although we may think we are free citizens with the requisite agency to control our destinies, the Foucauldian point is that we are much more circumscribed than we realise. The constraints we are subjected to encompass both our capacity to formulate certain thoughts, beliefs, and desires, as well as our ability to act on them. Therefore, Foucault concludes that because of the discursively produced human predisposition to unreflexively assent to and reproduce dominant societal norms, our chains cut deeper than we would like to acknowledge (Foucault, 1977).

Using Foucault's work as a blueprint, I developed a similar typology to act as a heuristic guide in trying to help explain the nature of the parental regime of care that most of the adults with Down syndrome I know are subjected to. This involves conceiving of the parents as 'reluctant jailors' and their sons and daughters as 'prisoners' of sorts—the use of such terminology is not meant to carry any negative connotations. In effect, I have augmented Foucault's claim that contemporary societies are surveillance societies to advance the conjecture that families that contain an adult with intellectual disability living in the parental home can be conceptualised as surveillance societies in their own right. This submission entails that the parents of intellectually disabled adults, in their role as gatekeepers to their son or daughters social and sexual lives, are, in metaphorical terms, the embodiment of Foucault's panopticon. In other words, as the reluctant jailors of their adult sons or daughters, they are the epitome of the normalizing power that their intellectually disabled offspring are subjected to (Foley, 2013). This is a state of affairs where both the parents and their adult children are always, either literally or metaphorically, being watched. In relation to the former, the gaze in question comes from within. The parent regulates their own actions by reference to the socially approved norms and standards regarding what it means to be a good parent. It is a subject position that, by the normative obligations it prescribes, dictates that the lives of their intellectually disabled adult children must be played out under the full visibility of the parental gaze.

To this end, part of the empirical element of this book will be to examine if and/or how the parents of adults with Down syndrome living in the parental home I spoke to negotiate the tension between trying to empower their impaired children to enjoy a sexual life while at the same time ensuring they come to no harm. Equally important though, given the critical analysis I will engage in throughout this book, is that the empirical data I have collected will also act as-a means-to a conceptual end. Namely, it will be used to explore the explanatory reach of the key insights deployed by the theorists mentioned previously. In addition, the use of the 'critical' prefix is designed to denote the fact that this book, in common with contemporary critical theory generally, is not simply setting out to describe and explain the workings of a given social phenomena, but is also offering prescriptions as to how it can be made better (Geuss, 1981; Kellner, 1990).

In the scholarly literature, the true genealogy of critical investigations into the nature of the social world is a matter of contention. Regarding the identification of possible progenitors some scholars invoke Socrates and Plato, while others locate the origins of the critical tradition as stemming from the enlightenment tradition of the 17th and 18th centuries as represented by such figures as John Locke and Immanuel Kant (Holub, 1991). However, from the post-world war two era until relevantly recently, critical theory was more narrowly defined by reference to 'pure' Marxism and its various offshoots such as those of the Frankfurt School or, staying within the field of disability itself, the social model of disability (Calhoun, 1995). This has changed, however, in the wake of the so-called 'linguistic turn' within the social sciences, which has seen the emergence and consolidation of post-structuralism as a legitimate mode of social investigation. Accordingly, at the time of writing, there exists a smorgasbord of critical frameworks predicated on different philosophical anthropologies. Nonetheless, the family resemblance that unites the language games played by contemporary critical theory, in all its various guises, is that in some form or another, their *raison d'être* is parasitic on Marx's exhortation that the purpose of critical social inquiry is not simply to interpret or to explain how the social world works but to offer prescriptions as to how to change it (Kellner, 1990; Geuss, 1991). Filmer captures the moral aspect of such a critical endeavour succinctly when he states that it involves the formulation of a social theory

> which seeks not only to explain the structure and practices of the society(ies) to which it refers, but also to provide a diagnosis of its/their organizational and ethical shortcomings, a design for an alternative and a proposal of the changes required to implement it.
>
> (1998:243)

It is this normative component that differentiates critical theory from traditional social science theory or positivism that sees the uninterested pursuit of knowledge as an intrinsically virtuous practice, and which thus limits itself to describing and explaining a given state of affairs from a supposedly value free or objective perspective (May, 1996). From the critical perspective, however, social inquiry is an inherently interpretive and evaluative enterprise. This insistence on making normative judgements regarding the nature of the social relations under investigation is partly derived from the initial decision to focus on problematic social arrangements in the first place. It also borne from a repudiation of the positivist contention that value neutrality and good social science go hand in hand. Within the critical tradition, the valorisation of the objective unbiased social scientist is not only a contradiction in terms but helps, especially from the Foucauldian perspective, perpetuate the fiction that social science insights play no considerable role in masking how power works and the concomitant legitimization of unequal and oppressive beliefs and practices.

As a point of reference for the reader, the remit I have set myself regarding this critical exercise in applied theoretical analysis is modelled on the approach adopted by Holland et al in their influential 1998 book *The Male in the Head: Young People, Heterosexuality and Power*. In this work, the authors, while using so-called qualitative research methods, embark on their field-work with a set of pre-established theoretical conjectures they set out to explore. The respondent's answers are then conceptualised or interpreted by reference to the author's theoretical framework. Finally, the authors offer a series of prescriptions as to how to solve the 'problems' they believe they have identified. Of crucial importance in this regard is that while the issues in question are deemed to arise from the data, the authors blueprints for change often transcend the data in question (Holland et al., 1998).

Ideological affiliations

It is important to state at the outset that in common with all social science inquiries—and their evaluation—I have certain ideological affiliations that have inevitably shaped the form and content of much of what is to follow. When it comes to the autonomy/paternalism debate generally, and specifically in relation to the focus of this book, my own view on the exercise of power, whether for paternalistic reasons or not, is parasitic both on C. Wright Mills' (1956) contention that a constitutive function of social theory is to criticise the workings of power and on Chomsky's (2009) formulation of hierarchical power relations. To wit, Chomsky states "power should always be questioned, it is not self-justifying: it carries a burden of proof" (2009:38). However, in relation to the subject matter of this book and without pre-empting what is to follow, I do not privilege in *a priori* fashion autonomy over paternalism or vice versa. In other words, this book is not another exercise in either 'parent', or more particularly, 'mother blaming' (Blum, 2007). Whether it involves a utilisation of the facilitated sex mechanism or not, for the parents of adults with intellectual disabilities, the autonomy/paternalism debate regarding increased sexual freedom for their sons and daughters is in many instances a paradigmatic case of being caught between the proverbial rock and a hard place.

Nonetheless, this book will also advance the normative argument that obstacles, be they legal or otherwise in nature, should not rob adults with intellectual disabilities of the opportunity of having genital sex—the justification for privileging this form of sexual interaction above all others will be explained in the following chapter—with others. Hence, the subject matter of the focus group, which all the mothers participated in, and which was designed to garner their views on the issue of facilitated sex. In addition, the penultimate chapter of this book will argue that liberal-minded parents—and all the mothers I spoke to characterised themselves as secular liberals—should subvert common-sense thinking and apply new rules of moral behaviour in their deployment of a new parental regime of care and at least consider the use of the facilitated sex mechanism to meeting this end.

This conclusion is in turn based on the premise that if secular liberals achieve praxis in relation to their stated ideological affinities, they are logically committed to agreeing with Singer when he states that "sex raises no unique moral issues at all...decisions about sex may involve considerations of honesty, concern for others, prudence, and so on, but there is nothing special about sex in this respect" (2005:5), and are 'obligated' to act accordingly. Hence, my contention that the facilitated sex option represents a genuinely liberal solution—taking the liberal understanding of sexual interaction to its logical conclusion—to the generic issues that constitute the autonomy/paternalism debate under investigation.

Conversely, if the sociological principle that one's views on the morality of sexual relationships is informed by one's ideological affinities is true, the preceding ideological qualification is necessary as it would be unrealistic for a secular liberal, with 'reason' on their side, to believe that the paternalistic regime of care adhered to, for example, by committed Catholic parents, is essentially credulous in nature and could be changed once they acquaint themselves with certain facts of the matter regarding the sexuality of their sons and daughters.

In addition, however, the argument for facilitated sex is also designed to address some of the very particular points made by the respondents. Of fundamental importance in this regard is that many of the adults with Down syndrome I spoke to do not consider other people with Down syndrome as objects of sexual desire, and thus would not entertain the notion of embarking on a sexual relationship with them. However, this is where a possible *Catch-22* situation arises. This refers to the following two findings, which as we shall see in future chapters, is also replicated in much of the relevant literature. Firstly, although all the parents I spoke to wanted their sons and daughters to enjoy a sexual relationship, they were adamant—to ensure a cognitive parity—that any partner would also have to have an intellectual disability, ideally somebody else with Down syndrome. Secondly, there is the fact that many people who do not have Down syndrome, even those who have some other form of intellectual impairment, do not find those with Down syndrome to be objects of sexual desire. Clearly, the use of the facilitated sex mechanism can act as an antidote to such *Catch-22* situations becoming institutionalised.

Fundamental to the argument that will be developed to ground such relativistic claims is the fact/value distinction. This is the proposition that you can't derive an 'ought' from an 'is', popularised by the Scottish philosopher David Hume in the 19th century, which has since become a basic tenet of meta-ethical thinking. This distinction is based on Hume's logically flawless insight that:

> ...in every system of morality, which I have hitherto met with I have always remarked, that the author proceeds for some time in the ordinary way of reasoning, and establishes the being of a God or makes observations concerning human affairs; when of a sudden I am surprised to find that, instead of the usual copulation of propositions, is and is not, I meet with no proposition that is not connected with an ought or an ought not.
>
> (1972:203)

If one assents to this conceptual distinction, the conclusion that follows is that no societal response logically follows from any given fact of the matter (Botros, 2006). Therefore, when the fact/value distinction is applied to the issues under investigation, the argument being advanced is that the fact that someone has an intellectual impairment like Down syndrome does not in and of itself logically lend itself to the formulation and/or implementation of a given social response. What happens in this respect is, arguably, decided ultimately by reference to a group's given ideological commitments and power to institutionalise their respective moral beliefs.

To sum up this reflexive section on my ideological affiliations, some words need to be said about my use of the personal pronoun throughout this book, the autobiographical material I will reveal, and by extension where I stand on the so-called 'insider-outsider' debates within sociology regarding the posited phenomenon that where the researcher is positioned or positions themselves in relation to this typology can affect how they carry out their research and the findings they arrive at.

To explain the relative absence of the autobiographical self in certain strands of sociological writing, Potts and Price state that "academic discourse in general isn't very good at acknowledging the materiality of its own production, the resources and labour that enables its existence" (1995:102). Although written more than twenty years ago, because there are, as explained above, different camps within sociology that privilege objectivity over subjectivity and vice versa, this conclusion still stands and will retain its status as a truism as long as sociology remains a heterogeneous discipline. Arguably, however, this stance has become somewhat inverted in relation to investigations into the subject matter of disability where it is becoming increasingly common for authors to locate themselves within their research and specify how this affects their position.

As readers will no doubt notice as they proceed, the personal pronoun has also been used extensively within this text. This decision to use 'I' as opposed to 'the author' and other such synonyms was taken for an array of reasons. Firstly, I had to ask myself what role having a sibling with Down syndrome play in this research? Due to this, I've spent more than thirty years socialising with other people with Down syndrome and their families. To my mind, the obvious answer to this question was that, in the phenomenological and observational sense, it made me more of an expert on the issue of the dilemmas facing such parents regarding whether, when, and how to privilege paternalism over autonomy or the other way around in relation to the sexual lives of their adult children with Down syndrome, than the 'usual suspects' already referred to. In addition, due to such experiential knowledge, and the fact that not only am I using the personal pronoun throughout but am adding aspects of my autobiographical self into the text, I also felt the need to situate myself in relation to the autobiographical reflexivity literature and address the 'insider/outsider' question therein—the following section will explore this process and set out the conclusions I have drawn. Secondly, and as already stated, I agree with the contention that "all research is ideological because no one can separate themselves from their world—from their values and opinions, from books they read, from the people they have spoken to and so on", and that the use of the personal pronoun makes this clearer than it might otherwise be (Letherby, 2003:5).

According to Etherington, researcher reflexivity refers to the "capacity of the researcher to acknowledge how their own experiences and contexts (which might be fluid and changing) inform the process and outcomes of inquiry" (2004:32). This issue of researcher reflexivity has become an increasingly significant theme in contemporary social research, and there is an ongoing debate about its meaning and value that transcends social science disciplinary boundaries, with some social researches wholly embracing the principle while others wholeheartedly reject it (Berg and Smith, 1998).

References to my own biographical story were employed with an intellectual objective in mind rather than a 'self-indulgent' end in itself (Bryman, 2008). In this fashion, my approach is parasitic on Behar's dictum that "the exposure of self who is also a spectator, has to take us somewhere we couldn't otherwise get…it has to be essential to the argument, not a decorative flourish, not exposure for its own sake" (1996:14). In effect, my use of biographical elements was to provide what I thought was necessary context and to substantiate some arguments made and conclusions I myself draw.

Gair states that

> the notion of insider/outsider status is understood to mean the degree to which a researcher is located either within or outside a group being researched, because of her or his common lived experience or status as a member of that group.
>
> (2012:137)

As with the tenets that underpin emancipatory research, the distinction between 'insider/outsider' statuses has its roots in a branch of feminist research and has now established itself as an article of faith amongst many proponents who adhere to the social model of disability. Regarding the former, it is deemed that women, by virtue of their gender, inhabit an 'insider' status when doing research with other women because they, unlike men, share a similar life-world that is somehow—usually unexplained in any coherent epistemological or ontological fashion—inaccessible to men.

As with most substantive conjectures in the social sciences this distinction, and the value of occupying either/or both positions, has been contested. For example, Serrent-Green states that "there appear to be as many arguments for outsider research as against, with the same issues able to be raised in support of outsider research, as against it" (Serrant-Green, 2002:38). In a similar vein Kanuha asserts:

> …for each of the ways that being an insider researcher enhances the depth and breadth of understanding a population that may not be accessible to a non-native scientist, questions about objectivity, reflexivity, and authenticity of a research project are raised because perhaps one knows too much or is too close to the project and may be too similar to those being studied.
>
> (2000:444)

Whilst Hammersley states:

> I do not believe that being an established participant in a situation provides access to valid knowledge that is not available to an outside researcher…There are no overwhelming advantages to being an insider or an outsider. Each position has advantages and disadvantages, though

these will take on slightly different weights depending on the particular circumstances and purposes of the research.

(1993:219)

However, in its weaker formulation, that is, the one that concerns me, the insider/outsider distinction is the conjecture that the researcher who shares relevant experiences with their respondents—in the sense that they concern the subject matter of the research—can be categorised as an 'insider': a classification, moreover, that may impact the research process in either a negative or positive manner. Hence, the purported need to be reflexive about one's position. Such scrutiny typically involves addressing such questions as "what is the appropriate relationship between the researcher and her or his research subjects"? And, "must the researcher be disinterested, dispassionate, and socially invisible to the subject?" (Harding, 2009:198).

As already explained, I have argued that my insider status not only helped me to access my research populations but also helped facilitate greater disclosure than if I was a complete outsider. Consequently, for now, I will concentrate on examining some of the main assertions regarding possible deleterious effects on the research process, and reflexively conclude whether I succumbed to such dangers. For example, Asselin (2003) has claimed that the 'insider/outsider' dual role can result in role confusion when the researcher responds to the participants or analyses the data from a perspective other than that of the more detached researcher. This is the assertion that due to the researcher's shared experiences with their respondents, close connections may be built up between the respective parties, which in turn may introduce an element of bias otherwise not present. In this context, researcher bias includes being "too close to the culture to be curious enough to raise provocative questions" (Merriam et al., 2001:411). In addition, however, insider research bias also refers "to the process whereby the researcher's personal beliefs, experiences, and values influence the study methodology, design, and/or results" (Greene, 2014:4). Hence, the author's warning that the insider researcher needs to "be wary of projecting one's own views onto participants or the data analysis" (Ibid.). Or as Aguilar puts it "subjective involvement [can act as a] deterrent to objective perception and analysis" (1981:15).

As an illustration of this danger, Jenkins states: "my role as an 'insider' meant I became emotionally connected to participants and concerned for their well-being", a state of affairs which he claimed "impacted on the methodological decisions I made throughout the study" (2013:378). He goes on to state that these relationships had become very important "as 'my story' and 'their story' had created a shared narrative in which both our lives had changed during the process of conducting the study" (Jenkins, 2013:380). Greene expresses similar sentiments when he states that "while I am always writing and reflecting on the process, it has proven difficult, largely as a result of my positioning as an intimate-insider, to gauge what level of involvement is 'enough' versus 'too much'" (2014:5).

In addition to such over-identification with one's respondents, there is another posited obstacle to producing 'authentic research' when occupying the insider role. This refers to a sense of alienation that may occur if the respondents do not validate your own experience of the allegedly emotionally fraught issues under investigation. To illustrate this point, Letherby and Zdrodowski explain how they "found that we feel a strong sense of identification with some of our respondents, whereas at other times we have found it difficult, if not impossible, to relate to their own personal definitions" (1995:586). This sense of cognitive dissonance was moreover not due "to differences of class, race, sexuality, and age… but to our different experiences of the research issue" (Ibid.). Letherby, in solo mode this time, ups the ante regarding the dangers of being a research insider when she states that with much of the research she has conducted, as well as feeling "empathy with my respondents I sometimes felt irritation or anger" (2003:111). In a similar fashion, Ramsay reports feeling similar negative emotions after interviewing somebody who did not share her worldview when she states: "when I left the office I was exhausted and unhappy about the interview. I had some good data but I colluded with a powerful man in recreating understandings about women sexuality and power" (Ramsay, 1996:138).

Because the notion of 'bias' regarding the factors that influence why we research the subject matter we do has already been dealt with, I will not repeat it here. However, with the aim of recognizing and acknowledging my own potential biases, specifically regarding the insider/outsider issue, let me explain my approach regarding the possible dangers outlined previously.

Firstly, I conceive of the distinction as that of a continuum rather than of binary opposites. I believed—and still do—that my insider status would solely play a role in facilitating access to both populations and in turn help gain greater disclosure than if this classification were absent. Regarding the issue of becoming overinvolved with my respondents and thus collapsing the insider/outsider distinction, I did not foresee this to be an issue, and as I write this in hindsight, I believe that this initial assumption has been vindicated. This intuition on my part was based on several factors. Firstly, I have been doing such research—albeit in a less systematic way—for most of my adult life. In other words, it has been a very rare occurrence in all my years of talking to people with Down syndrome and their families about issues that are of concern to them, that I have been asked, or have asked, my interlocutor to become 'my friend' based on a few hours conversing. Somebody with their own biases regarding how empathy works and human connections are formed, may say that I, and all those others, should therefore be deserving of some mental health classification, but I would beg to differ. In the social world I inhabit, which is similar to those I have talked to, both informally, and for more formal academic purposes, people are already leading busy lives and do not assume that informal conversations are a prelude to the formation of intimate friendships.

This does not mean that I did not identify and empathise with the respondent's various predicaments: I most certainly did. However, while such experiences are under-represented in academia, based on my experiential knowledge, most of the accounts I heard contained nothing factually new, as, I had already had first-hand experience of them previously. Nonetheless, even if this had not been the case, I find the notion that the insider experience will—again seemingly by definition—impact on methodological decisions or in some way taint the analysis of the findings puzzling from an epistemological perspective. Perhaps, this is because much of this debate refers to the more ethnographic aspects of qualitative research, where one is in the 'field' for extended periods of time, and grounded theory is typically the analytical framework being employed.

However, this is not the case with the empirical research carried out for this book. In fact, I would go further and state that such research is, à la the Holland et al. book already referred to, qualitative research by default. In other words, because the theoretical work this book engages in is just as important as the empirical findings it has produced, the use of semi-structured interviews and a focus group were conceived of as mechanisms to produce the quasi-Socratic type debates I deemed necessary to collect the quality of data I needed. To this end, my approach was to "consider 'hypotheses' rather than 'respondents' as the subject matter of research" (Pawson, 2000:41). Consequently, when it came to utilising my research samples to answer my research questions I conceived, as Pawson does, that "the research subject as an 'informant', passing judgement through their own eyes on the researcher's theory" (2000:42).

As an extension of this point, regarding the fear that insider status can result in 'alienation' from one's respondents if they as fellow insiders say something you do not agree with, and thus cannot 'relate' to, I have three responses. Firstly, such a reaction surely depends on how 'involved' a researcher is and how prejudiced they are—and particularly what forms their prejudices take. For instance, does their prejudice extend to the belief that there is an objective definition of something called *sensitive research* that demands that the researcher experience certain emotions or entertains certain thoughts or not (Rogers, 2003)? Regarding my own relevant prejudices, there are two to note. One of them is informed by the insight attributed to the ancient Roman playwright Terence to the effect that 'I am a human being; nothing human can be alien to me'. The other is Montaigne's assertion that 'there is no conversation more boring than the one where everybody agrees'. In other words, when conversing with friends or acquaintances, I do not judge them on their political views. Instead, I judge them on how they support or justify what they say. This same principle applies to the mind-set—this is mind-set in the singular, as unlike Reinharz (1997) and those who share her prejudices, I did not bring multiple selves, never mind 'twenty', to either the research interaction or the analysis of my findings—I adopted when conversing with the respondents who participated in this project.

Namely, I informed them that I did not care if what they said was 'politically incorrect' (or some such epithet) if what they were saying was an answer to a question I asked or bore some relationship to the research questions this book is trying to answer. Consequently, all things being equal, unlike many of the 'experts' cited previously, I do not need people to agree with me to empathise, understand, or 'relate' to them. Rather, as the focus group on the issue of facilitated sex hopefully demonstrates, such disagreement tends to pique my curiosity.

In addition, the fact that 'I do not have an emotional dog in this fight' regarding what my respondents say or whether theory X has more explanatory reach than theory Y has another consequence in relation to where I position myself in relation to my insider/outsider status. That is, as explained previously and throughout this book, while I have a normative concern with the fact that many adults with Down syndrome living in the parental home are leading celibate lives, I do not have a fixed *a priori* answer to the question as to whether their parents should privilege paternalism over more self-determination in the sexual realm or vice versa. The parents in question are grappling with important and infinitely perplexing moral dilemmas and I do not know what I would do in their situation. Moreover, if I find myself in this situation—which I will if my sister outlives our parents—I imagine I will remain in this Hamlet-like state. This same conclusion needless also extends to the issue of availing of facilitated sex but for different reasons. Namely—and this comes back to the recurring theme throughout this book regarding a conflict between the head and the heart on the part of the mothers—while I do believe, intellectually at least, that this mechanism should become part of a parental regime of care, I do not know that put in the position of being—to quote one of the mothers—my sister's 'pimp' (in terms of arranging who she has sex with, how much money is to be exchanged, and so on), I could achieve praxis where such intellectual convictions are concerned.

Finally, to sum up this chapter and to avoid any confusion in the reader's mind regarding the remit of this book, it is necessary to explicitly state that the general/particular distinction alluded to in relation to the argument for facilitated sex will be conceptually accounted for as necessary. In other words, while much of the analysis engaged in is grounded in the empirical data collected, its content is not exhausted by reference to the respondent's views. Rather, the scholarly obligation to engage with relevant literature that offers diametrically opposed views and arguments to those expressed by the respondents, but that are germane to a critical investigation of the autonomy/paternalism debate generally, is one which will also be met.

2 The autonomy/paternalism debate

Introduction

The autonomy/paternalism debate regarding the issue of increased sexual self-determination for intellectually disabled adults revolves around the question of rights, both positive and negative as well as legal and moral. The reason such a debate exists is based on the following proposition: namely that, because of the cognitive characteristics that constitute the intellectual disability classification, members of this population—regardless of age—cannot exercise the degree of self-determination that is considered normal for their non-intellectually disabled contemporaries. Consequently, the best of paternalistic reasons are invoked for denying them the right to control their sexuality—whether this is a legal right they possess or not. Therefore, to understand better the legal and moral landscape parents of intellectually disabled adults and their families must navigate when it comes to these issues, it is necessary to provide some detailed context regarding the nature of this rights debate, and explain why sexual expression for certain populations is deemed to be an autonomy/paternalism issue in the first place.

The autonomy/paternalism debate

Autonomy/paternalism debates revolve around the question as to whether it is ever justifiable for a state or a particular third party to paternalistically restrict the liberty of an individual or a class of individuals (Dworkin, 2005). According to Sneddon, "to act paternalistically is to do something for the good of another person but without, or even against, that person's will" (2013:119). It is paternalism, which for example, provides the logic for anti-drug legislation, enforced wearing of seat-belts, compulsory schooling, and so on (Feinberg, 1986). However, while certain paternalistic practices apply to everybody equally, the form of paternalism this book is investigating is the form of paternalism that discriminates between different groups of people based on their ontological status as a specific instance of a 'social kind'. The concept of a social kind refers to the fact that all contemporary liberal democracies taxonomize their populations into different kinds of people—child/adult, normal/abnormal, and so on (Hacking, 1999). How one is classified determines whether and how the paternalistic practices you are subjected to differ in degree and/or kind from those enjoying a different ontological status. For example, it is because many intellectually disabled adults (due to their cognitive impairment) are ascribed an inferior ontological status, which explains why they do not enjoy the legal right to control their own sexuality (Foley, 2012).

According to O'Neill, autonomous action "is the action of agents who can understand and choose what they do" (1984:173). This self-authorship form of individual liberty, where the autonomous individual in their guise as rational agents, gets to 'write the story of his or her life'—albeit within the structural parameters bestowed by society in its role as the eponymous 'editor'—is a foundational concept underpinning the structure of contemporary western liberal democracies (Mendus, 2000). One of the canonical explanations as to why this should be the case was offered by John Stuart Mill. In *On Liberty* (1859), Mill set out and defended his thesis "that each person is the best judge of his or her own happiness and that autonomous pursuit of goals is itself a major source of happiness" (O'Neill, 1984:173). Conversely, Mill argued that "happiness could seldom be maximised by action which thwarted or disregarded others' goals, or took over securing them" (Ibid.).

In liberal democracies, those deemed to be autonomous enjoy the legal rights to do what they want without third-party interference if what they want to do is not illegal. In legal terminology, and specifically in relation to the autonomy/paternalism issue under scrutiny, the autonomous individual is said to possess the legal capacity to control his or her sexuality (Murphy, 2003). This capacity is in turn defined by reference to the ability to engage in a rational process of means-end reasoning regarding both the ranking of one's beliefs and desires hierarchically, and the implementation of effective strategies to realise them (Christman, 2009). Hence, the nature of the legal rights' one possesses is based on how autonomous one is deemed to be. This state of affairs in turn explains the rationale behind the notion of legal capacity. The legal capacity concept is designed to balance the right to protection from harm and the right to freedom of decision-making (Murphy and O'Callaghan, 2004). This distinction corresponds to the important difference between social or positive rights and civil or negative rights. In relation to the sexual realm, civil rights legally empower the individual to act autonomously while social rights paternalistically protect from sexual exploitation those who are deemed to lack autonomy.

The dilemma in relation to the autonomy/paternalism debate regarding the sexual rights of intellectually disabled people is that it creates a conflict "between the ideological wish to facilitate appropriate sexual expression while also guarding against exploitation and abuse when cognitive impairment interferes with the ability to make informed decisions" (Dukes and McGuire, 2009:727). In other words, if the threshold for capacity/consent is set too high, it restricts, or in the worst-case scenario makes it illegal, for people with intellectual disabilities to control their own sexuality. Conversely, if the threshold is set too low, arguably it runs the risk of failing to adequately protect vulnerable individuals from being taken advantage of.

The 'if capacity allows' qualification regarding the specific focus on the rights of adults with Down syndrome to embark on, and/or not be prevented by a third party, from embarking on a sexual relationship is important. As already hinted at, this book is not arguing from a radical social constructionist perspective to the effect that an intellectual impairment such as Down syndrome is a discursive fiction whose ontological status is a linguistic invention that can be argued away. Rather, my perspective aligns with the conventional wisdom that states that meeting a cognitive threshold is a necessary condition to consent to a sexual relationship. However, given that all definitions of what constitutes capacity are both arbitrary and normative in nature, I, like the mothers I interviewed, would make a distinction between adults with Down syndrome having sex with other adults with Down syndrome in the context of a boyfriend/girlfriend relationship, and members of this population having sex with non-intellectually disabled adults in the context of a boyfriend/girlfriend relationship. In the former case I, again in common with the mothers I interviewed, believe that capacity should either be assumed or deemed not relevant. However, in a situation involving intellectually disabled adults having sexual relations with non-intellectually disabled adults, things are more complicated. In my view, the major complications of such a relationship are twofold. Firstly, the cognitive differential between the parties does constitute a difference that could lend itself to the non-intellectually disabled adult exploiting their partner in the sense that they are simply being used as means to the other's sexual gratification. Secondly, and again in concurrence with the conventional wisdom regarding such relationships, I hold the scholarly supported view (which may be deemed 'offensive' or some such epithet by some), which is also shared by all the mothers I spoke to, that most non-intellectually disabled adults would not, if they had the choice, choose to sexually interact with an adult with Down syndrome for non-nefarious ends (Millar, 2000; Green, 2008).

This suspicion of normalising boyfriend/girlfriend relationships between intellectually disabled adults and their non-intellectually disabled counterparts should not however be considered as a contradiction regarding my advocacy of parents availing of the facilitated sex mechanism for their intellectually disabled sons and daughters. While both involve adults without an intellectual disability having sex with adults who have an intellectual disability, this is where the similarities begin and end. The facilitated sex relationship is a professional one, and in addition, as I conceive of its use, would be deployed as part of the existing paternalistic regime of care. Given the existence of such checks and balances, the possibility of the professional in question, if they do not want to be charged with a criminal offence, abusing the intellectually disabled adult in any way is thus rendered very low.

To sum up where I stand regarding the issue of capacity as being the key for the opening of one's sexual autonomy, I take issue with both the legislation (such as that which currently pertains in some European countries and some American states) and the views I have heard expressed when socializing with many parents and siblings regarding the *a priori* assumption that adults with Down syndrome, do not, by definition of their impairment, possess such abilities. Furthermore, even if it can be 'demonstrated' that many adults with Down syndrome do not possess the requisite degree of capacity to meet what is ultimately an arbitrary legal measure, this does not in itself lead to the conclusion that in order to prevent exploitation taking place, all forms of sexual relationships must be denied them. This latter point will be developed in the penultimate chapter when I put forward the normative argument that regardless of cognitive capacity, the recourse to facilitated sex can/should become an integral component of the paternalistic regime of care adopted by liberal-minded parents towards their adult sons and daughters.

Whether the rights one possesses are negative or positive in nature, to be conferred with a legal right is *ipso facto* to possess an advantage over those who do not possess the same right. For example, what differentiates an appeal to one's legal rights from other moral discourses (such as some parents' perceived moral duty to institute a particular regime of care) is that the wrong committed when one's legal rights are violated is a wrong which can, in principle, be rectified by an appeal to the law (Freeman, 2011).

According to Sneddon, "autonomy is a threshold phenomenon", one in which "we go from not having it to having it on the basis of the level of development of certain capacities" (2013:12). For non-intellectually disabled individuals over the age of sexual consent, this cognitive threshold is more metaphorical than real in the sense that there is no formal test that one must pass to be deemed autonomous. Rather, autonomy is considered to be a by-product of reaching a certain age. However, this is not always the case for intellectually disabled adults. Instead, when it comes to many members of this population, the legal burden of proof is on them to prove they are autonomous and not the other way around (Johnson et al., 2010).

In addition to the question as to who enjoys what competing legal rights, in jurisprudence, the important distinction between legal rights and moral rights—which is central to the autonomy/paternalism debate as it relates to the subject matter of this book—is usually made. Legal rights are those that are enshrined and therefore enforceable in law. Moral rights, meanwhile, such as the belief on the part of a parent that they have a moral obligation to subject their adult son or daughter with Down syndrome to a paternalistic regime of care, denote moral claims that have yet to be legally institutionalised and are consequently not binding on the respective state or any given individual to recognise. Since the emergence of legal systems, enforceable laws have always been met with resistance in some quarters on the basis that a law is unjust by violating a more fundamental moral principle (Rainbolt, 2006).

Indeed, this is the normative stance taken by many disability activists—a population to which all the mothers who participated in this project belong. In addition, it is also a cornerstone of the social model of disability and the philosophy of normalisation/Social Role Valorisation (SRV). Both these approaches to conceptualising disability invoke the notion of moral rights to ground their claims that the current legal status quo, which discriminates between people with disabilities and those without, is unjust and should be overhauled accordingly (Cameron, 2014). A salient example of the all-too-frequent clash between legal and moral rights would be a situation where, although an intellectually disabled adult has both the desire and the legal right to engage in a sexual relationship, because their parents believe they have a moral right to paternalistically prevent such a relationship occurring, the possibility of said adult having such rights legally enforced in the face of such parental obstacles may be limited in the extreme (Foley, 2012).

Such a scenario becomes a distinct possibility in countries that have ratified the Convention on the Rights of Persons with Disabilities or CRPD. This legal document is seen by many disability scholars as a 'game changer' when it comes to furthering the rights of people with disability (Harpur, 2012). For instance, Richards et al state:

> there is a long history of sexual denial that requires immediate attention and it is the goal of the Convention on the Rights of Persons with Disabilities to assert that people with intellectual disabilities are equally worthy of the same rights that have been taken for granted by most others.
>
> (Richards et al., 2012:104)

From this international perspective, which does not require a cognitive threshold to be met for one to possess civil rights, adults with intellectual disabilities have the negative right to control their own sexuality. This granting of legal personhood or capacity provides adults with intellectual disability with a formal legal status that Quinn likens to a shield that "helps persons fend off decisions made against them or otherwise 'for' them by third parties" (2010:10).

Most noteworthy in this respect are Article 12 and Article 23 of the CRPD. The former states "that persons with disabilities have the right to recognition everywhere as persons before the law: persons with disabilities enjoy legal capacity on an equal basis with others in all aspects of life" (CRPD, 2006). This includes the need to respect the autonomy of people with disabilities on an "equal basis with others" (CRPD, 2006). According to Quinn, Article 12, in relation to securing increased autonomy for people with disability, "is the vehicle that enables us to complete the non-discrimination journey which protects people against the behaviour of third parties by giving voice back to people to direct their own lives" (2009:5). Article 23 meanwhile states: "State parties shall take effective and appropriate measures to eliminate discrimination against persons with disabilities in all matters relating to marriage, family, parenthood and relationships, on an equal basis with others" (CRPD, 2006).

However, to conclude this section, a note of caution should be introduced regarding the power of the CRPD to usher in a paradigm shift in the empowerment of people with intellectual disability as it relates to the specific focus of the autonomy/paternalism debate this book is concerned with. That is, the question of 'who knows best'—the adult with intellectual disability, their parents, or the state—and how to resolve any clash between moral and legal rights that may break out between these interested parties (Foley, 2012). This conclusion will be explored in further detail in the analysis chapters.

Historical and cultural discourses of sexuality

From the Foucauldian perspective, the concept of sexuality is of political interest as it is constructed within fields of power. This states that sexuality in its contemporary guise is entangled in a web of constitutive discursive forces, be they religious, moral, economic, familial, medical, or juridical in nature. According to Weeks, "amongst the most crucial forms of mediation are the categories, concepts and languages which organise social life, which tell us what is 'good' or 'bad', 'evil' or 'healthy', 'normal' or 'abnormal', 'appropriate' or 'inappropriate' behaviour" (1985:7). As a result of such normalising power, the sexuality concept has become the chief catalyst for the self and other policing we deploy regarding who can have sex and what kinds of sex they can have. This explains the rationale underpinning Foucault's call to those who feel oppressed by such injunctions to resist sexuality's hegemonic power to control thoughts and deeds by co-opting its meaning for their own ends. With this strategy in mind, the Foucauldian understanding of the sexuality concept is one that, while retaining the link with actual sexual practices, attempts to deconstruct the common-sense notion that human beings possess an essential sexual identity. An essential sexual identity in this context is predicated on the notion that sexuality essentially speaks its own truth in the sense that while one is born a heterosexual one is, in some form or another, forced to become a homosexual, that intellectually disabled people are asexual/sexually indiscriminate, and so on (Jackson and Scott, 2010). Such an account, in its extreme forms, has led some to believe that a social constructionist view of sexuality is committed to the conclusion that there are no innate sexual desires or drives. This is a strategy seemingly designed to undercut biological understandings of sexuality that have been appropriated by reactionary social forces to argue that because, for example, homosexual forms of sexual expression are not 'natural' they are therefore 'wrong'. While one can debate the usefulness of the rhetorical claim that a pre-discursive conception of sexual desire is a contradiction in terms, there are easier ways of deconstructing the 'because it's natural it's good' form of reasoning, namely by recourse to Hume's fact/value distinction explicated in the first chapter.

Consequently, a reductive social constructionist perspective will not be the interpretation this book is utilising to argue that increased sexual emancipation for adults with intellectual disabilities will constitute a form of social change which, if it ever comes to pass, will be conducive to the well-being of this population. Rather, the philosophical anthropology employed is one that conceives of human beings as simply another form of embodied animal. What follows from this is that we are neither demigods nor are we blank slates. Rather, we come into the social world predisposed to find certain experiences more pleasurable than others (Pinker, 2003). Hence, in the same way that it is a physiological fact that all things being equal, most human beings do not find the experience of getting sick a physically pleasurable sensation, all things being equal, it also seems to be a physiological fact that most men and women enjoy having their genitals stimulated by a sexual partner of their choice. Consequently, in common with much of Foucault's own work on sexuality, my application of social constructionist insights is concerned primarily with the use and abuse of sexuality as an instrument of social control; with who gets to say what people can and should do with each other in a sexual context; and what such actions say about the 'essential' you (Foucault, 1978).

The focus on genital sex explained

As outlined previously, I have a normative concern that many intellectually disabled living in the parental home are unwillingly leading celibate lives. Hence, my stipulative definition of sex as being synonymous with different forms of genital sex should be self-explanatory. In addition to this concern, the focus on genital forms of sexual interaction is crucial to exploring the autonomy/paternalism debate where the issue of sexual expression is concerned. Again, to invoke both my own experiential knowledge of the parent/adult with Down syndrome child relationship and the empirical evidence collected for this project, most such parents do not have a problem with their intellectually disabled adult sons and daughters having boyfriends/girlfriends and would no doubt be relieved of many of their worries about the nature of such relationships if genital contact was not an issue. Consequently, if their offspring, either consciously or unconsciously were 'queering' conventional notions of sexual expression and were sexually satisfied with just holding hands or some other form of non-genital contact, then the problem of the sexuality of adults with intellectual disabilities would not be much of a problem at all. However, because in contemporary liberal societies, the right to engage in genital sex is a marker of adulthood, and conversely for certain populations the issue of genital sex constitutes both a taboo and a social problem—one partly 'solved' by such institutional practices such as a legal age of sexual consent and so on—it is genital sex that is the focus of this book (Jackson and Scott, 2010). Obviously, this is not to deny that forms of sexual expression via the medium of sexual relationships do not by definition have to include genital contact, nor is it to ignore the role that self-masturbation can play in achieving sexual pleasure: It is simply to state that such practices are not the concern of this book. For similar reasons, the binary distinction between heterosexuality and homosexuality and the hegemonic status still enjoyed by hetero-normative notions of sexual expression will not be explored.

The dangerous discourse of sexual expression

If the historical record is anything to go by, the question of who can sexually interact with whom has always been, in some form or another, an autonomy/paternalism issue. Hence, it seems to be the case that from time immemorial, every human society has put in place rules regulating "the age, gender, legal, and kin relationships between sexual actors, as well as setting limits on the sites of behaviour and the connections between organs" (Gagnon and Simon, 1973:4). While a cross-cultural analysis of why such sexual ethics exist is beyond the scope of this book, due to my concern with the sexuality of intellectually disabled adults, a brief genealogy of the roots of such regulation, both legal and moral as they pertain to western societies, will be undertaken.

When analysing the West's suspicion of certain populations expressing themselves sexually and why the issue of sexuality in general exists within a moral and political battlefield, it is necessary to start with the power and influence exercised by the Christian religion. The Judeo-Christian tradition adopts a default view of what constitutes legitimate sexual expression. This is the stipulation that only procreational sex meets its moral strictures and that sexual gratification as an end-in-itself is deemed sinful (Genovesi, 1997). Working within the Foucauldian framework, a genealogical argument can be advanced that the dominant 'regime of truth' regulating who can have what kind of sex with whom, which has seen many intellectually disabled adults ascribed a subject position that constructs them as disembodied, desexualized legal subjects, is partly a result of this Judeo-Christian influence (McDonnell, 2007).

Somewhat ironically, given the Christian opposition to such policies, the other form of 'bio-power' that has had immense influence in the control and regulation of the sexuality of people with intellectual disability is that of the ideologies propounded by the eugenics movement (McDonnell, 2007). Bio-power is Foucault's oft used concept—first introduced in *The History of Sexuality Volume 1* (1978)—that denotes a state's use of productive power to manage the health of its population at large (Mills, 2008; Taylor, 2011). One manifestation of such power in action can be seen in the use of state power to contain and cure disease and define and manage so-called 'perverted' forms of sexual expression by normalising sexual practices and regulating who can engage in them (Foucault, 1978). In contradistinction to the Christian discourse, which conceived of people with intellectual disabilities as eternal children, the eugenics movement takes a diametrically opposite view of their sexuality. This is the belief that people with intellectual disabilities people are not only highly sexed, but in addition are essentially indiscriminate when it comes to the expression of their sexuality (Galvin, 2006). While the eugenics movement reached its apogee with Nazi Germany's systemic murder of thousands of intellectually disabled people, its advocates transcended the left/right political divide. In fact, the discrimination against anomalous forms of corporeality can, in the history of western culture, be traced back to the Greeks and their institutionalised practice of infanticide. To wit, it is important to note that both Plato and Aristotle—the founders of western philosophy—gave their imprimatur to such policies. For example, Hughes states that the latter, "preached abortion and argued that deformed children should not live" (2000:560).

The term 'eugenics', coined by Francis Galton, a cousin of Charles Darwin, did not come into existence until the 19th century. The philosophy itself is effectively an application of Darwin's insight regarding how the driving force behind his theory of evolution by natural selection is the notion of the 'survival of the fittest', where the teleology underpinning 'progress' is the elimination of the weak. Eugenics as a form of social Darwinism is predicted on the belief in the normal/abnormal distinction. It advocates that those who are deemed intellectually 'abnormal' or 'corporeally abject', such as people with intellectual disabilities, needed to be prevented from reproducing, for fear that to bring more of their 'kind' into the world would lead to a degeneration of the whole human race (Scheerenburger, 1983). Actually, the official nomenclature of the time used by enlightened liberals for people with intellectual disabilities like Down syndrome included labels such as 'imbecile'/'feeble-minded'/'idiot'/'mental defectives'/'retard' and so on (Scheerenburger, 1983). Unlike the practices engaged in by Nazi Germany, the relevant western democracies stopped short of the outright murder of people with intellectual disabilities. Rather, their favoured policy of choice to stop this population reproducing was that of forced sterilization. While such language would not be used today, in public at any rate, the logic behind the compulsory sterilisation of people with intellectual disabilities was powerfully captured in the eminent 'liberal' US Supreme Court Justice Oliver Wendell Holmes' infamous phrase justifying his imposition of such practices. Namely, that "three generations of imbeciles are enough" (Lombardo, 2010).

Liberal society and changing sexual mores

Because of the secularisation processes that western societies experienced during the twentieth century—and continue to experience—the stranglehold exercised by Judeo-Christian teaching regarding who can have sex and what kind of sex they can have has lost much of its grip, especially for those who self-identify as secular liberals (Jackson and Scott, 2010). While a basic tenet of Christian teaching is that sex is an inherently 'sinful' business, from the secular liberal perspective, this formulation is inverted (Genovesi, 1997). This secular liberal classification refers to those liberals who, if they are to be true to their chosen ideological affiliation, assent to the proposition that 'God is dead', subscribe to a secular or humanist ethical code, and who implicitly or explicitly employ John Stuart's Mill's anti-paternalistic 'principal of harm' criterion as a normative guide as to how one's sexual life should be led (Donner, 1991). It is a worldview predicated on the idea that sexual behaviour has no *intrinsic* meaning. Rather, it is simply another set of practices—raising no unique moral dilemmas—that human beings may choose to engage in, or not, as they see fit (Russell, 1929; Goldman, 1977). Consequently, with the twin constitutive concepts of God and sin jettisoned, and specifically in relation to the specific instance of the autonomy/paternalism debate under scrutiny, the primary question the secular liberal must concern themselves with answering is: if X is allowed to embark on a sexual relationship, will it harm them in some way?

The belief that certain forms of sexual expression, if engaged in by certain populations, can be harmful is one that unites both theists and secular liberals alike—hence the consensus regarding the need for a legal age of sexual consent. However, the ontological commitments and the reasoning employed to reach their respective conclusions differs dramatically between the two opposing ideological camps. From the secular liberal perspective, the possible harm caused by engaging in sexual relations is not to the soul but rather to the psychological well-being of vulnerable populations; that is, those who cannot or have yet to reach a certain degree of emotional/cognitive maturity. Thus, in relation to policing the boundaries that distinguish vulnerable populations from fully fledged autonomous adults the contention that "the modern child has become the focus of innumerable projects that purport to safeguard it from physical, sexual and moral danger" (Rose, 1989:121), can equally be applied to the surveillance many intellectually disabled adults are subjected to.

However, to conclude this section, it will suffice for the reader to be cognisant of the following two facts. Firstly, the age of consent is a paternalistic policy based on the notion that non-intellectually disabled teenagers, but who are below a given country's age of sexual consent, lack the autonomy to control their sexuality. Secondly, based on both the empirical research carried out for this book and the experiential knowledge I have acquired by virtue of having a sister with Down syndrome and as a result of thirty years socialising with other people with Down syndrome and their families, the consensus view amongst such parents, is that their adult children with Down syndrome, regardless of their age, do not, and cannot, possess either the emotional or cognitive maturity of the average non-intellectually disabled teenager.

The parental perspective

One of the most common themes in the literature in relation to mothering a child with disability concerns the negative—initially at any rate—thoughts and emotions experienced by the mother on hearing the news that their newborn son or daughter is impaired in some way (Read, 2001; Hodapp, 2002). Although there is no necessary connection between the nature and extent of such feelings and whether the impairment is physical or intellectual in nature, the widespread agreement in the literature reflects the common-sense assumption that there exists a positive correlation between the initial sense of disappointment and the severity of the impairment (Lloyd and Hastings, 2009; Hogan, 2012). The answer as to why this should be the case is again the obvious one. This is the fact that many parents have certain hopes and expectations regarding the kind of child they desire, and that all things being equal, this does not include having a child with impairments that are intrinsically disabling regardless of how society is organised. To illustrate this state of affairs, Rogers states that "in thinking about mothering and care, it is important to recognise that expectations (particularly in Western cultures) during pregnancy and beyond can be full of hopes and dreams for a child's future" (2013:132). She then goes on to make the crucial point that such hopes and dreams typically involve mothers seeing their children becoming more independent and autonomous (Rogers, 2013). However, as this book demonstrates, it is this expected trajectory from dependence to independence (in relation to that what is deemed typical for their non-intellectually disabled contemporaries) that much of the literature dealing specifically with intellectual disability constitutes a destination that members of this population can never arrive at. For instance, while most people have been subjected to parental paternalistic intervention as children, one of the defining features of adulthood is that while parents may retain the power to influence some of the decisions we make, they no longer in a legal sense have, or typically want, the right to make us do things we do not want to do (Feinberg, 1986). However, the transition to adulthood for individuals with an intellectual disability is a much more problematic affair (Cuskelly and Bryde, 2004; Rogers, 2009). While Rogers states that the onus is on parents to find the 'right' balance between supporting "liberation and autonomy to pursue an intimate and sexual life" while at the same time ensuring "protection from potentially harmful and potentially abusive events in their children's lives" (2009:206), much of the available evidence shows such parents privileging the precautionary principle over its correlative. For example, when it comes to parents of intellectually disabled children trying to manage the autonomy/paternalism dilemmas such relationships invariably throw up, it is typically the case that "dependency, obedience, and child-like behaviours" are promoted rather than "independence, self-direction, and the assumption of responsibility and greater autonomy" (Mill et al., 2009:196).

In relation to the subject matter under scrutiny, one of the defining features of adulthood for non-intellectually disabled adults in contemporary Western societies is the legal right to choose whether to embark on a sexual relationship (Feinberg, 1986). As we have already seen, this legal right, embodied in the concept of legal capacity, remains one that is denied to many adults with an intellectual disability. However, in addition to their inferior legal status, and as alluded to previously, many adults with an intellectual disability also have the extra obstacle of ongoing parental intervention into aspects of their lives, a phenomenon that is particularly acute when it comes to the regulation of their sexuality (Cunningham, 2006; Carr, 2008; Hamilton, 2009). For instance, research evidence has demonstrated that intellectually disabled adults have the same sexual needs as their non-intellectually disabled counterparts. Yet, studies continue to find that many parents view and treat their adult children with and without an intellectual disability in quite different ways when it comes to the area of sexual relationships (May and Simpson, 2003; Priestley, 2003; Valenti-Hein and Choinski, 2007). Many such parents, who otherwise encourage and try to facilitate their adult son or daughter with an intellectual disability to become more independent in most areas of their lives, greet the prospect of extending such freedoms to the sexual realm with alarm (May and Simpson, 2003; Priestley, 2003; Valenti-Hein and Choinski, 2007).

To illustrate this last point, both Carr (2000) and Docherty and Reid (2009) in their respective studies gauging the attitudes of parents of adults with Down syndrome towards their offspring's ability to exercise more autonomy over their lives, found a consensus among their respondents in relation to their felt need to adopt the role of gatekeepers toward their adult children's social/sexual lives. Moreover, this response seems to be the rule rather than the exception. In all the academic research this book has referenced that deals specifically with the nature of the lives led by adults with Down syndrome in the parental home, the recurring motif is this clash between the head and the heart on the part of the parents in question. This is a conflict over how they would in principle like to act and how in practice they do in fact act when it comes to answering the question as to where they should locate themselves on the empowerment/protection continuum in relation to the possibility of their adult son or daughter enjoying a non-celibate sexual life. While some of the parental attitudes cited differ in terms of the degree and forms of control they believe they must exercise over their adult children in this regard, the basic belief that they have a moral responsibility to play the gatekeeper role, at least in the initial stages of any putative sexual relationship, was unanimous.

Consequently, when it comes to the issue of sexual relations, many parents of intellectually disabled adults living in the parental home prioritise the perceived cognitive capacity of their adult son or daughter over that of their physical development. They conclude that embarking on a sexual relationship, which may constitute a possible danger to their son or daughter's emotional and/or physical well-being is an experience their adult children are not cognitively equipped to cope with, and consequently must be protected from (Griffiths, 2007; Evans et al., 2009). A key precept underpinning the paternalistic position adopted by such parents is articulated by McCarthy and Thompson when they state that when it comes to parents of adults with an intellectual disability "the only right that they are interested in is the right to protect their mentally handicapped son or daughter" (1997:120).

However, from a human rights perspective, as represented by social model thinking and the CRPD, "substitute or decision-making by proxy is never appropriate in decisions on consent to sexual relations, these are intrinsically individual matters as recognised in human rights law" (NDA, 2009:5). Thus, the danger is that when some parents privilege paternalism over autonomy for their intellectually disabled adult son or daughter, they run the risk of perpetuating a situation where, in guaranteeing the physical and emotional safety of their child, they inadvertently create a situation that leaves "the quality of their lives diminished, their aspirations unfulfilled and their human needs unmet"; a state of affairs where they effectively "become protected prisoners" (Caffrey, 2004:105).

Facilitated sex

According to Shildrick, facilitated sex "raises the question of how far is it justifiable to exclude certain people from the expression of their sexuality when the situation could be easily alleviated" (2007:57). Due to the work of many scholars, the topic of facilitated sex has effectively lost its taboo status within disability studies, at least where the sexual needs of adults with a physical disability are concerned. Furthermore, if the success of the 2012 Academy Award-nominated movie 'The Sessions' can be used as a barometer of changing societal attitudes towards this subject, it seems to be the case, at least amongst those individuals who self-identify as sexually liberal, that the logic justifying the physical disability/facilitated sex equation enjoys a widespread validity regarding both theory and praxis. For example, in relation to practices on the ground, Sanders reports that "men with physical and sensory impairments are a core group of clients that visit commercial female sex workers" (2007:439). Earle, in referring to how such practices are perceived, states that "for some disabled people, facilitated sex is qualitatively no different to other forms of assistance, such as help with washing, dressing and elimination needs" (2001:438).

However, the issue of facilitated sex has yet to gain anything like the same currency when the debate turns to how to best meet the sexual needs of adults with an intellectual disability (Appel, 2010). This is a state of affairs that vindicates the insight that in many instances the barriers to the sexual fulfilment of disabled people "do not reside in the impairments of the body but in the restrictions of our society" (Shakespeare et al., 1996:12). Regarding such restrictive structures, the previous reference to those who identify as sexually liberal is a necessary qualification to make, as not everybody—including those who believe that disabled people have the right to a sexual life—would condone the use of facilitated sex to that end. The primary rationale behind such objections is that if one accepts the proposition that facilitated sex is a mechanism that can be utilised to ensure that the sexual needs of people with disabilities are met, one is effectively condoning prostitution, thereby reproducing the exploitation of the men and women who provide such services (Di Nucci, 2011).

An example of this prohibitive stance is provided by Jeffreys, who states that "prostitution and 'facilitated sex' teach a depersonalised, objectifying form of sexuality to men with disabilities that requires that a woman suffers emotional and/or physical abuse" (2008:334). While such arguments in relation to people with disabilities—where the focus is nearly on adults with a physical disability—are sometimes prefaced by the 'speaking as a feminist' phrase, such attempts at sophistry are largely redundant as those who identify as feminists are equally divided on the rights and wrongs of prostitution (O'Connell-Davidson, 2002; Weitzer, 2009). As Sanders and Campbell explain the competing perspectives "fall broadly between the abolitionists who seek to eradicate prostitution and those that believe that selling sex can be a form of labour" (2007:2). To unpack this distinction, they state:

> the former contends that prostitution is always oppressive, perpetuating male patriarchal privilege and subjugating women to suffering and victimization, the latter have moved beyond the victim perspective arguing that abolitionism denies the agency that women have to make choices about entering the sex industry.
>
> (Ibid.)

As should be clear from my advocacy for the normalisation of the use of facilitated sex, my ideological position aligns with the view there is nothing *intrinsically* objectionable or exploitative in selling one's body for sex and thus believe that prostitution should be viewed as a perfectly legitimate form of labour. In addition, I agree with the argument advanced by Sanders (2005, 2007) and Nussbaum (1998) that unless one holds what they deem to be 'irrational' or 'prudish' attitudes towards sexuality and sexual interaction, the most relevant factor that explains why some prostitutes/sex workers are subjected to emotional and physical harm by their clients is that the practices they engage in are not legally protected. In effect, I concur with the standpoint that argues that prostitution/sex work "should be recognised as a legitimate form of labour and commercial service work one which requires survival strategies similar to conventional service work, and where regulation of the industry would offer sex workers legal, political and civil rights" (Liddiard, 2014:841). In other words, legalisation of such practices provides practitioners protection from exploitation they do not currently possess. That is, that they are not exploited over and above the 'exploitation' that from certain ideological perspectives is constitutive of being 'forced'— in the Marxist sense—to sell one's labour to do certain jobs one would not otherwise choose to do (Nussbaum, 1998).

This reference to Marx is particularly appropriate when discussing the debate around the legitimacy of facilitated sex as this issue is essentially another variation on the autonomy/paternalism debate. The 'abolitionist' camp is ultimately making a paternalistic argument that is, at some level, parasitic on the Marxist notion of false consciousness. For many of its critics, because this concept denies certain people privileged—obviously, the analyst levelling such charges is exempt from such indoctrination— access to their own reasons for action, it robs them of any agency in the process. In other words, they are arguing that those who 'choose' to adopt the prostitute subject position are acting in a way that is incompatible with their 'real interests' and should be prevented from doing so (Nussbaum, 1998). Conversely, when arguing the pros and cons regarding this issue, it is important to invoke Hume's fact/value distinction to restate the ethical truism that where normative issues are concerned, one simply cannot logically derive an 'ought' from an 'is'. Consequently, just as there is no objective right way to solve the autonomy/paternalism debate as it relates to the subject matter of this book, there is also no objective right way to resolve the question of whether prostitution/facilitated sex is a legitimate social practice to engage in and that should enjoy the full protection of the law (Schroeder, 2010). Rather, they constitute a case of the opposing camps playing incommensurable language games with the effect that where one stands is determined by one's ideological commitments—or indeed ignorance of other ideological views—as opposed to an appeal to reason *qua* reason (Mackie, 1977).

To sum up this section it is important to note, as alluded to above, that most of the literature, both for and against facilitated sex for people with disabilities, examines it in relation to the sexual rights of men with a physical disability. Consequently, regarding the emotional/physical harm to the sex worker argument, it is apposite to restate points previously made. Firstly, the facilitated sex relationship is a professional one. Secondly, if utilised at all by parents, it would be deployed as part of the existing paternalistic regime of care with all that entails regarding a system of checks and balances in place. Therefore, there is virtually no possibility of the adult with Down syndrome (a population that, let us remind ourselves, is renowned for its malleability in the face of third-party pressures) abusing the sex worker they are interacting with in any way. While the same 'guarantee' cannot be offered regarding other intellectual impairments, because such an arrangement would entail intensive parental involvement, the argument that such practices limit the possibility of 'client' abuse in a way that is not possible when one is speaking about men with a physical disability acting autonomously still stands.

Conceptualising disability

In the preceding sections, reference has been made to the social model of disability and the philosophy of normalisation/SRV as approaches to conceptualising disability that have helped to usher in a new rights based discourse regarding how to close the gap between the lives that many disabled people are living and the lives that they and/or their family members want them to live. Thus, at this stage, it is appropriate to look in more detail at these frameworks to examine where they stand, either implicitly or explicitly, in relation to the autonomy/paternalism debate as it pertains to the subject matter of this book.

According to Harpur, the social model of disability "was formed as a radical Marxist model that identifies capitalism as a major cause of the oppression of persons with disabilities" (2012:326). He goes on to state that a key tenet of social model thinking is that people with disabilities "will never be free of their oppression until capitalism is replaced with a more humane system" (Ibid.). By extension, from the social model understanding, many of the problems facing disabled people is due to the dominance of the medical model or 'personal tragedy' model of understanding disability (Oliver and Barnes, 2012). In the eyes of its social model critics, one of the dangers in adhering to a medical model view of disability is that it reduces people who are so labelled to their medical classifications, thereby tacitly supporting the negative exclusionary consequences that typically follow when an individual's identity is defined in such a one-dimensional fashion. According to Hughes (2000), such medical labels act as "powerful cultural distinctions which promote and reinforce social hierarchies and sort people into the bare 'essentials' of identity", a social/ideological process that in turn reinforces the widely-held view that disabled people are different in kind—paradigmatic instances of alterity—rather than different in degree from their non-disabled counterparts (Hughes:558). Similarly, Humphrey (2000) has argued that in its focus on the disabled individual, the medical model has effectively "erased the experiences of disabled people from the medical map" (2000:65). Apropos such disputable exclusionary practices, Lang also makes the factual claim that it is the medical model that has the power to determine whether people with disabilities are provided with help from the state in the form of benefits and access to other material resources. To wit, he states

> the medical profession still has a great deal of influence in the manner in which disabled people live, invariably being seconded by agencies of the state to make assessment of their needs and abilities, often in areas which have little to do with the application of medical science.
>
> (Lang, 2001:14–15)

However, for the purposes of this book it is the charge by McRuer and Wilkinson regarding the medical model's creation of a state of affairs where "disabled people are infantilised, constructed as helpless and viewed as asexual" which is of most relevance (McRuer and Wilkerson, 2003:10).

The medical model is considered individualistic/tragic because it propagates the notions that it is 'tragic' for one to have a disability—defined as a "defect or a failure of a bodily system that is inherently abnormal and pathological"– in the first place (Goodley, 2011:7). Also, and most contentiously for its social model critics, the medical model assumes both that disability exists regardless of whether it has been diagnosed, and that it can be intrinsically disabling regardless of how society is structured (Williams, 2001). This question regarding the ontological status of the classification that is Down syndrome and whether it is intrinsically disabling will be discussed in more detail in the following chapters.

From the social model perspective, by reducing all explanations of disability to the physical workings of the body, the medical model provides a reductive and depoliticized answer to the question as to how society should cope with difference. In effect, it allegedly propagates the potentially reactionary theme that 'biology is destiny'. A discourse that is said to absolve society of its role in the disabling process (Barnes, 2012). Accordingly, Davis has argued that: "when we think of bodies in a society where the concept of the norm is operative then people with disabilities will be thought of as deviants" (1995:290). In other words, and as the eugenics movement proved, the medical model can be used to give a degree of scientific legitimacy to the ideological construction of people with disability as the despised 'other'. Regarding the notion of what constitutes physical and mental normality, the social model perspective utilises a social constructionist understanding. This entails that definitions of normality not only change over time and culture, but are also normative constructions rather than value-free discoveries (Oliver and Barnes, 2012).

As already briefly mentioned, one of the primary objectives of the social model is to radically change the current asymmetrical power relations that pertain between disabled and non-disabled people. This involves a paradigm shift in both thought and deed designed to change the perception and treatment of people with disabilities from 'objects' of charity, medical treatment and social protection to 'subjects' with rights who are in control of their own destinies. Consequently, the social model sees all discrimination against disabled people as wrong even if the justification for such differential treatment is paternalistic in nature. For example, Oliver and Barnes state:

> ...there are numerous texts advising on how to empower and conferences where the powerful talk endlessly about how to empower the disempowered. The contradiction in all this is that empowerment is only something that people can do for themselves because, ultimately, deciding to empower someone else, whether they want it or not, is the most disempowering thing that can be done to them.
>
> (1998:10)

Similar sentiments are expressed by Morris, who asserts that

> people who are said to need caring for are assumed to be unable to exert choice and control. One cannot, therefore, have care and empowerment, for it is the ideology and the practice of caring which has led to the perception of disabled people as powerless.
>
> (Morris, 1997:54)

As these statements make clear, the social model of disability is fiercely anti-paternalistic—nominally at any rate. This is a necessary qualification to make as whilst the social model has its conceptual roots in Marxist theory (which means it should not adopt a principled anti-paternalistic stance) it frequently fails to respect the rights of people with disabilities who do not subscribe to its normative agenda.

In relation to autonomy/paternalism issues, the social model always argues for an equalisation of the legal rights enjoyed by disabled and non-disabled people. For example, from the social model perspective, the legislation that denies many intellectually disabled adults the civil rights to control their sexuality would be classified as a form of social exclusion that should be challenged and changed accordingly. In its attempt to further such societal changes, the social model "is a deliberate attempt to shift attention away from the functional limitations of individuals with impairments onto the problems causing disabling environments, barriers and cultures" (Barnes, 2012:18). From this perspective, the individual and collective disadvantage endured by disabled people is due to a complex form of individual and institutional discrimination, termed 'disablism', as fundamental to our society as sexism, racism, or homophobia. A corollary of the claim that it is a disablist society that disables certain forms of difference is the social model's insistence on "separating out 'impairment' (that is, the functional limitations of our bodies and minds) from 'disability'" (Morris, 2001:2). Regarding the impairment/disability distinction, the argument advanced by social model theorists is that while impairment—defined as a "form of biological, cognitive, sensory or psychological difference"—may be a human constant 'disability' is not (Goodley, 2011:8). Thus, the conclusion reached is that disability is not an intrinsic feature of a given individual's difference, but is rather "centrally structured by social oppression, inequality and exclusion" (Thomas, 2004:570).

While the social model has been the dominant paradigm in researching and understanding disability in recent years—especially in British academic circles—it continues to be subject to an array of criticisms. In relation to the facet of the autonomy/paternalism debate under investigation, one of the most important of these is the charge that it has refused to systematically engage with the issue of intellectual impairment. For instance, Walmsley states that "people who write about the social model do not always consider impairments which are located in the brain rather than the body" (2005:726).

The danger of this failure on the part of social model proponents to engage with the issue of impairments located in the brain is noted by Shakespeare. He argues that in its failure "to include the social and cultural dimensions of embodiment" (Shakespeare, 2004:17) it paradoxically concedes that when it comes to understanding the nature of such intellectual impairments the medical model has the last word on the subject. As an attempt to ward off this threat, Shakespeare and Watson argue for an "embodied ontology" of disability or a "materialist ontology of embodiment" (2001:9–10). At the heart of this critique is the claim that the clear distinction between impairment and disability is no longer sustainable. Rather, Shakespeare and Watson state the reality of the situation is that "people are disabled both by social barriers and by their bodies" (2001:17). In relation to this debate over the ontological status of the impairment/disability distinction, I agree with the conclusion reached by Shakespeare and Watson that "impairment and disability are not dichotomous, but describe different places on a continuum" (2001:22). As I understand it, the idea that to privilege one over the other automatically has negative consequences for a population with impairments involves a wholesale collapse of Hume's fact/value distinction. For example, the fact that people with Down syndrome have a cognitive impairment in no way determines how they should be viewed and treated when it comes to the issues this book is concerned with. By extension, I also agree with Wasserman when he claims that "the understandings of impairments as sources of functional limitations is fully compatible with the recognition of impairment as stigma and with the endorsement of environmental reconstruction and social reform as the primary responses to disability" (2001:222). With these insights in mind, my conclusion, and as the data will demonstrate, this is shared with all the mothers I spoke to, is that Down syndrome constitutes both a real functional limitation that objectively limits the subject positions that people with Down syndrome can occupy and a social signifier that can induce certain negative social responses on the part of a given third-party.

Finally, there are also problems, which will be explored in more detail later in this chapter, regarding where the social model nominally stands in relation to the rights debate, its sometimes-brutal condemnation of disabled people who refuse to follow its normative agenda, and its approach to the issue that is at the heart of this book: the contention that people with intellectual disabilities sometimes need third parties to 'care' for them, a practice that may, in some situations—such as that of limiting their freedom in the sexual realm—reduce their autonomy in the process.

Normalisation/SRV

In common with the social model of disability, the philosophy of normalisation and its later mutation into Social Role Valorisation (SRV)—the two terms will be used interchangeably throughout this book—is a normative theory designed to change the negative perceptions and treatment of people with disabilities. Unlike the social model however, the populations that are the object of its concern are solely those subsumed under the intellectual disability umbrella term. With its emphasis on valued and de-valued social roles, and the power of such labels to determine first and third-party definitions of those thus labelled, the theoretical foundations of normalisation/SRV are rooted in the deviance or labelling school of sociology (Flynn and Lemay, 1999).

Normalisation/SRV is not a static theory. For example, two of its key theorists, Bengt Nirje and Wolf Wolfensberger, differ as to what its key tenets should be. However, all its various formulations assent to the proposition that the needs of intellectually disabled people are "basically the same as those of ordinary people, with the difference that they may not be able to meet these needs unaided or as independently as other people can" (Ryan and Thomas, 1987:129).

The chief premise informing normalisation/SRV is that people with intellectual disabilities constitute an oppressed and marginalised social group occupying some of the most devalued roles in contemporary western societies. The conclusion reached by its proponents is that the primary way of changing such negative perceptions and the discriminatory practices that follow is to ensure that mechanisms, such as legal rights, which will allow people with intellectual disabilities to occupy socially valued roles are put in place. To this end, normalisation/SRV has "provided the ideological backbone for anti-institutionalisation and for the campaigning mission of families and professionals working for the inclusion of people with intellectual difficulties in the mainstream" (Shakespeare, 2004:10). In the minds of its advocates, normalisation/SRV offers people with intellectual disabilities the opportunity to be given valued social roles in an unequal society that values some such roles more than others. As with the social model, the legal ramifications of this commitment to equality is the principled view that people with intellectual disabilities are entitled to the same rights, including the right to express their sexuality in whatever manner they choose, as those enjoyed by the non-disabled segment of the population. However, unlike the social model and its unconditional advocacy for equal civil rights for disabled people, normalisation/SRV adds the proviso that the intellectually disabled person should have the right to direct their own life in as much as that is possible, depending on the nature of the cognitive impairment they have (Wolfensberger, 2002).

Since its inception, the philosophy of normalisation/SRV has been subjected to an array of criticisms. For the purposes of this book, one of the most important of these is the social model charge that because it sometimes argues in favour of paternalism, it fails to respect individual freedom and consequently reproduces the power imbalance between non-intellectually disabled third parties—including family members—and people with intellectual disabilities (Race et al., 2005). As such attacks make clear, the social model attack on caregiving is not exclusively limited to the institutions of the state. Rather because social model proponents "view care as a category that pathologises those who are defined as its recipients" and characterises "non-disabled parents of disabled children as part of the problem" (McLaughlin, 2006:2), it also includes the subject matter of this book, namely informal family care. In the eyes of some, such familial practices constitute a "variant of 'community care'" which "by no means guarantees greater independence and autonomy for disabled people" (Thomas, 2007:97).

The notion that parents of children with disabilities can be part of the 'problem', once both the problem and one's ideological affiliations are clearly stated, is obviously at the heart of the autonomy/paternalism debate as it concerns the increased sexual autonomy of intellectually disabled adults. However, the conclusions reached by such social model advocates do raise the question that if an impairment is suitably severe to restrict an individual's autonomy, in some, or all aspects of their lives, then who should care for those whose intellectual impairments are intrinsically disempowering. For example, and perhaps this can be explained by its penchant for implicitly privileging the plight of those with a physical disability, there is virtually no debate about such issues in the social model literature. As a result, there are no coherent answers to the proposition that while "the home may not always be 'a haven in a heartless world'...for the very vulnerable, connections with family members are often the only shield against the slings and arrows of an uncaring society" (Kittay, 2001:571).

As already indicated, it should also be noted that from a conceptual perspective this *a priori* privileging of individual choice over third-party influence on the part of the social model is philosophically confusing. For example, as already explained, the social model utilises Marxist insights to explain why people with disabilities face the obstacles they do (Harpur, 2012). However, all versions of Marxism take issue with the *laissez-faire* view of freedom which states that one is free in so far as one can do what one wants. This explains the Marxist focus on the value of positive rights/paternalistic state practices. For the Marxist, freedom is much more than simply being allowed to follow one's caprice. Consequently, all branches of Marxism question why we have the preferences we have and why we want the things we want. Such scrutiny is predicated on the belief that the capitalist system colonizes our consciousness to such an extent that it fools us into thinking—via the process of false consciousness—that our 'choices' are 'freely chosen' rather than the product of systemic conditioning (Gray, 1991; Boucher, 2012). Yet, the paradox is that when social model theorising is applied to critiquing normalisation/SRV and/or paternalistic intervention into the lives of people with disabilities generally, one of the main tenets of Marxist thought—the notion of false consciousness—is often simply ignored.

Another related and equally relevant criticism of normalisation/SRV—as it challenges one of the key empirical findings this project has produced—is that it is intent on changing people with intellectual disabilities to make them more like 'normal' people. This is the contention that "the assimilationist aspect of normalisation/SRV is at odds with the type of empowerment strategy used by other devalued groups (ethnic minorities, women, people with disabilities, gay) who have instead glorified their differences and openly congregated" (Culham and Nind, 2003:71). Campbell makes similar claims when she argues that the problem with normalisation/SRV is that they reproduce the politics of ableism (2009, 2012). She states: "a chief feature of an ableist viewpoint is a belief that impairment (irrespective of 'type') is inherently negative which should, if the opportunity presents itself, be ameliorated, cured or indeed eliminated" (Campbell, 2008:253). The claimed effect of such discourses in shaping the thinking of disabled people is the creation of a state of 'internalised ableism'. This refers to the phenomenon where "to emulate the norm, the individual with disability is required to embrace, indeed to assume, an 'identity' other than one's own" (Campbell, 2009:21).

To sum up this section, however, I want to return in a little more detail to two of the main social model critiques against a medical model understanding of disability and offer some suggestions as to how to clarify the somewhat muddy nature of the ongoing debate. Firstly, the criticism made by some social model proponents that medical classifications are constitutively disempowering is one I find contentious. In my view, the truth of the matter does not lend itself to such a simplistic dichotomous condemnation. Rather, the reality of the situation is a somewhat more complicated affair. This is to say that sometimes medical classifications are intrinsically disempowering and sometimes they are not. Given the logical structure of such statements, their epistemological status must be established empirically and not in an *a priori* fashion. For example, and again this specifically relates to people with Down syndrome, my argument is that even in the absence of any such official medical classifications, people with Down syndrome would be discriminated against solely on their basis of their physical appearance and their relative cognitive limitations. At face value, because this is society doing the disabling, this conclusion is in line with social model thinking. However, the crucial distinction between my views on certain forms of discrimination against people with intellectual disabilities is that I hold a wider view of what constitutes such discrimination, and am less optimistic that it can ever be overcome. To make explicit in what was implied in my critique of social model attacks on normalisation/SRV, my definition of discrimination against people with an intellectual disability like Down syndrome includes the reluctance on the part of non-intellectually disabled people to have their contemporaries with Down syndrome as best friends and sexual partners. However, regardless of whether one accepts this wider definition as to what constitutes discrimination or not, the point remains that the discrimination (as conventionally understood) and disempowerment that people with Down syndrome face cannot be explained solely by reference to institutionally sanctioned medical classifications in tandem with socio-economic factors. Rather, one needs to also invoke cultural and psychic factors to explain why many people—disabled or otherwise—sometimes respond to people with Down syndrome in a negative fashion. Conversely, where socio-economic factors are concerned, the social model criticism that it is medical definitions that determine who gets what, if any, state benefit obviously raises the question as to what alternative criteria should be used when it comes to the distribution of such resources. Social model theorists are conspicuous by their absence in answering such questions. One may not like it, but Rothman (2010) states a political truism when she tells us that in order "to access needed resources and services, the individual, medical model is a social necessity" (2010:195). Why this is the case should be self-evident to anybody with even a cursory knowledge of the workings of capitalistic western liberal democracies. But to explicate the obvious, when there is conflict, as there is in most such societies, among the populace as to who gets what state benefit, eligibility therefore "necessitates some form of criteria, some gatekeeping function, which preserves the resources for those who have a legitimate claim to them" (Rothman, 2010:195–96).

While I do agree with another of the criticisms levelled by the social model against the medical model—that it justifies the asymmetrical power relations between professionals and people with disabilities—I think its importance is overstated, at least in relation to my own experiential knowledge of how my sister with Down syndrome has being treated by medical/health professionals. For example, my sister (who gave me permission to reveal this information) is sterilized. This decision—not an easy one to arrive at—was the result of a series of discussions that took place between my mother, my sister, and my sister's doctor. Both family members informed me that at no time during these consultations did the doctor act in a patronising, disempowering manner. Rather, the pros and cons of being sterilized, in addition to the use of other less 'extreme' forms of contraception, were gone into in a detailed fashion. This involved the doctor constantly pausing to check whether my sister understood what was being said, seeking her views on the issues, and so on. The final advice given by the doctor to my sister was that she had to think about this by herself—while discussing it with significant others—and that she had to make up her own mind on the issue. While I cannot generalise from my sister's experience to the population of people with Down syndrome as a whole, thereby falling prey to a mode of reasoning too often employed by social model advocates, I can report that such encounters are in no way unusual within the social milieu that I inhabit. Clearly, such meetings in and of themselves refute the absolutist charge that medical model practitioners devalue, as a matter of course, the sexuality of people with intellectual disabilities or do not take the social context of people with intellectual disabilities into account.

I hold a similar view regarding the charge that the medical model wants to fix the individual rather than society. The propositional content of such claims is invariably context-dependent and should be evaluated as such.

In effect, they depend on what the impairment is, and what the individual with the impairment wants. For example, my sister has seen a speech and language therapist since she was young. While the initial decision for her to do so was made by my mother, when my sister turned 18, the decision whether to continue seeing this 'expert' was put in her hands. She made the decision to continue to see the speech and language therapist because she wanted to improve her communicative abilities—albeit defined by reference to a contingent norm regarding appropriate modes of communication. Her decision in this regard is to my mind analogous to the decisions I have made to take advantage of the numerous course offered by the Universities I have taught at designed to help lecturers improve their lecturing skills—albeit defined by reference to a contingent norm regarding appropriate modes of communication. Therefore, I agree with the medical model that sometimes people with disabilities—in common with their non-disabled contemporaries—need the support offered by members of the professional classes. The one proviso to be made is that such decisions—once the requisite degree of autonomy is present—are to be left in the hands of people with disabilities themselves.

This stipulation brings us to one of the major contradictions that inform social model thinking: namely, the imperative to empower disabled people to take control of their lives while also implying they are cultural dupes when the decisions they make adhere to a so-called normalisation agenda. This sloppy thinking is one which too often seems to characterise this whole debate. Arguably, a more logical approach to adopt when discussing the medical model is to make a distinction between the theories underpinning its claims, which allow it to situate itself as a body of objective scientific knowledge, and the practices carried out by the members of the medical and its allied professions. However, this is very rarely done. Consequently, it is in many cases uncertain as to what the 'medical model' label actually refers to. Is it a set of codified propositions that determines what medical and health professionals say and do to disabled people or is to be seen as an umbrella term referring to a general mind-set shared by many non-disabled people?

If it is the former, I would suggest several steps should be followed. Firstly, the epistemological status of a specific medical claim needs to be examined in isolation to establish its propositional content, if any. Secondly, we need to be mindful of employing umbrella terms such as the 'medical model' in the first place. In effect, a disciplinary distinction needs to be made between the sciences that form the basis of the claim under question. For example, the claim predicated on the biological sciences that people with Down syndrome cannot process information and/or think in the abstract fashion that is considered 'normal' for their non-disabled counter-parts seems to me to enjoy a greater epistemological status than psychologically informed claims that an inability for an adult to demonstrate that they can give 'informed consent' to enter a sexual relationship means that they should be prevented from doing so. In short, the first claim maintains the fact/value distinction, while the second collapses it. Apropos of not conflating descriptive and normative claims, a distinction also needs to be made regarding scientific claims made about people with Down syndrome and what governments, disability service providers, and indeed society at large does with such information. Alternatively, if the 'medical model' term is being used to refer to a mind-set, and if the cash value of such a mind-set is that non-disabled people, either individually or in terms of public policy, have no responsibility to change either their negative attitudes/policies towards people with disabilities, then clearly the social model approach is offering a body of necessary normative truths. Society does indeed need to change its attitudes and practices towards people with disabilities and stop contributing to their disablement.

My conceptual framework

As briefly touched on in the introduction chapter, the conceptual frameworks I have chosen to interpret and contextualise the responses provided by the respondents will draw on Michel Foucault's productive conception of power (1977, 1978), the concept of abjection developed by the psychoanalyst Julia Kristeva (1982) and the theory advanced by the Disability Studies scholar Margrit Shildrick (2007, 2009) that anomalous forms of embodiment, such as those inhabited by people with Down syndrome, sometimes become figures of abjection for a given third party—including siblings and parents of people with Down syndrome.

The Foucauldian framework

Essential to the Foucauldian aspect of the analysis I will be deploying is Foucault's claim that the social subject is a discursive construction. This is to say that subjectification or our sense of who we are occurs through discourse. Within this framework, discourse refers to a structured or rule governed way of talking—even to one's self—about a given subject that determines which statements are accepted as meaningful and 'true' in a particular historical epoch. While this notion of a set of unwritten rules dictating what can and cannot be thought or said does include strategic subjects cognisant of how the social game is played and who think and act accordingly, it is not exhausted by such a definition. Rather, it also denotes the power of social forces to produce the conventional wisdom lenses through which we view the world while working at a subterranean or precognitive level. The reason why the word true in this paragraph is in inverted commas brings us to Foucault's insistence that power and knowledge are inextricably entangled. Thus, he states:

> Truth is a thing of this world: it is produced only by virtue of multiple forms of constraint. And it induces regular effects of power. Each society

has its régime of truth, its 'general politics' of truth: that is, the types of discourse which it accepts and makes function as true; the mechanisms and instances which enable one to distinguish true and false statements, the means by which each is sanctioned, the techniques and procedures accorded value in the acquisition of truth; the status of those who are charged with saying what counts as true.

(Foucault, 1980:131)

In substantive terms, this statement proffers that "regimes of power define what counts as a meaningful utterance, what topics are to be investigated, how facts are to be produced, and the like" (Bevir, 1999:66). Equally, however, because all regimes of power are constituted by discursive formations, it also follows that "regimes of knowledge define who does and who does not have the intellectual authority to decide issues, how information should be gathered about who and by who, and the like" (Ibid.). In one of his many formulations in which he repeats this same point, Foucault himself states that "power produces knowledge", that "power and knowledge directly imply one another", and that consequently, "there is no power relationship without the correlative constitution of a field of knowledge, nor any knowledge that does not presuppose and constitute at the same time power relations" (Foucault, 1977:27). While there are many ramifications to such audacious ontological commitments, for my purposes there are two that are especially noteworthy. Firstly, the nature of such an incestuous relationship entails that what we sometimes blithely take to be self-evidently true may not truly deserve such an elevated epistemological status. Secondly, this power/knowledge connection also means that what passes as the conventional wisdom—which is parasitic on what is unsayable and unthinkable—on a given issue, such as the rights of people with intellectual disability to express their sexuality, is the result of a power struggle (which need not be contemporaneous) between competing social forces. Another example of such processes in action is noted by Mills when she observes "that what is studied in schools and universities" did not fall from the sky but is very often "the result of struggles over whose version of events is sanctioned" (2008:21). In short, and if not taken too literally, Foucault's contention regarding the role played by power, particularly in its disparate institutional forms, in the production and regulation of socially sanctioned knowledge, can usefully be conceptualised as a variation on the 'history is written by the victors' principle regarding why our beliefs and desires take their current form.

Accordingly, within the Foucauldian framework, it is discourse, via its vehicle of the power/knowledge nexus, which explains "how the knowledge which a particular discourse produces connects with power, regulates conduct, makes up or constructs identities and subjectivities, and defines the way certain things are represented, thought about, practised or studied" (Hall, 1997:6). To this end, and as foreshadowed in the introductory chapter, to explicate the parent/adult child with Down syndrome relationship regarding the issue of increased sexual self-determination the notion of 'panoptic power' as developed by Foucault in *Discipline and Punish* (1977) will form a crucial component of the analysis.

Much of Foucault's work on the inter-related themes of discourse, the construction of subject positions, and the power/knowledge nexus is given over to an interrogation of the classificatory schemes contemporary societies employ to put people into manageable boxes based on where they are aligned on the normal/abnormal continuum. These categorisations, which work through rules of inclusion and exclusion, are then arranged hierarchically when it comes to the distribution and rationing of the goods, such as formal legal rights and sexual citizenship status, that societies have to offer (Dews, 1987). To illustrate such binary mechanisms at play, Horowitz explains how our assent to one subject position is always at the expense of another in the sense that "any definition of self immediately posits nonself, the other of the self, which is excluded from the self by definition" (Horowitz, 1987:62).

In contradistinction to traditional notions of power, which focus on overt coercion, repression, and prohibition—where X is said to have power over Y if X can make Y do something they would not otherwise do—Foucault argued that "we must cease once and for all to describe the effects of power in negative terms: it 'excludes', it 'represses', it 'censors', it 'abstracts', it 'masks', it 'conceals'" (1977:194). Instead, he advanced the thesis that "power produces; it produces reality; it produces domains of objects and rituals of truth. The individual and the knowledge that may be gained of him belong to this production" (Ibid). While not denying instances of sovereign power, Foucault argues that the dominant form of power at work in contemporary societies is this productive power that manifests itself primarily through the vehicle of normalizing discourses. Such discourses govern the variety of ways it is possible to think about something and which thus "make it difficult, if not impossible, to think and act outside them" (Allen, 2003:18). As stated by Bauman, this form of power acts "to regulate, to legislate, to tell the right from wrong, the norm from deviance" and, referring to Hume's fact/value distinction, the "ought from the is" (1982:41).

This new formulation of discursive power has its origins in the human sciences and their alleged ability to tell us the truth about who we are and what we need to do and say to become or remain 'normal'. These bodies of knowledge are in turn utilised by people to make sense of themselves and others. In effect, they act as metaphorical rulebooks delineating the parameters as to what one can legitimately think, say, and do. This recourse to so-called experts regarding the right way to live, in terms of how we relate to ourselves and others, holds out "the hope that problems of regulation can remove themselves from the disputed terrain of politics and relocate onto the tranquil yet seductive territory of truth" (Millar and Rose, 2008:69). As reference to metaphorical rulebooks imply, I am not arguing that the mothers I interviewed have actually read such works and reflexively assented to their conclusions. Rather, the Foucauldian claim is that they do not have to in order to be subject to their discursive strictures. In this respect, it is not inappropriate to conceive of the workings of a dominant discourse as akin to Jung's notion of a collective unconscious or Hegel's notion of the Zeitgeist. Namely, that a dominant discourse's power to define and defend the borders between the thinkable and the unthinkable goes "right down to the depths of society" (Foucault, 1977:27). In effect, the power of these discourses is such that they constitute the air we breathe and are as necessary to the workings of the social body as oxygen is to the natural (Dews, 1987).

The psychoanalytical framework

While the work of Foucault has become a widely-used framework to interrogate issues of disability and impairment, the same cannot be said for psychoanalysis generally, and the work of Kristeva in particular (Goodley, 2011). In my view, this is an oversight. As the Frankfurt School, amongst others, has shown, an interdisciplinary approach that utilises psychoanalytical insights can lead to illuminating conjectures as to why the social world takes the forms it does. In this respect, I agree with Goodley's claim that one of the primary values of employing a psychoanalytic approach to investigate the workings of disabling societies lies in its ability to shed light on the prevalence of non-disabled people to "characterise, construct, gaze at, project, split off, react, repress and direct images of impairment and disability in ways that subjugate and, at times, terrorise disabled people whilst upholding the precarious autonomy of non-disabled people" (2011:2). In addition, for the purposes of this book, another important component of the psychoanalytical framework and its privileging of unconscious over conscious factors in shaping our subjectivity is the contention that unbeknownst "to our conscious selves, we can think and feel very differently from what we believe or say" (Sarup, 2002:46). This psychological need to remain strangers to ourselves has in turn knock-on consequences regarding our unwitting complicity in the marginalisation of difference via categorising certain populations as a manifestation of the other and acting accordingly.

In relation to the subject matter at hand, where one of the guiding theoretical assumptions is that discrimination against disabled people is a response to physical differences or anomalous forms of embodiment, both Kristeva and Shildrick's work is particularly apposite as it provides a necessary augmentation to the limitations of adopting a purely Foucauldian approach. Foucault's work, while crucial, only takes us so far as it remains hampered by his wilful refusal to critically engage with questions of interiority. Due to this failure to put flesh on the bones of the real material body, Foucault fails to provide an adequate answer to the question of why, when 'hailed', we respond to some forms of discourses rather than others. For example, one can convincingly argue that the normalising, humanistic discourses invoked by Foucault would have embraced the belief that sexual expression for adults with an intellectual disability is a legitimate aspiration. This is particularly the case for those with Down syndrome, who in almost every other aspect of their lives are living more 'normal' lives. Given that this has not yet happened, we need to ask why not? The Foucauldian approach, which ignores the "permeability of internal and external worlds, and downgrades the individual to a mere cipher in the reproduction of the larger social world" (Elliott, 2008:86) is limited in its ability to answer this question. On a related point, the predominant social response to anomalous bodies engaging in sexual activity, one which is well captured by reference to the so-called 'yuck factor' response, is not only cross-cultural but also predates both the birth of the human sciences and the power/knowledge nexus that is Foucault's primary explanatory factor in deconstructing hegemonic conceptions of identity.

Consequently, to adequately deal with the poverty of the stimulus-type objections levelled against Foucault's contribution, a fruitful hypothesis to employ is that the so-called 'yuck factor' has its origins in something more primordial/pre-discursive in nature. While the Foucauldian self can be likened to an empty space waiting to be filled by societal discourses, psychoanalysis is predicated on the belief that it is a mistake to see the content of the subject's psychic life as merely the internalisation of norms or "the distorted effect of an oppressive social world" (Rose, 1986:10). Hence the positing of the unconscious to act as a mechanism that partly explains why people exposed to the same external stimuli will, nevertheless, respond by emotionally investing in different subject positions. This is where Kristeva's contribution comes in. In her ontology, the corporeal is more than an infinitely malleable *tabula rasa*. Unlike Foucault, she argues that there is a psychical reality. Its roots lie in the infant child's attempt to differentiate itself from its parents, a struggle whose transformative effects on the adult psyche and subsequent behaviour is as profound and as long-lasting as that of any irreducibly sociological phenomenon (Keltner, 2011).

In *Powers of Horror*, Kristeva defines abjection as

> ...an extremely strong feeling which is at once somatic and symbolic, and which is above all a revolt of the person against an external menace from which one wants to keep at a distance, but of which one has the impression that it is not only an external menace but that it may menace us from inside. So it is a desire for separation, for something autonomous and also the feeling of an impossibility of doing so.
>
> (1982:135–36)

Furthermore, Kristeva goes on to state that it is not a "lack of cleanliness or health that causes abjection but what disturbs identity, system, order" (Kristeva, 1982:4). It is my contention that adults with Down syndrome are in this sense an object of abjection for many disabled and non-disabled people alike. Consequently, I want to argue that the answer in terms of how and why the latter respond to the former is in many respects to be found at the psychic level. In effect, we project on to certain disabled bodies the vulnerable part of ourselves we wish to but cannot fully disavow. This conclusion is predicated on the theory that in "signifying disease, trauma and decay, the anomalous body is an uncomfortable reminder that the normative, 'healthy', body, despite its appearance of successful self-determination, is highly vulnerable to disruption and breakdown" (Shildrick, 2007:66). To thwart such dangers, and thus retain our delusional sense of who we really are, the 'normal' third party deploys defence mechanisms such as abjection when in the presence of people with intellectual disabilities like Down syndrome. It is via the deployment of such defence mechanisms that the psychoanalytical approach bridges the gap between the individual and the social, and the internal and the external, by positing the existence of a 'cultural imaginary' that leaves very little room for anything other than heteronormative sexuality (Elliott, 2008).

The concept of a defence mechanism clearly begs the question as to what we are trying to protect ourselves from. The psychoanalytical answer concerns the nature of human subjectivity and the price paid for entrance into the symbolic world of language/human society (Homer, 2005). This is the proposition that to function as mature adults in this realm, the 'big lie' that needs to be fortified at every turn is that to be, is to be a self-subsisting autonomous whole self—where the borders that individuate us are sharply defined and strictly policed. In 'reality', however, this is not the case. Rather, the situation is such that the self does not have a fixed or unitary identity. That we think otherwise is a necessary story we need to tell ourselves about ourselves in order to fortify our insecure ontological status.

With the previously discussed theorists in mind, several key assumptions will inform the conceptual avenues this book will explore. Firstly, there is the proposition that the formation of one's social identity is a process involving social groups defining themselves in relation to other social groups. However, this is not a politically or morally neutral endeavour. Rather, as Hall correctly states, the marking of such differences "leads us, symbolically, to close ranks, shore up culture and to stigmatise and expel anything which is defined as impure, abnormal" (Hall, 1997:237). Consequently, the deployment of such dichotomising classifications needs to be seen as an exercise of power that is both exclusive and oppositional in nature. In effect, when we define ourselves via value-laden binary oppositions such as normal/abnormal, healthy/pathological, acceptable/taboo, we create an us/them hierarchical relationship involving an inferior 'other' who we define ourselves in opposition to. This view is summed up by Canguilhem when he claims that "that which diverges from the preferable in a given area of evaluation is not the indifferent but the repulsive or more exactly, the repulsed, the detestable" (1991:240). By extension, this means that "the disabled body and the 'normal' body always exist in a diametrically opposed relationship with one another, dependent on the other for meaning" (Gray, 2009:120). Secondly, and in contradistinction to a social model ontology, we need to see the superstructure as somewhat autonomous and hence invoke the notion of the 'cultural imaginary' as an equally pertinent factor in the production and reproduction of discrimination against people with an intellectual disability. This concept of the cultural imaginary, which posits a constitutive connection between the psychic and the social, refers to "those vast networks interlinking discursive themes, images, motifs and narrative forms that are publicly available at a given culture at any one time, and articulate its psychic and social dimensions" (Dawson, 1994:48).

Consequently, the argument I am advancing is that in addition to the various sociological components at play, there also exists a plethora of important psychological and psychoanalytical factors that explain the disablism that people with intellectual disabilities are subjected to on a day-to-day basis. Primary amongst these is the conjecture that it is prejudicial attitudes, that transcend political ideology, and which very often have their origin in the unconscious—a manifestation of psychic anxiety on the part of the non-intellectually disabled section of the population towards people with intellectual disabilities—which go some way in explaining the ongoing plight of the latter population.

This conclusion is based on the premise that those with an intellectual disability such as Down syndrome have been symbolically marked as 'other'; that is, they have become victims of an essentialist identity. This third-party ascription, where people with Down syndrome are reductively defined by reference to their physical appearance and intellectual impairment, is a constitutive part of the processes that create minority population subgroups as 'other' and therefore not part of 'we' or 'us'. As a result of being symbolically marked in this way, it follows that in a sense the impairment that is Down syndrome is constructed, rather than discovered, in the non-disabled gaze. Thus, the invalidation of impaired bodies is not simply an economic and cultural response to them, but also arises in the mode of perception—an extension of the 'eugenic gaze'—which visualises and articulates them as manifestations of the monstrous other. In other words, because the bodies of people with Down syndrome breach normative standards of embodiment, they are met with largely ambivalent responses—too often negative in nature –from third parties whose bodies do not (Hughes, 1999; Shildrick, 2003).

In relation to the psychic status of the adult with an intellectual disability vis-à-vis possible unconscious parental responses, the contention is that the former represent "all the irresolvable ambiguity of the abject: neither wholly part of the subject, nor safely outside; disavowed, yet disturbingly familiar" (Shildrick, 2007:232). Consequently, I want to argue that the nature of the paternalistic regime of care is shaped by this inability on the part of the parent with a son or daughter with an intellectual disability to always see themselves in their child and thus engage in the kind of parental narcissism that is taken for granted with 'normal' children. In addition, it is this intermingling of fear and fascination and love and hate in the presence of the abject that also makes it a useful concept to apply when trying to understand the preferred sexual object choice expressed by many of the respondents with Down syndrome.

3 Research findings and analysis
The parental perspective

Introduction

As explained previously, the analysis of the empirical data involves applying key insights/concepts drawn from the Foucauldian framework and the psychoanalytical approach employed by Kristeva and Shildrick to the data. To briefly recap what this entails, the fundamental premise underlying the Foucauldian framework I am utilising is that there are two meanings of what it is to be a social subject. These are to be subject "to someone else's control and dependence" and to be "tied to one's own identity by a conscience and self-knowledge". Both of these "meanings suggest a form of power which subjugates and makes subject to" (Foucault, 1980:212). Although Foucault does not employ the same terminology, in terms of propositional content, such a typology clearly identifies two of the defining features of the autonomy/paternalism debate as it relates to the subject matter under scrutiny. As the analysis will show, in regards to how they negotiate the tricky moral terrain that constitutes the relationship they have with their intellectually disabled adult children when issues of sexual self-determination are at stake, the respondents primarily embody the latter definition of what it is for one's subjectivity to be discursively produced, while their sons and daughters generally fall into the former.

Thus, we will see that the mothers, in their embodiment of the 'good parent' subject position, are tied to this identity by a moral imperative to 'do the right thing' by their adult children with Down syndrome. The paternalistic regime of care that ensues is therefore, almost by definition, the combined effect of both conscience and self-knowledge in action. This perceived need to subject their intellectually disabled sons and daughters to 'someone else's control and dependence' will in turn be explained by reference to the cognitive limitations that are a constitutive component of the Down syndrome classification. This then is coupled by the fact that in contemporary liberal societies, sexual interaction, rather than being viewed as just another ordinary form of life, retains, for some populations at least, its quasi-transcendental status as a Dionysian set of practices signifying both danger and morality in equal measure (Singer, 2005).

To this end, the classification I have given to this aspect of the analysis is to conceive of it as a form of Foucauldian critical discourse analysis—broadly understood. This somewhat ambiguous definition is unfortunate, but necessary, as the concept of Foucauldian critical discourse analysis suffers from the problem that afflicts discourse analysis in its own right. Namely, that "the term discourse analysis covers a great number of different social science practices and ideas" (Yates, 2004:233). Consequently, I use the moniker of 'Foucauldian critical discourse analyses' for two reasons. Firstly, the data analysed takes the form of discourse. Secondly, the analytical framework is predicated on the assumption that the respondents in their guise as social subjects are discursively produced. This is the contention that in terms of propositional content, people do not come into the social world with *a priori* knowledge of themselves and others. Rather, such knowledge is produced and disseminated via the power/knowledge nexus.

The logic of the Foucauldian framework, which conceives of the production of social knowledge as inter-textual in nature, dictates that such accounts are and can only be derived by reference to respondents' interpretative repertoires. These are defined as a "collection of ideas, concepts and terms which are used to define and evaluate experiences and events" (Wetherell and Potter, 1988:175), the origins of which are to be found in the social identity one occupies at a given place in time. Moreover, because the Foucauldian perspective is based on the proposition that who we are is an effect of the discourses culturally available to us, in order to make sense of respondents' replies they need to be contextualised by reference to the wider discursive resources of which they are an instance. When translated into question form, such inquiries can be formulated to ask what kinds of discourses respondents avail themselves of to produce their respective explanations as to why they think and act in the way they do.

According to Wetherell, a defining characteristic of discourse analysis is that it involves "the study of language in use" (2001:3). However, as the notion of 'language use' has numerous, sometimes contradictory, connotations within the sciences, it needs to be clarified that my analysis is not an exercise in any form of linguistics, applied or otherwise. Therefore, the formal properties of the language used by the respondents—such as the nature of the semantic, grammatical, lexical, or phonological relations—are of no interest to my inquiry. Hence, the focus is not on language use *per se*. Rather, the focus is on the beliefs and desires expressed by the respondents, through the medium of language. The reason this form of data is being privileged is predicated on the assumption that when human beings answer questions addressed to them—a process which typically involves them 'using language'—the third-party garners insights regarding the subject positions they occupy and the nature of the society they are a part of, which in turn help explain the respondent's thoughts and actions regarding the questions asked of them. In other words, the language used by the respondent's acts as a mirror into the psycho-social world they inhabit allows for a macro-analysis of the nature of such realms—which is the only form of analysis this book is engaged in. In effect, the Foucauldian element of my analysis involves "making speculative claims about interview talk—discourse in a micro sense—as saying something about Discourse, i.e., a mode of reasoning about and shaping the world that structures language use and experience" (Alvesson, 2002:117).

From this perspective, the answer to the question of how one should view the interview data provided by the respondents is to see it "as the outcome of the discourses that are present" [which constitute] "the subject and her talk" (Alvesson, 2002:116). By extension, because the respondents occupy subject positions that are discursively produced, their subjectively meaningful responses "are mainly of interest as indications of the discourses at play and the powers over the individual subject" (Ibid.). Thus, while the respondent's answers constitute a true account of why they think and act the way they do in relation to the issues raised by the research questions, why they do in fact think and act in the way they describe is, at least partly, to be explained and accounted for through the discursive rules and themes that predominate in a given socio-historical context (Prado, 2005).

The application of the psychoanalytical model involves the utilisation of Kristeva's concept of abjection—a psychic defence mechanism guarding our exposure to and contact with certain configurations of matter. In addition, Shildrick's appropriation of this concept (2003, 2009), which argues that the non-normative disabled body is an object of abjection—particularly in its guise as a manifestation of the 'monstrous other'—is also employed.

The point made previously by Alvesson (2002) regarding the speculative nature of social analysis also applies to the epistemological status of any claims I make when using the psychoanalytic framework. Consequently, this book's conception as to what constitutes a sociological 'explanation' has less grandiose epistemic connotations than those associated with the positivist framework. Instead, and in common with the critical tradition generally, the use of the term 'explain' is coterminous with offering a theoretically informed interpretation/reading as to why the empirical data takes the form it does. This qualification is designed to alert the reader that regardless of my own epistemological aspirations, or indeed any application of sociological theory to a body of empirical data, the findings in question will remain rightly classified as theoretically informed conjectures as opposed to a set of indubitable truths (Bishop, 2007).

However, the fact that the theorising I will engage in to 'explain' why the respondents think and act the way they do will take the form of a subjective interpretation rather than reference to some kind of objective 'covering law' favoured by positivists, where to explain an event is "to be able to deductively subsume it under covering laws, i.e. universal empirical generalizations" (Bhaskar and Danermark, 2006:283) does not mean that there are no epistemic standards from which to evaluate such conclusion, but simply to note that they are relativistic rather than 'objective' in nature. What this means is that while "within a given theoretical framework one can ask whether this is true, or whether that is a fact" one cannot ask which theoretical explanation "is more correct or in better accordance with the facts than the other" (Pratt, 1993:58). Consequently, given that "much of what is currently put forward as social scientific knowledge is open to serious dispute" (Hammersley, 2009:4), the test of a given theoretical interpretation is established by asking whether the conclusions reached are logically consistent with the theoretical frameworks themselves as opposed to asking whether the theoretical framework is itself true (Harrington, 2005).

Interviews with the mothers and analysis of the findings

Theme 1: Parental perception of what it means to be normal—the rationale behind the paternalistic regime of care

The question of what it means to be 'normal' and what follows from such a categorization for their adult sons and daughters with Down syndrome is a dominant theme throughout all the interviews that took place with the population of mothers. For example, Mary expressed both her surprise and the subsequent disappointment she felt when finding out that her child had Down syndrome—as she 'never for a minute thought anything would be wrong with him'. In addition, there is also the fact that the respondent did not immediately tell her other children that their new brother had Down syndrome because she 'didn't want him treated as abnormal' but rather wanted 'them to get to know him as a person' before she told them the truth of their brother's impairment. Yet on the other hand, we see her disgusted response to the doctor's suggestion that her child was so 'abnormal' that she would not want to and would not have to take care of her newborn child with Down syndrome.

Mary stated that her son:

> ...was only a few minutes born when my doctor came in and told me my child had Down syndrome and that he would have a flat head...small squinty eyes...and he would probably have a heart condition ...all doom and gloom. And I lay there thinking to myself "this is not my son" ...my child is beautiful and he doesn't look anything like that. We were told then later on in the day that we didn't have to bring him home...that we could put him in a home...but ah...X's dad was not impressed with that and it took the security guard to stop him from you know saying "a few words" to the doctor.

The sense of disappointment on Mary's part (which was shared by all the mothers) on realizing that her newborn baby was intellectually impaired is a common theme in the literature. For instance, Blacher et al state: "whether an act of God or fate, chance mutation, or the inevitably of a genetic blueprint, having a child with an intellectual disability is rarely a welcome event" (2007:303). In a similar vein, Ryan and Runswick-Cole state: "for many mothers having a disabled child is unexpected or undesired and can involve a journey on a different route to that anticipated" (2008:203). This sense of parental loss, of what could have been, is invariably induced by the fact that while becoming a parent remains a dream come true for many, having a disabled child, particularly one with an intellectual impairment like Down syndrome, is in the words of Kittay "difficult to celebrate" (2001). As the data I have collected clearly demonstrates, this perceived lesser value, at least initially, in having a baby with Down syndrome when the desire was for a child without an intellectual disability is clearly reflected in the respective mother's descriptions—with use of words like 'shock', 'loss', 'grief' and 'anger'—of their initial reaction after learning about their child's impairment.

This ambivalence on the part of Mary as to how, when, and where she locates her son with Down syndrome on the normal/abnormal continuum continues right up to the present day. One instance of this tension in action is exemplified during her son's teenage years. At this stage, the conscious attempts on the part of the parents to ensure their son had a normal social life went hand in hand with a sense of paternalism that frequently saw them accompanying their son and his friends to a given venue. This belief on the part of the parents that 'we had to be very careful...so we would always stay in the background' ensured that the degree of freedom they extended to their son in relation to how he spent his leisure time was limited, hence the fact that such outings nearly always took the form of supervised socialising. This privileging of the precautionary principle in relation to her son's social life has continued as he has got older and become an adult. For example, Mary recounts how on turning 18, her son's self-image changed as he began to actively define himself as an adult and began to question the discrepancy that existed between his life and that enjoyed by many of his non-intellectually disabled contemporaries—especially where the social lives of his brothers were concerned. In her own words, Mary explained:

> I suppose as he got older, when he reached 18...well he himself would have been very aware that he was 18 and that he was now an 'adult'... and it kind of hit home a little bit then because your baby is no longer a baby he has turned into an adult and he expects to be able to do the same things that the rest of the family is doing. For example, Y (his brother) is a year younger and X would say "why is Y allowed to do these things and I'm not?" I think I found that part of his life the bit that hurt me the most, because he wanted to get married, he wanted to have children, he wanted to buy a car, he wanted to move out...and you got a lot of 'why'...and I found that part of his life really hard.

According to Mary, her reluctance to explain to her son 'that you have Down syndrome and you just can't do these things', coupled with her realization that the struggle to find what she considered the appropriate balance between empowering and protecting him was to be an ongoing conflict, often saw her crying at night, asking 'why did this happen to my son'?

In some of her responses, Angela also displayed a similar ambivalence in relation to the different attitudes she adopted towards her daughter regarding her changing status as sometimes normal and sometimes not. For example, in recounting the extent of her daughter's social life as a young teenager, she acknowledged her popularity and the fact that her daughter seemed to have a lot of friends. On the other hand, however, she expressed her belief that maybe this was more because the individuals concerned were really her son's friends. This puzzle led the respondent to pose the question as to whether her daughter 'would have had the same number of people coming in and out of the house...or if she would have had the same interaction' if this had not been the case. However, when asked whether she believed that some of the individuals were taking pity on her daughter, she responded in the negative. The reasoning offered to support this conclusion was a variation on the notion that while the normal/abnormal binary describes a very real material state of affairs, its importance is time- and context-dependent. Hence, her contention that 'children at that age don't realise...they kind of sense that something is wrong...that the person is slower...but that they don't see them as somebody that they should be alienated from or put out there as somebody totally different'. When asked whether the distinct facial appearance of people with Down syndrome would mark members of this population as different—a difference moreover that is characterised as a deficit and responded to accordingly by a third party—Angela remained committed to her original conclusion; namely, that there is a difference between the pre-teen's perception and response to such differences and that of older people. Thus, she stated:

> Children at a young age...say up to 12/13...when they go in to secondary school say, might ask their parents what was different....maybe her friends asked what was different about my daughter or they may have heard their parents talk about my daughter in a different fashion...she could have been in and out of their houses and would have been in and out of their houses so then children get to understand there's a difference and why there's a difference...but generally speaking I wouldn't have thought a pity thing came into it at that stage.

When asked, Sofia recounted a similar, broadly positive, experience in relation to how her son was perceived as a pre-pubescent. However, when it came to the teenage years and beyond, Sofia did express the view that pity plays a more central role in explaining the less than ideal nature of the socialising between her son and her non-intellectually disabled contemporaries. According to Sofia: 'I definitely noticed a change in how X was treated by those people he would have viewed as his friends'. When asked to expand on what she meant, she stated: 'Well, I mean that practically all of his 'normal' friends effectively abandoned him once they hit a certain age and the issue of being 'cool' became important to them'. In response to my question, Sofia explained that the phrase 'being cool' revolved around a concern with how her son's former friends would negotiate the new lifestyle opportunities that went hand-in-hand with 'a fascination with girls, being allowed to stay out later and all that kind of stuff'. When I asked Sofia whether she felt resentment at what happened to her son in this respect, she answered: 'No, not really. Obviously, I felt very sad for X, but on the other hand it is probably asking too much for 'normal' teenagers to include somebody with Down syndrome in such activities'. As to why she believed this to be the case, Sofia clarified by stating:

> It's obvious...people with Down syndrome, such as my son, are not 'cool' and they can't be, at least not to other teenagers that don't have Down syndrome. Like I said, it's sad but that's how the world works, and I can't judge other people for holding such views as I was never faced with that situation when I was their age. If I was, I have a feeling that I wouldn't have acted any differently.

Pre-empting a follow-up question, Sofia than asked me had I ever seen the film *Mean Girls*—a commentary on the cliquish behaviour engaged in by 'normal' teenagers of being evaluated by (and in turn evaluating) those you socialise with, your physical appearance, and so on. When I replied that I had, Sofia stated:

> Well that's what it's like at that stage...and I don't think it gets much better as we get older. In other words, we discriminate when it comes to who we want to be friends with based on shared interests, you know, sense of humour and all the rest of it. So, it's not surprising to me or any of the other parents I've spoken to who are in the same boat that it would be a very rare person, a 'normal' teenager or an adult, to have somebody with an intellectual disability like Down syndrome as a best friend.

With Rebecca, the recurring theme of how parents conceive of their adult sons and daughters with Down syndrome in relation to the normal/abnormal continuum is a trope that runs throughout this interview. For example, when I asked Rebecca how she felt on first hearing that her daughter had Down syndrome, she replied 'it was a surprise...actually it was a shock as I never for a moment thought we would have a handicapped child'. When asked whether she felt disappointed that her daughter had Down syndrome, she admitted:

> Yeah I was...I know that's an awful thing to say but I was devastated when I heard the news. She was the third of my five kids...the first two

were completely normal and my pregnancy with X went fine...so it just never occurred to me that anything would go wrong...God I hate myself for saying this...but it was the way I... well in fact it was the way me and my husband felt...for far too long unfortunately.

When asked about her daughter's social life as a teenager—did she have many friends at this stage of her life—Rebecca replied 'yes and no'. She then went on to clarify what she meant by explaining that her daughter 'was very popular on our street...and the neighbours were always very friendly', because of which her daughter 'would spend hours in their houses just chatting away'. But, according to the respondent, things were a little different when it came to her daughter forming friendships with non-disabled teenagers of her own age such as those of her neighbour's children and/or the friends of her siblings. In Rebecca's view, it was in relation to her daughter forming friendships with her non-disabled contemporaries 'where the problems always lay', adding 'it's strange the way that was handled, or developed, or whatever the right word is'. Regarding her daughter, Rebecca went on to explain how her 'kids are all quite close in age so her brothers would have hung around with the neighbour's kids, both boys' and girls'. At the same time her daughter 'would have talked to her brother's friends, particularly the girls, on the assumption that they were her friends as well'. According to Rebecca, the reality of the situation was 'they weren't...not really'. Thus, while 'some of the other kids could be quite nice and nobody ever ignored her', Rebecca believed that because her daughter has Down syndrome and was therefore considered abnormal, 'there were real limits on how much they included her in the things they would do'. When asked if she could give an example of such discrimination in action, she stated:

> Yeah loads unfortunately. I suppose the main thing was that it was very rare for any of them to spend 'one on one' time with her...so you never had a situation where one of them would hang out with her on her own...either one of the brothers had to be there or else X had to be in one of the friends' houses...but when that happened it was more often the mother or father paying her the attention....they were the ones paying her "genuine attention".

Based on her experience, Katy also agreed with the contention that people with Down syndrome are typically seen as 'abnormal' by their non-intellectually disabled contemporaries, including those in their immediate family. After stating that her son was very popular in his workplace, Katy was asked whether she thinks he has made any friendships with any of the non-disabled staff. To this, she replied:

> Ah...well this is always a tricky issue to make a judgement on.... I suppose it depends on what you mean by 'friendship'? You can probably

relate to this given you have a sister with Down syndrome but from my experience it is very rare that anyone without Down syndrome will want to have someone with Down syndrome as a true friend.

When I then asked why she thought this was the case, she stated: 'I suppose my theory would be that because Down syndrome is an intellectual disability most people without Down syndrome don't find people with Down syndrome all that interesting. I think that's basically the long and short of it'. When subsequently asked whether the brothers of her son with Down syndrome (who are approximately two years younger and older) tried to include him in their socialising, Katy, in common with most of the other interviewees regarding the question of sibling interaction, replied that yes, they did, but that such socialising was heavily context-dependent. She stated: 'While both of his brothers did make an effort to include him in what they were doing, they also started to push him away as they got older'. When asked for her explanation why this occurred, Katy replied: 'I think it's basically for the same reasons that X hasn't made normal friends', namely that from her perspective, 'people with Down syndrome can be a bit of a burden'. Prefacing her final response to the specific question with the statement that 'this is a horrible thing to say but I think it's true', Katy concluded by adding that people with Down syndrome can also be 'a bit of a bore as they can't really understand what's going on or join in to the same extent as normal people'. In relation to the context-dependent nature of the socialising that did go on with her son with Down syndrome and his brothers, Katy clarified that while X was still 'welcome to socialise with his brothers and their friends during the daytime, the problem was more to do with them feeling he was a hindrance when it came to their hanging about at night'. When Katy was asked to explain the different criteria her other sons used in relation to the daytime/night-time distinction, she replied that it was 'for all the obvious reasons'; namely, 'at this stage they would have been hanging around with girls...drinking and stuff like that'. Because of the changing nature of the socialising that occurred as her non-intellectually disabled sons got older, Katy explained how they would have complained 'that X was "cramping their style" and that they didn't always want to have to be minding him when they were trying to enjoy themselves'.

While not all similar aged non-intellectually disabled siblings enjoy close friendships, or socialise together, the accounts given by some of the mothers regarding how non-intellectually disabled teenagers negatively perceive their intellectually disabled sibling and the context-dependent nature of the socialising that does take place corresponds to much of the literature on this issue (Stoneman, 2005). For example, as stated by Kramer et al, the 'burden' trope is frequently invoked by non-disabled brothers or sisters to characterise their intellectually disabled sibling, and thereby justify or explain why the socialising they engage in takes the forms it does. This leads them to conclude that "among siblings of a brother or sister with IDD [intellectual development disorders], these relationships tend to be more 'asymmetric' in reciprocity, with nondisabled siblings providing more support to siblings with IDD than they receive from those siblings" (2013:483).

When Claire was asked how she felt when she realized her son had Down syndrome, she describes feeling 'quite shocked'. This reaction was based on the fact that he was her third child and that she 'just assumed that he would be a normal healthy baby'. Hence, when she heard 'he wasn't', she felt, while acknowledging that it might be a 'horrible thing to say', 'very disappointed to be honest...disappointed and sad'. This contention on the part of Claire that Down syndrome is a difference with negative consequences for those so labelled and their family is one that she maintains to this day. Invoking hindsight, she went on to state: 'Looking back on it now I think many of my feelings at the time have been vindicated in a way'. She concluded that her 'initial gut reaction that to have Down syndrome is a tragedy of sorts has been proved right'. This conclusion was based on the respondent's view that 'to have Down syndrome is to be dependent for the rest of your life'. For Claire, this state of affairs means that her son 'won't be able to stand on his own two feet', which in turn 'means he will never be able to have some of the things he wants and some of the things we want for him, the stuff that the rest of us take for granted'. In other words, Claire believes that although her son 'is 37 years of age, he is, in many ways, in terms of what he can and can't do, basically a child'.

Theme 1: Analysis

The master concept, in the discursive repertoires that all the respondents draw upon to justify how they think and act towards their sons and daughters with Down syndrome and from which everything else stems regarding the existence and the nature of their paternalistic regimes of care, is the notion of what it means to be normal. Given the inter-textual nature of the discourses that circulate in contemporary western societies, it is clear that the parents are subject to an array of these, sometimes overlapping, sometimes in conflict with each other, which influence the nature of the regimes of care they deploy. The most relevant of these discourses is the discourse of the good mother, the discourse that ties personal autonomy with cognitive ability, and the discourse around what constitutes legitimate and illegitimate forms of sexual expression. In practice, we see the respondents constantly fluctuating as to where, when, and why they position their adult children with Down syndrome on the normal/abnormal continuum in these various aspects.

As with all subject positions, the 'good mother' role (which can be both empowering and disempowering depending on the context and one's ideological affiliations) is one that puts limits on the respondents' discursive practices or possibilities of action, if they are to stay convincingly within such an identity concept. Thus, the subject position of 'good mother' in warranting certain discursive practices also puts an embargo on alternative modes of being. For example, Woollett and Nicolson state that "good/normal mothers' are always available to give their children love, time and attention, they are calm, patient, and in control of their own emotions, and hence able to put children first" (1998:3). My use of this concept, which is primarily descriptive in nature (based as it is on the mothers' responses), in the following analysis, differs slightly from the preceding quotation. Instead, my conception of the good mother subject position does not entail putting one's children first, calmness, patience or undue control of one's emotions. Rather, my use of this concept denotes that mothers, who love their adult sons and daughters with Down syndrome, believe themselves to have a moral obligation to subject their adult children to a paternalistic regime of care. In addition, my application of this concept is also used to advance the conjecture that such mothers (in common with mothers of children without intellectual disability under the age of consent) have internalised normalising discourses governing what constitutes legitimate sexual interaction and who can engage in it. As a result, they are limited in reflexively engaging with questions of whether the subject position they embody is also that one that entails a moral obligation to question such dominant discourses.

With this definition in mind, from the Foucauldian perspective, it is no surprise to find the respondents in their roles as good mothers drawing on the cognitive ability/autonomy continuum to justify the parental regimes of care they deploy because, as demonstrated in the 'sexuality and its discontents' section of the literature review chapter, this discourse is fundamental to the structuring of most contemporary liberal democracies. As well as being a lynchpin of legal systems the world over—without it, the age of consent and criminal liability would dissolve—it is the constitutive concept on which the hierarchical parent-child relationship is built (Dworkin, 2005). This relationship is one in which the parent/s of a child—defined by reference to age and/or cognitive capacity—are given the legal authority to restrict the liberty of their children, even if this means overriding their expressed wishes, in order to further their so-called best interests (Conly, 2013).

From a Foucauldian perspective, the cognitive ability/autonomy discourse—a variation of the exclusionary distinction between madness and reason discussed in *Discipline and Punish* (1977)—can be conceived of as the dominant discourse that constructs and reproduces empowered/disempowered subject-positions. As this state-sanctioned normative definition of 'normalcy' is concerned with the inability of certain classes of people to meet a set of required standards, it can be characterised as a primary instance of Foucault's concept of biopower in action (Taylor, 2011). The failure to reach a contingent social definition of what it means to be normal means that those who are stigmatized accordingly have their subjectivity devalued and their freedom curtailed (Foucault, 1978). However, unlike the 'deviant'—such as the 'mad' and 'bad'—described in *Discipline and Punishment* (1977) whose behaviour can, in principle, be reformed via the application of suitable reconditioning techniques, the normalisation strategies deployed to ensure that the 'deviant', that is, the adult with Down syndrome, does not stray too far from the path of normal behaviour dictates they remain under the tutelage of a relevant expert. In the context under scrutiny, the individual playing the role of relevant expert is the parent. This state of affairs vindicates another one of Foucault's most important insights: namely, that knowledge and power are inextricably linked. Consequently, and as the data demonstrates, because of the cognitive, and by extension knowledge, differential that exists between the mothers and their sons and daughters with Down syndrome, it is the former—by recourse to the dominant discourse regarding the innate vulnerability of people with Down syndrome—who regulate and control the lives of the latter.

When it comes to the mothers' use of the cognitive normal/abnormal continuum, we can see its deployment is not meant, in any conscious way, to devalue their sons and daughters with Down syndrome. Rather, it seems to be used in a solely descriptive sense. Referring back to the section on conceptualising disability within Chapter 2, it can be categorised as an adherence to the so-called medical model ontology. That is, the respondents perceive the intellectual impairment of Down syndrome as an objective biological difference that differentiates their intellectually disabled offspring from their non-intellectually disabled contemporaries. This distinction moreover is one that the mothers believe constitutes a state of affairs that means that in many respects the adult child with Down syndrome is deemed to be different in kind from the 'normal' adult and must be treated accordingly. For the mothers interviewed for this project the primary instance of how the difference of Down syndrome is to be treated manifests itself in the paternalistic practices to which they subject their sons and daughters. For the purposes of this study, the most relevant of these is the role they play as gatekeepers into their adult children's social and/or sexual lives. For example, in their roles as 'good mothers', all the respondents stated that their parental regimes of care necessarily entailed knowing where there sons and daughters were and what they were doing at all times. Hence, all the socialising their adult sons and daughters with Down syndrome engaged in was in some form or another monitored and regulated by non-disabled third parties.

This perceived need on the part of the parents to maintain a panopticon-like gaze on their adult children was explained by reference to the cognitive normal/abnormal continuum. Although the respondents formulated their responses somewhat differently, they all assented to the proposition that cognitive ability is a constitutive component of being allowed to act autonomously. As the mothers' responses exemplify, for the status of self-governance to be ascribed, it is not enough to be able to express or communicate a desire, which adults with Down syndrome clearly can do. In addition, one needs something extra to be deemed a proper self-regulating subject capable of making 'independent choices'. This something extra is the set of cognitive skills that enables one to not only acquire and process information in a rational manner, but also encompasses the ability to respond rationally to such external stimuli. According to this dominant discourse, the optimal response required in terms of what differentiates the rational human being from his or her less rational counterparts is the capacity to engage in a process of instrumental reasoning. This is a form of reasoning where one understands the choices one has and the consequences that will, or may, ensue when choice X rather than choice Y is decided as the goal or objective to be pursued (Christman, 2009). From the mothers' perspective, their adult sons and daughters with Down syndrome, because of their impairment, lack the requisite volitional abilities to govern themselves in this fashion. This inability to transcend a certain cognitive threshold means that the respondents, in common with the Irish legal system (Johnson et al., 2009), feel justified in denying them the right of self-determination in relation to their sexuality and to have those rights respected by all third parties. While not all the respondents were as explicit as Claire, who in talking about her thirty-seven-year-old son stated that when it comes to 'what he can and can't do he is still basically a child', in terms of categorising the propositional content of the views they expressed, the child/adult Down syndrome analogy is one that all the parents at some level subscribe to. Consequently, they view the cognitive difference of Down syndrome as a deficit, and one which shapes, if not wholly determines, the regime of care they deploy towards their adult sons and daughters with Down syndrome.

Obviously, this stance on the part of the mothers raises the question as to whether they are right in their conclusion that their adult sons and daughters have a biologically impaired ability to reason in the fashion that is deemed normal for their non-intellectually disabled contemporaries and which is deemed necessary—per the relevant legislation—for one to give valid consent to entering a sexual relationship. Ironically enough, given the theoretical frameworks I am using to analyse the data, many theorists who draw on Foucault, and "have demanded the reformulation of 'impairment' in purely socio-cultural terms" (Thomas, 2007:180) would say, or at the very least imply, that they are in fact wrong in their estimation that there is a cognitive threshold that adults with Down syndrome will never be able to transcend. For example, according to Tremain, "a Foucauldian approach to disability would hold that the governmental practices into which the subject is inducted and divided from others produce the illusion that they have a prediscursive, or natural, antecedent (impairment)" (2005:11). From this Foucauldian perspective, such ontological commitments are deemed problematic as "this allegedly 'real' entity is in fact a historically contingent effect of modern power" (Tremain, 2002:34). As such quotes demonstrate, Tremain is attempting to theorise impairment *qua impairment* and not 'merely' society's response to impairment. Therefore, to claim that something is socially constructed, as Tremain does, is to hold out the hope that that which is socially constructed can be otherwise (Kukla, 2000). In this regard, Hacking correctly states, "social constructionists about X tend to hold that X need not have existed, or need not be at all as it is. X or X as it is at present, is not determined by the nature of things; it is not inevitable" (Hacking, 1999:6). Apropos of this definition, in relation to the critiques levelled against the realist ontological commitments of medical model classifications of intellectual impairments, the key logical point to bear in mind is that to claim that an intellectual impairment like Down syndrome is a social construction or a discursive invention is to imply that the current cognitive differences between people with Down syndrome and their non-intellectually disabled contemporaries can be equalised.

There is a temptation at this point to invoke Jennifer's wholly representative statement when, after invoking the Down syndrome classification to justify her paternalistic regime of care, she was asked to respond to the contention that with the right amount of societal help, the adult with Down syndrome could over time learn to be as autonomous as their contemporaries without intellectual disability. To wit, Jennifer states:

> I'm pretty familiar with this notion as a result of the activism I've been engaged in, all the conferences I've attended, the presentations by academics I've sat through...or been made to sit through (she laughs) and I find it all pretty ridiculous. You know, whatever about other intellectual disabilities, most of which I know very little about, when it comes to Down syndrome I'm an expert. And when it comes to Down syndrome there is no chance in hell of somebody like my son becoming as smart, autonomous, rational...or whatever the right word is, as for example his cousin, who is 15, never mind other 'normal' adults his own age. Yeah, sorry but I get quite angry about stuff like this, it's just so stupid (said with emphasis) given all that we know about Down syndrome. I also take offence at the implication...you know that it's the parents fault, they didn't send him to the right school, they didn't encourage him enough, they didn't spend the right amount of time educating him and all the rest of it. No...I just wish people like that would, sorry I'm going to have to swear...but I just wish they would F off and stop talking such shite. (We both laugh.)

However, such an approach would be to ignore the remit I have set myself regarding the general/particular tension outlined in the introductory chapter. In other words, while much of the analysis I am engaging in is grounded in the empirical data I have collected, its content is not exhausted by reference to the respondent's views. Rather, there is also a scholarly obligation to grapple with relevant literature that advances arguments diametrically opposed to the views expressed by those who participated in this project, but that are nevertheless important to engage with in a critical scrutiny of the autonomy/paternalism debate.

With this objective in mind, and as the realism/anti-realism debate has a long history in both the natural and social sciences, there are a number of standard conceptual moves that can be made to refute claims such as those made by Tremain (Searle, 1996; Boghossian, 2006). For example, one can accept the premise that language is in no way transparent, agree with the conclusion that it does not simply hold up a mirror to nature and in a sense constructs reality, but still go on to argue that the fact that we use our conceptual apparatus to carve up the world based on human interests does not do the logical work certain poststructuralists think. Thus, there may well be "normative, social and thereby political judgements on normality and abnormality that underlie the search for neuronal differences of people with syndromes associated with intellectual disability" (Altermark, 2014:1468). However, just because something is interest dependent (for example, an instance of biopower, the product of the power/knowledge nexus etc.), does not mean it has a nominal ontological status. To claim it does simply on *a priori* grounds is to commit the 'genetic fallacy'. For example, just because the diagnostic category of Down syndrome is a recent social or discursive construction, it does not follow that the cognitive limitations and by extension the set of behaviours that differentiate those who have Down syndrome from those who do not did not have an objective existence that preceded the invention of the actual concept.

The fundamental discursive/pre-discursive distinction is well made by Vehmas and Makela, who state

> ...the diagnosis of Trisomy 21 (or Down syndrome) has a social history and it has had various social consequences to the lives of those with that diagnosis. However, despite the fact that Trisomy 21 is a construction, an invented term for a certain phenomenon, it is a term for an existing physical fact. Irrespective of any construction or representation, someone either has or has not an extra chromosome 21. And the fact that someone has an extra chromosome 21 does not have a social history; it has a mere biological history. In other words, the diagnosis 'Down syndrome' is not a sole creation of anatomy and physiology whereas the existence of an extra chromosome 21 is.
>
> (2008:94)

Hence, what makes the claim that adults with Down syndrome have an impaired cognitive ability relative to those without such an intellectual disability true is that it corresponds to one aspect of reality. While the terms 'truth' and 'reality' are in principle ripe for deconstruction, how far one can go with such an endeavour depends on the application of such concepts. In the current literature, we see time and time again the reproduction of the old canard that poststructuralists who utilise the work of Foucault—whether Foucault himself can be characterised as a poststructuralist is an irrelevance for the concerns of this book—do not believe in an objective truth or an objective reality (Prado, 2005). If such extreme scepticism really exists, one can be sure that it ends when the academic in question turns off their computer and leaves their office. We will leave to one side the objective reality and the various facts of the matter that need to pertain for such practices to be engaged in at all and concentrate on the substantive point. That is, that once the distinctions between truth and truth claims, fact and assertions of fact, and knowledge with pretensions to knowledge are made, it follows that poststructuralists do in fact believe in an objective material reality and they do in fact adhere to a correspondence or objective theory of truth. If they did not, they would be guilty of engaging in a performative contradiction. In other words, as with the 'liar's paradox', the necessary question to ask of such committed sceptics relates to the epistemological status of the very claim that there are no truths: Is this claim itself true or false? The epistemological, ontological, and moral relativism that is rightly associated with the poststructuralist/Foucauldian perspective (which in terms of propositional content bears a close resemblance to Hume's fact/value distinction) concerns the status of value judgements or normative claims in themselves and/or making value judgements or normative claims based on true empirical facts (Hicks, 2004).

References to a set of behaviours that are constitutive of a given impairment clearly beg the question as to which behaviours are caused by biology and which are caused by the classification thereof—and how we delineate between the two. For those, who adhere to a realist understanding of Down syndrome, such as the mothers who participated in this project, the relevant different behaviour—the inability to process and act on information to the same level that is deemed typical for their non-intellectually disabled contemporaries—is biologically caused (Wright, 2011). From the specific poststructuralist perspective being referred to, there are two possible responses to this posited "biology equals behaviour" equation. One is to claim that there is no connection, which as we have seen is a vacuous proposition. The second is to say that there is a connection and that biology does play a role in producing the cognitive limitations that are constitutive of the Down syndrome classification, but then to go on to make the normative argument that the cognitive limitations in question should not be used as a reason to treat people with Down syndrome differently from their non-intellectually disabled counterparts. In other words, this is to implicitly take one side of the autonomy/paternalism debate without really treating this debate with the seriousness it deserves. However, as alluded to in the introduction to this section, when nominally attempting to theorise impairment *qua impairment*, to concede the point that the cognitive difference has a real ontological status and limit one's social constructionist claim to how society responds to it, is in theoretical terms, to engage in the propagation of sociological or conceptual truisms. For example, how is the autonomy/paternalism debate advanced even if consensus is reached regarding claims such as "pathology is not something that science can 'discover', as it does not exist independently of presumptions and normative frames, but is something that is constructed with the aid of normative assumptions" (Altermark, 2014:1465)? Or, "what differs between people with intellectual disability and people that are extremely talented in mathematics is precisely the judgement that the former constitutes pathology while the latter does not" (Altermark, 2014:1468).

However, for fear that the competing perspectives are playing incommensurable language games, this section will conclude by simply seeking answers from the poststructuralists who are attempting to theorise impairment *qua impairment*—and indeed those who privilege autonomy over paternalism in an *a priori* fashion regardless of their theoretical proclivities—to the following fundamental questions:

1   Do they agree with Noam Chomsky's contention that "thought and language are properties of organized matter—in this case, mostly the brain, not the kidney or the foot" (2007:85) or are they positing some Cartesian like mysterious, supernatural substance, to explain the human ability to think?
2   If the ability to think is brain-dependent, does it not logically follow that if the brain is structured non-normatively, this will impact on a person's ability to think 'rationally'?
3   Is the proposition that human beings who are born with an intellectual disability like Down syndrome have an impaired ability to think 'rationally'—to formulate the range of sophisticated beliefs, desires, goals and objectives that are considered typical for their non-intellectually disabled contemporaries—a true proposition or not?
4   If the preceding proposition is true, does it not logically follow that the adult with an intellectual disability like Down syndrome enjoys a more limited capacity to exercise the kind of control over their lives that their non-intellectually disabled counterparts can?

With these questions in mind attention can then be paid to the facts on the ground. Namely, that certain populations subsumed under the umbrella term of intellectual disability—such as those with Down syndrome—do not enjoy the same ability to exercise the degree of autonomy over their lives that their non-intellectually disabled contemporaries take for granted (Pueschel, 2006).

Given what the mothers have actually said in relation to the autonomy/ paternalism tensions under scrutiny, and by extension the question as to whether the impairment of Down syndrome is discovered or constructed, I do not think it is unfair to attribute to them the view that the social constructionist claims they subscribe to are entirely to do with the societal response to those biological givens. In effect, they take issue with the pseudo-authoritative claims made by those authorities, who 'with truth on their side' claim that because someone has Down syndrome they can be characterised as 'useless eaters', second-class citizens, have their sexuality devalued and denied, and so on.

However, the responses by the mothers also illustrate an interesting ambivalence to this issue of cognitive capacity being a necessary condition to be met for them to 'allow' their sons and daughters with Down syndrome to embark on a sexual relationship. The tension in question revolves around 'expert' definitions of capacity as embodied in current legislation, their own evaluations of the relative autonomy their adult's sons and daughters enjoy, and most crucially of all the ontological status of any potential sexual partner, and the likelihood of that partner being able to harm their child in any way. Consequently, one reading of their responses would be to conclude that the mothers' view aligns with the conventional wisdom which states that meeting a cognitive threshold is a necessary condition to consent to a sexual relationship. However, given that all definitions of capacity are by their very definition both arbitrary and normative in nature, they make a distinction between their sons and daughters embarking on a sexual relationship with other adults with Down syndrome in the context of a boyfriend/girlfriend relationship, and those who would enjoy the 'upper cognitive hand' over their adult children. As the research findings demonstrate, from the mothers' perspective, this rules out people without an intellectual impairment, but may also include other populations subsumed under the "intellectual disability" umbrella term. Based on what the mothers have said, one can conclude that when it comes to their sons and daughters having a boyfriend/girlfriend with Down syndrome, they believe that capacity should either be assumed or deemed not relevant. However, in a situation involving their sons and daughters having sexual relations with non-intellectually disabled adults and/or other intellectually disabled adults who may possess the 'cognitive upper hand', things are more complicated. Firstly, from the mothers' perspective, any substantial cognitive differential between the parties constitutes a difference that could lend itself to their sons and daughters being exploited in some way. Secondly, and again in concurrence with the conventional wisdom regarding such relationships, they hold the perhaps 'politically incorrect' view that most non-intellectually disabled adults would not, if they had the choice, choose to sexually interact with an adult with Down syndrome for non-nefarious reasons. This issue will be returned to in the penultimate chapter of this book.

Theme 2: Parental refutation of the charge that their regime of care is to 'blame' for the celibate lives led by some of the adult children with Down syndrome

When Jennifer was asked whether she erred on the side of caution when trying to find the right balance between protecting her son from possible harm as opposed to facilitating her son's autonomy around forming sexual relationships she replied, 'no, not at all'. She went on to explain that while she and her husband 'have always been protective of X, much more protective of him than of his two brothers—one of whom is a year or two older and one a year or two younger', the rationale behind such a parental regime of care was 'because he has Down syndrome he is more vulnerable to abuse, or being taken advantage of'. In terms of the parental regime of care deployed, this meant that there were numerous things that her son was not allowed to do that his brothers were, for example 'in terms of socializing, going out drinking in pubs and clubs and that kind of stuff'. However, Jennifer explained she and her husband 'were always relatively liberal when it came to encouraging him to socialize with friends [albeit] in a supervised setting'. Summing up the role she played in this respect, she stated: 'As his mother I will willingly hold my hands up and say if I had another chance at bringing him up I would do a million and one things differently'; however, subsequently she stated 'I don't think it's fair to suggest that the reason why he hasn't had a girlfriend is because we as parents were over-protective in that area'. From her vantage point, they were not. In addition, Jennifer went on to explain that from her perspective, her son's celibate life was not to be blamed on the parental regime of care, but rather on her son's own criteria as to whom he wants to have a sexual relationship with. According to Jennifer, her son 'can also be quite judgmental too when it comes to the people he considers to be girlfriend material'. As a manifestation of her son's criteria in action, the respondent recounts how it seems to be the case 'that girls with Down syndrome are not people he generally finds sexy'. When asked to expand on what she meant, in terms of giving examples of this behaviour in practice, she stated 'there have been occasions down through the years when he would have told us that a certain girl with Down syndrome fancies him, and has sometimes even asked him to be her boyfriend, and he has always said no'. According to Jennifer, the main reason why her son has always said no to such requests is because he believes that women with Down syndrome 'are ugly'. Jennifer then explained that when her son uses the term 'ugly' he means they are '"too fat', 'not sexy' and all that kind of stuff'. Due to her son's use of such criteria, Jennifer concludes 'it's not really fair to say that he hasn't had opportunities to form relationships, it's just that from his perspective they are with 'the wrong kind of people'. When asked if she had ever tried to change his mind on this issue, and encourage him to 'take a chance' with one of these girls, Jennifer replied 'yes I would have'. However, given that this advice has not worked in the past, Jennifer expressed a feeling of impotence because from her perspective 'there was no changing his mind', leaving her to ask, 'so what can I do in those circumstances—I can't make him like somebody he doesn't, I can't make him choose a girlfriend he thinks is 'ugly'—can I?' Jennifer's account of why her son has never crossed the sexual relationship barrier proved to be very illuminating, and corresponds to the views held by many of the mothers who were interviewed.

When Susan was asked the question—referring to a debate within the academic literature—on whether parents can be 'held responsible' for the fact that many adults with Down syndrome have never had a sexual relationship because they are too protective of them, her initial response was one of surprise. In her own words, she replied 'well that's new.... I've never been asked that before'. After a moment's reflection—during which she asked aloud the question 'am I to blame that my son hasn't had many girlfriends?'—Susan concluded 'no, I don't think so'. She went on to state that although 'I sometimes treated him, and maybe still do at times like a child of sorts', she does not think that such practices have prevented him from forming relationships with girls. This paternalistic stance on Susan's part was to her mind a necessary one to adopt because her son 'does have Down syndrome'. From her perspective, this fact 'means he needs somebody to watch out for him'. As a result, she stated 'we have put lots of restrictions as to him going out alone'. To illustrate her point, she explained

> we wouldn't let him, even now, just walk out of the house at night time without knowing where he is going, who he is going to meet, when he would be coming home and how he would be getting home,

She went on to add that to her mind this 'is just a very normal way of caring for somebody with Down syndrome'. After another moment's pause, Susan concluded her point by stating that she did not 'see the connection between taking care of him in this way and preventing him from forming relationships, sexual or otherwise'.

When I asked Eimer whether her thirty-three-year-old son has a girlfriend, she responded: 'Nope he has never had a girlfriend....and God knows he has wanted one.... or more' (she laughs). In response to my question as to why she thought this was the case, she replied:

> Yeah that is the million-dollar question...why not indeed! Well to return to the earlier point about normal people not finding people with Down syndrome particularly interesting...I think that view is multiplied in spades when it comes to the idea of going out with someone with Down syndrome...so some of the girls he fancied would have been friends of his brothers...so obviously that stuff was a non-starter.

When I then inquired about the possibility of a girl with Down syndrome being 'girlfriend material', Eimer stated:

> Yeah that issue seems to be much more complicated...although you would think it would be so much easier wouldn't you? So why no Down syndrome girlfriend? I suppose I don't really know. He did tell us that he would have fancied some of the girls with Down's in his group but nothing ever came from it.

In response to my question as to why nothing ever came from her son's interest in the aforementioned girls, she stated:

> I don't know...there was one incident I can give you some details about... this was where I would have talked to the parent of one of the girls in

question and asked her if my son asked her daughter out and she said yes, if she would support that kind of relationship, but she said, and I suppose you have to respect her frankness... "no she wouldn't" so that didn't go any further.

When I asked if this mother explained her reasoning, Eimer stated: 'Well kind of, she basically felt her daughter, who was 24 at the time, was too immature to be involved in a sexual relationship, so obviously, that put an end to that'. My next question, prefaced by acknowledging that the account offered by Eimer explains why that potential boyfriend/girlfriend was never actualised as such, returned to the subject of why she thought her son has never had a girlfriend with Down syndrome. To this, she responded:

> I honestly don't know why there hasn't been anybody so far, although from my own experience I do think that many parents with daughters with Down syndrome are very protective when it comes to this whole area of relationships, so I think that's definitely an issue. But I don't think that is the complete answer to your question, I also think there may be something in this notion that some people with Down syndrome don't actually find other people with Down syndrome that sexually attractive.

When I asked Eimer if she found this was also sometimes the case with her son, she stated:

> Yeah definitely, there have been a few incidences where the shoe was on the other foot and some of the girls would have expressed an interest in X becoming their boyfriend but he would have brushed such advances off by explaining that so and so was just a friend and on other occasions he would have been less than gentlemanly in basically saying that he didn't fancy them so....

However, this did not mean that Eimer denied that her parental regime of care towards her son was a paternalistic one, just that there was no connection between this and the fact that he has yet to have a sexual relationship. Eimer stated, 'in terms of controlling his social life to the extent that I have...I do it because I need to, it's purely in terms of looking out for his interests.' She then went on to explain that certain things follow from the fact that her son has Down syndrome. In her own words, she stated:

> He has Down syndrome, and this, and I don't care what anybody who doesn't have a child with Down syndrome thinks about this issue, means that his ability to think is and always be in many ways similar to that of a child. So, in the same way that most parents control the social lives of their children I think a similar principle applies to me and the fact that I can't let my son just do or go wherever he wants. That would

be too dangerous; I have a duty to protect my son from being taken advantage of, which I think is unfortunately a real possibility given the world we live in. So yes, there has being lots of overseeing his social life and all that kind of stuff, but that never applied to preventing him from socialising with other people with Down syndrome. So, no I don't think it's fair to blame me for the fact that he hasn't had a girlfriend, like I've tried to explain he has had opportunities so...

In relation to the issue of her son expressing his sexuality via the medium of a sexual relationship, Eimer summed up her position by stating 'I don't think there is anything wrong with my son having a sexual relationship with somebody else with Down syndrome'.

The contention that a paternalistic parental regime of care cannot be blamed *a priori* for the celibate lives led by many adults with Down syndrome living in the parental home continued to be a reoccurring trope during the interview with Angela. Thus, in response to the question as to whether she believed that the regime of care she deployed regarding her daughter's social and/or sexual life was a contributing factor in explaining why her daughter has yet to be involved in a sexual relationship, the respondent replied: 'I'm not too sure it's fair to blame the parents in that way'. The fact is that Angela wants her daughter to have a boyfriend; that this has yet to happen is, in her own words, 'all very sad'. However, and in common with the accounts offered by many of the other respondents, Angela maintained 'the reason why my daughter has never been in a relationship is because she has Down syndrome and not because anything that I've done'. According to the Angela, she has no regrets that that she did not allow her daughter to 'do what normal people her age do such as go to clubs, stay out all night, get drunk, take drugs and all that kind of stuff'. After a moment's pause, Angela went on to explain that 'the fact that my daughter has an intellectual disability means that she is not like "normal people"'. For the respondent, this means that her daughter 'is very vulnerable to being taken advantage of'. Because of such status, Angela stated unambiguously:

> There was never a chance in hell of me letting her do whatever she wanted regardless of the age she is, to let her do whatever she wanted even though she has Down syndrome would to my mind be a form of child abuse.

The conclusion on Angela's part, that it is not the regime of care, but rather the intellectual impairment, that is the primary explanation accounting for the celibate lives lived by many adults with Down syndrome is based, once again, on the notion that her daughter has her own criteria as to whom she wants as a boyfriend. From Angela's experience, this is someone who is 'normal' rather than an individual with a visible disability like Down syndrome. To illustrate this phenomenon in action, Angela gave the example of how her daughter would react when somebody with Down syndrome would appear on the television. According to the respondent, more often than not her daughter 'would say "yuck, turn it off" or words to that effect'. Such behaviours led Angela to conclude that when it came to forming or trying to form friendships and/or sexual relationships, her daughter would always privilege trying to connect with 'normal people' over those with Down syndrome. In Angela's own words, her daughter 'wanted to be "normal", she wanted to have "normal friends"'.

In response to a specific question about her daughter embarking on a sexual relationship with somebody with Down syndrome, Angela repeated her earlier theory, namely that because of her daughter's 'prejudice about other people with Downs', such an eventuality was 'extremely unlikely'. When then asked whether she thought her daughter had ever had such an opportunity, she stated that 'yes', she had. To illustrate this fact, Angela gave the example of how her daughter would often 'come home with stories about people in the Downs group asking her to be their girlfriend', sometimes even going so far as to try 'to touch her inappropriately'. Such events led Angela to state unequivocally, that from her perspective, her daughter 'had the chance of having a boyfriend with Downs if she had wanted to'. As to such relationship inertia ever changing for her daughter, Angela said that she did not know, but that if a suitor appeared then 'obviously, it would have to be with someone else with Downs'. But there the rub lies, as Angela believes that unless her daughter 'changes her attitude than maybe it will never happen at all'.

Mary responded to my inquiry as to whether she believed there was any link between her paternalistic regime of care and the fact that her son is, as far as she knows, still a virgin by stating:

> Wow, that's a tough question...I don't think I have ever thought about it in those terms before. Like I said before, we have treated him differently where his social life is concerned, but that can't be helped, he has got Down syndrome so he is more vulnerable than normal people his age. But on the other hand, he has had girlfriends in the past...and he does have a fairly hectic social life so...To tell you the truth I don't know how to answer that.

Mary then clarified that her son has had one girlfriend since he turned 18— an age when according to the respondent, her son began to actively define himself as an adult, and who wanted to be allowed do what other adults do. When asked to describe what her son and his girlfriend would do together, she gave the following example:

> Well we would let them go to the pictures together...and let them have their pizza after...and then they would go their separate ways.... sometimes we would bring her home to her parents and then drive back home

sometimes her parents would pick her up.... but she also went to some of our family parties.

I then asked her why she felt she or her husband had to be present or nearby when her son was on a date. She responded by stating: 'Well we wouldn't have been invading their privacy, but within X [she names the mall where they would usually meet] there are lots of shops, it's a big place. Plus, he wouldn't have been able to get home otherwise'. Regarding my follow-up inquiry regarding her son possibly getting a taxi home, Mary said: 'He probably could have...but I don't know why we didn't let him do that [she laughs] ...I don't know why, we just did'. Mary then added: 'Perhaps we were too careful looking back on it'. When asked to clarify why she felt this need to be extra careful in comparison to how she treated her other non-intellectually disabled children, she stated 'I think there is just something in here [points to her heart] that tells me I have the mind the "little guy" no matter how old he is' [she laughs]. Returning to the issue of her son's relationship with the girl mentioned previously, my final question on this subject was whether Mary tried to encourage the relationship to deepen in a way that it more resembled a typical boyfriend/girlfriend relationship. In response, she stated: 'Well nothing happened if you know what I mean, but we didn't try and stop anything happening.... we didn't stop him from going out with her...and he was the one who actually broke it off so...'

When I asked Aileen, on the back of her explaining that she has, and still does, treat her daughter in a more paternalistic fashion than her siblings, whether this regime of care may have had a deleterious effect on her daughter forming boyfriend/girlfriend relationships earlier than she did, she responded in the negative. In her own words, she stated:

No I don't think so...at least where other people with Down syndrome are concerned. As I've been saying, we put a lot of limits on where she was going and who she was going with when she was younger. So she didn't have the social life her brothers had at the same age, she didn't go out to clubs, she didn't go out and get drunk and all the usual stuff "normal people" do when they are teenagers or in their twenties...so maybe you could say that because of the restrictions we put on her, she didn't have a sexual relationship at that stage...but only if we are talking about her having a sexual relationship with somebody who didn't have Down syndrome.

When asked to explain further what she meant by this, she replied:

I mean the restrictions we put on her in terms of going out on her own and all the other kind of stuff I mentioned didn't affect the opportunities she had to form a relationship with somebody with Down syndrome. Her social life in that respect was very busy and like I told you we didn't have a problem with her having a boyfriend...quite the opposite, in fact. So, while we had to be careful, I don't think we were unduly restrictive. The proof is in the pudding in fact...so again like I told you already she did have quite a serious boyfriend in her twenties and as you know she is currently engaged to another chap with Down syndrome so...

As this book has conclusively demonstrated, in relation to both the literature cited and the original empirical data collected, the existence of a paternalistic regime of care regarding the social and sexual lives of their respective sons or daughters is an extremely common practice among parents of adults with Down syndrome who are still living in the parental home. There is also a correspondence between the literature and how the mothers I spoke to justified their reasons for acting in such a manner: namely, by reference to the inner conflict they experienced regarding their desire to promote autonomy while also guarding against the possibility of their adult sons and daughters being harmed in some way (Wright, 2011). This theme of a perceived moral duty on the part of parents to deploy a paternalistic regime of care that is based on the existence of a dialectical relationship between the intrinsic vulnerability of the intellectually disabled adult and the threats posed by the external world is also mirrored in a study by Saaltink et al. (2012). The authors claim that the rationale behind the parental regime of care is based on "the degree to which young people were perceived to require protection and thus were able to participate in decision making seemed to be driven by their personal characteristics, which in turn interacted with external threats to well-being" (Saaltink et al, 2012:1080). They go on to state that, "in terms of personal characteristics, parents often described their children with ID as lacking flexibility and complex decision-making skills, as not being able to discern between 'right and wrong'", hence the need for their intervention (ibid.).

Theme 2: Analysis

The contention that as parents they sometimes had to act as if they were reluctant jailors when it came to the nature of the parental regimes they deployed towards their adult sons and daughters with Down syndrome was something that all the mothers assented to. However, when it came to the specific issue of those mothers whose adult children were not and have never been in a boyfriend/girlfriend relationship, any posited connection between these two variables was vigorously disputed. Due to the mothers' acceptance of the cognitive capacity/autonomy discourse that positions adults with Down syndrome as members of a vulnerable population—more liable than their non-intellectually disabled contemporaries to be sexually exploited and/or abused, for example—they, occupying the subject position of 'the good mother', deemed it necessary to put restrictions on the nature of their social life.

Thus, based on their responses, the mothers would, to a greater or lesser extent, no doubt agree with the social model charge that views the kind of family care they are involved as something that "by no means guarantees greater independence and autonomy for disabled people" (Thomas, 2007:97). However, as their responses also demonstrate, they take issue with the notion that their sons and daughters actually possess the cognitive wherewithal to act autonomously in the first place. This conclusion on the mothers' part is based on their belief that when it comes to where they stand on the specific instance of the autonomy/paternalism debate under perusal, impairment matters. Consequently, the reasons why the normative 'force' of the assertion made by Thomas, which are typical of the social model perspective generally, do not have the effect on the mothers (all of whom informed me that as political activists they were extremely familiar with the social model of disability) that they have in other quarters is due to one of the major criticisms of the social model approach. Namely, that much of its claims, whether descriptive, normative or rhetorical in nature, privilege the plight of physically disabled people over the plight of intellectually disabled people, where the question of reduced autonomy and the need for third party intervention is a very real-life issue. For instance, as the mothers' responses exemplify, the autonomy/paternalism debate as it relates to the right, or not, of intellectually disabled people to control their sexuality is a crucial one to engage with for those who are concerned with the sexual well-being of adults with Down syndrome. Conversely, it has little relevance for those who are concerned with the sexual well-being of those whose impairments are purely physical in nature and whose capacity for consent within a sexual relationship is not called into question.

However, the mothers, while unwilling to recant the need to deploy a paternalistic regime of care, were equally adamant that in saying 'no' to one form of life for their adult sons and daughters they were not closing down all possibilities for the expression of their sexuality via the medium of a sexual relationship. Hence, the consensus view on the part of the respondents was that even in such circumscribed circumstances, there were still opportunities for their charges to meet a boyfriend/girlfriend. This position is encapsulated by Susan, who stated:

> I don't agree with the notion that because we are more 'paternalistic' with X than we are with his siblings that he hasn't had the opportunity to find a girlfriend—he has. Obviously, the fact that he has Down syndrome means that we can't let him just do whatever he wants when he wants, but that doesn't mean that he has no social life and no opportunities to socialize with members of the opposite sex. In a certain sense his social life has always been very full, and it always involved socializing with members of the opposite sex. Of course, they would have had some kind of intellectual disability as well...mainly Down syndrome...but my point is that although we are very protective of him, opportunities for him to find a girlfriend have always existed.

It is also clear that the mothers' attitudes towards their perceived need to care for their sons and daughters via the paternalistic regimes they deploy is not one they see as inherently disabling—the predominant view espoused by disciples of the social model theorists. Rather, their approach seems to take the exact opposite view; that is, the care they show towards their children is a means to their empowerment. Arguably, the preponderance of the data leads one to believe that, whether they could formulate it in such explicit terms or not, the mothers in their relationships with their sons and daughters are in behavioural terms acting out of the basic tenets that inform normalisation/SRV. That is, they assent to the proposition that the needs of people with intellectual disability are "basically the same as those of ordinary people, with the difference that they may not be able to meet these needs unaided or as independently as other people can" (Ryan and Thomas, 1997:129) and are trying to act accordingly.

Consequently, despite the paternalistic regimes of care in place, the adult sons and daughters of the mothers are not wholly wrapped in cotton wool and thus denied the dignity that many argue comes with being allowed to engage in 'risk-taking' behaviour (Brown and Brown, 2009; Hollomotz, 2009, 2011). The essence of this 'risk-taking equals increased autonomy argument' is advanced by Deeley and Hollomotz respectively. The former states that while parents may wish to protect their disabled sons and daughters from 'unpleasant' experiences, "it is these very experiences that help towards human growth" (2002:32). The latter, on the other hand, makes a dangerously flawed analogy between the sometimes less than rational decisions made by non-intellectually disabled people and their intellectually disabled contemporaries asserts: "seeing through the consequences of ill-advised decisions…teaches a person that their choices have real consequences", a process which in turn "can increase autonomy and cultivate the ability to manage risks more independently" (Hollomotz, 2014:248).

As we have seen, all the adults with Down syndrome I spoke to work part-time, and many of them are allowed make their way to and from their workplace on their own, which entails negotiating public transport, amongst other things. This state of affairs contrasts strongly with the research, involving interviews with adults with Down syndrome and family members undertaken by Carr, which found that "over a quarter of the people with Down syndrome were said never to be left in the house alone for more than half an hour, and just over half were never allowed out alone beyond the garden" (2008:393).

To those who are ignorant of the cognitive limitations that accompany the intellectual impairment of Down syndrome, there may not seem much 'risk' involved in such endeavours, but as someone who does know something of such cognitive limitations, let me state categorically that there is. To use a personal example, my sister passed with flying colours the training course she attended designed to empower adults with Down syndrome with the requisite skills to get from A to B via public transport. Yet, it took her over a month to finally master the process of getting the two buses involved and getting off at the right stop—an endeavour that I and my non-intellectually disabled friends had mastered instantly as pre-pubescent children. Moreover, the interim period in question was characterised by numerous phone calls by my sister—and sometimes strangers she had asked for assistance (despite also taking courses dealing with the issue of 'stranger danger') calling on her behalf—to her parents and/or siblings asking for help as she had taken the wrong bus and was now lost, or that she had taken the right bus but had got off at the wrong stop and was now lost. Again, from my experience, such occurrences are not isolated. In fact, the anecdotal evidence I have offered in relation to my sister could be repeated numerous times over in relation to the stories I have heard from other family members of adults with Down syndrome, many of which had very unfortunate consequences for the individuals involved. However, to return to Carr's study regarding those adults with Down syndrome who were allowed to venture outside their respective gardens on their own:

> ...11 people with Down syndrome had at some time been lost, some for several hours, some involving wrong bus or train rides, and eventual return by the police, of whom the parents spoke warmly. Only two, both women, had had potentially sexual encounters: one, walking home from where she was dropped off the coach bringing her back from her day centre, was repeatedly found to have sweets and money that could not be accounted for and which she eventually said had been given to her by 'a man like Grandad'—after this the coach dropped her off at her door; the other met some young men in a pub, went back to their flat for the night and next morning went to the police, but she had not been assaulted or harmed.
>
> (2008:394)

In allowing their adult children with Down syndrome to engage in such practices—and similar instances could be drawn from the data provided in relation to their social lives—the mothers have demonstrated they while they are risk-averse in relation to the specific aspect of the autonomy/ paternalism debate under scrutiny, they are not completely so in general. This distinction is based on the wider societal typology that differentiates between the risks involved in making 'mundane' and important choices, such as control of one's social and sexual life, and the cognitive conditions that have to be met to be allowed act accordingly (Conly, 2013). In addition, however, this stance on the part of the mothers is also informed by their belief that the autonomy their adult sons and daughters enjoy, regardless of the learning they are exposed to, will, due to their cognitive impairment, always be a relative one. The following quote by Jennifer perfectly illustrates their stance vis-à-vis the question of how autonomous an adult with Down syndrome can become. According to Jennifer:

He has Down syndrome, and this—and I don't care what anybody who doesn't have a child with Down syndrome thinks about this issue –means that his ability to think is, and always will be in many ways, similar to that of a child. So, in the same way that most parents control the social lives of their children, I think a similar principle applies to me and the fact that I can't let my son just do or go wherever he wants.

This belief on the part of the mothers regarding the cognitive abilities of their adult sons and daughters with Down syndrome is also mirrored in the study by Carr, who reports:

In the case of independence, while carer attitudes may have imposed restrictions in some cases, the dominant factor was the person's level of cognitive ability. Parents and carers restricted the independence of those they judged to be less able to cope with the demands that independence makes, fearing, in most cases, for their safety: these fears cannot be lightly dismissed.

(2008:396)

Such conclusions are in stark contrast to the views propagated by many of those who argue from a 'human rights perspective', as understood in certain scholarly circles. This classification refers to those who swear allegiance to the social model and/or invoke the CRPD to ground their privileging of the empowerment principle over that of its paternalistic counterpart (Hollomotz, 2009:2014: Richards et al, 2012). Although often formulated in different ways, such a stance is predicated on the belief that

…the ever-present legacy of the idea that those with intellectual disabilities require protection in areas of sexuality has hindered the full embrace of ensuring the empowerment of individuals and must be replaced with a proactive strategy of teaching the concept of freedom and necessary skill of assertion to make sexual decisions independently.

(Richards et al., 2012:112)

However, such ploys assume that the oppressed interlocutor has the cognitive capacity to process the information and act accordingly. But herein lays the problem for such human rights advocates: Their strategies for increased autonomy presuppose a degree of agency that many intellectually disabled people, unlike other oppressed groups they are often compared to, can never possess. As already detailed, according to the mothers interviewed and the relevant literature cited, this is especially the case when the intellectual disability is that of Down syndrome. However, at no stage of their critiques—whether implied or explicit—of those who apply the paternalistic principle to justify their contention that intellectually disabled adults should not enjoy carte blanche to decide how they express their sexuality, do these social model advocates explicate the necessary and sufficient conditions that must be met for such agency to be ascribed to a given individual with intellectual disability. Kittay sums up this theory/praxis confusion when she states:

> ...advocates of disability rights have insisted that the independence and productivity that are essential to being considered equal citizens in a liberal society are no less attainable for the disabled than for the non-disabled. They have argued that their impairments are only disabling in an environment that is hostile to their differences and that has been constructed to exclude them. Yet, the impairment of mental retardation is not easily addressed by physical changes in the environment.
>
> (2001:558)

With Kittay's insight acting as the premise, the conclusion I draw is that the authors in question, in advancing their respective normative arguments, albeit nominally based on empirical claims regarding the potential of all people with 'intellectual disabilities'—as they all employ this umbrella term—are begging the question at hand. Namely, is there, as the mothers I spoke to believe, an isomorphic relationship between specific intellectual impairments and a congenital inability to learn such intellectual self-defence skills in the first place? While not exactly self-evident, in the logical sense at least, the answer to this question—which is indeed yes—can, if the term is used colloquially, be deemed to be a self-evident truth for anybody who knows anything about the various impairments subsumed under the "intellectual disability" umbrella term. To illustrate this conclusion, we can point to the entitlement to positive welfare rights and services (such as a disability benefit) for everybody with Down syndrome living in Ireland. Such provisions are an implicit recognition that such individuals lack the requisite autonomy to exercise the degree of self-determination that is considered normal for their counterparts without intellectual disability. This is because if adults with Down syndrome "were able to be fully independent and to make important life choices without support then they would not be receiving such state-funded services in the first place" (Fyson and Kitson, 2007:434). To cite just one empirical instance to support this claim (as already extensively documented throughout this book), one of the chief findings from an in-depth study of the proceedings of a 'parliament' for intellectually disabled people in an English local authority concerns the "limits of an approach to empowering learning disabled individuals that is cast too exclusively in terms drawn from liberal models of citizenship that prioritise voice over care, security, and wellbeing" (Redley and Weinberg, 2007:767). Thus, Fyson and Cromby, in stating that

> the heterogeneous nature of the ID population means that individual capacities for reasoning will vary hugely: the capacity for decision making

> and independent living of someone with mild or borderline ID may be little different from that of the average citizen, while that of an individual with profound ID is likely to be severely limited.

are essentially repeating a well verified platitude (2013:1166). It is for these reasons, and those offered in the previous section on the ontology of impairment (particularly the series of questions I set out) that the familiar analogy referred to previously—essentially a cognitive version on the notion that we are all temporarily able-bodied—regarding a generalised irrationality is an extremely flawed and misleading one. The fact that *homo economicus* is a myth and that non-intellectually disabled adults sometimes make less than rational decisions has no bearing on the factual claim that the cognitive disparity which differentiates people with intellectual disabilities from their non-intellectually disabled counterparts raises different autonomy/paternalism issues for the former than it does for the latter.

Regarding the differences in relation to cognitive capacity that characterise the various populations subsumed under the "intellectual/learning disability" umbrella terms, it is worth nothing that Richards et al (2012), when not deploying such umbrella terms, make brief references to autism and dyslexia to support their claims. It is also worth noting that among those who have been retrospectively diagnosed as autistic by clinicians, academics, and biographers include Ludwig Wittgenstein—considered by many to be one of the most important and influential philosophers who has ever lived—and Albert Einstein (Monk, 1990). Fyson and Cromby (2013) offer a possible explanation for the conflation of political goals with scholarly argumentation when they contend that the reason for "this lack of balance between permissive and protective rights is that the loudest voices within the self-advocacy movement are, perhaps inevitably, those of well-connected individuals with mild ID" (2013:1169).

From the responses provided by the mothers, we can conclude that the various dilemmas they face regarding how they respond to the autonomy/paternalism issues raised by the fact that they are caring for adult sons and daughters with Down syndrome is based on their belief that their respective charges enjoy an ambiguous ontological status in the sense that although they inhabit physically mature bodies, they retain, in the most part, the minds of pre-pubescent children. To illustrate this stance, it is worth quoting Aileen, as her views—in terms of propositional content—are mirrored by all the mothers I spoke to.

> The fact that my daughter has Down syndrome means she is very vulnerable to being taken advantage of. So, there was never a chance in hell of me letting her do whatever she wanted regardless of the age she is, to let her do whatever she wanted even though she has Down syndrome would to my mind be a form of child abuse.

However, while there is a recognition that identity is relational in the sense that we are who we are by reference to who we are not (Jenkins, 2008), the 'us and them' dynamic that exists between the mothers and their adult children with Down syndrome and that underpins the power relations and the exclusionary practices that follow, is not of 'an all or nothing' nature. Hence, the mothers positioning of their adult children as vulnerable was not in and of itself an acceptance of the discourse that propagates the fiction that adults with Down syndrome are asexual. As already stated in the mothers' acknowledgement that their adult children are sexual beings, they have illustrated they are not cultural dupes, and are, within certain parameters, capable of resisting certain normalising discourses and the subject positions that accompany them. When it came to disentangling any linkage between the paternalistic regimes of care they deployed and the fact that their sons and daughters have never been in a boyfriend/girlfriend relationship, the mothers, again demonstrating their ambiguous relationship to the normal/ abnormal continuum when it came to ascribing different subject positions to their adult children, made reference to the fact that people with Down syndrome, like non-intellectually disabled adults everywhere, operate with certain criteria as to who is deemed boyfriend/girlfriend material. As a result, and as explained previously, according to the relevant mothers, their sons and daughters with Down syndrome seemed for the most part to find non-intellectually disabled adults normal more sexually desirable than their contemporaries with Down syndrome.

Theme 3: Parental view of their adult sons and daughters with Down syndrome as sexual beings—and the desire that they find a girlfriend/boyfriend

When it came to the issue of whether the respondent viewed their adult sons and daughters with Down syndrome as sexual beings with similar sexual desires to that of their contemporaries without intellectual disability, the responses they provided were interestingly ambiguous. For example, in response to a specific question on whether she wanted her teenage daughter to have a boyfriend or whether that was a non-issue, Aileen replied that while her daughter was below the age of seventeen, she *'wasn't particularly thinking along those lines'*. She went on to add: *'I was always open to the idea that there was no reason that my daughter wouldn't want to have a boyfriend, just like other girls of her age'*. Hence, the issue of her daughter entering what would presumably be a sexual relationship was not something that Aileen *'was against per se'*, rather the dilemma was one born out of a sense of fear as to *'how that could be dealt with'*. This was a fear on Aileen's part of how she would be able *'to guarantee that her daughter would have a boyfriend that would respect her'*. In formulating a tentative answer to this question, she drew once again on the normal/abnormal continuum, thinking aloud about whether such security could only come if her nominal boyfriend came *'from the same background'* as her daughter—in the sense of he too having Down syndrome—or whether a sexual relationship involving her daughter with *'somebody who didn't have a disability'* was in any way feasible or healthy from her daughter's perspective. Her conclusion on where she stands on such issues was nominally inconclusive with the respondent claiming that she *'never knew'* the right answer and still does not.

The contention by Aileen that the prospect of her daughter embarking on a sexual relationship with someone without an intellectual disability is one she finds more problematic than if a potential suitor was intellectually disabled is one that has been replicated in the extant literature. For example, in my own published work on the autonomy/paternalism debate as it relates to increased sexual self-determination for adults with Down syndrome (Foley, 2013), when I asked the respondents (made up of both fathers and mothers of adults with Down syndrome) to consider the hypothetical scenario of their son or daughter entering into a sexual relationship with somebody without an intellectual disability—where there would be an asymmetry in relation to cognitive capacity between the parties. The consensus view on the part of the respondents was that such a relationship was one they could not, and would not, condone. A stance they maintained even if it turned out that their son or daughter 'was in love with the individual concerned'. For instance, one of the fathers stated that such a situation would be exploitative given the power differential he deemed would necessarily follow from the cognitive imbalance between his son and a suitor without an intellectual disability. To this end, he stated:

> as far as I'm concerned someone who doesn't have an intellectual disability has control over him and I wouldn't allow it, no matter how much he loves him, no way. I see my son having a relationship with someone of his own ability.
>
> (Foley, 2013:5)

In a similar fashion, one of the mothers, when talking about the possibility of her daughter with Down syndrome becoming sexually involved with a man without an intellectual disability, stated: 'I wouldn't be able to get my head around it'; 'the question I would be asking is 'why'? What apart from the obvious, apart from simply using her for sex would he want, what else would he get out of such a relationship?' (ibid).

Regarding the issue as to whether sexual relationships were ever a topic of conversation between her and her daughter. Aileen stated that, yes they were, and that typically the subject was initiated by her daughter. When asked to explain why she thought this subject matter had become a recurring topic between the two of them, Aileen replied that it was simply because her daughter *'was dying to have a boyfriend'*. When asked to expand on what she thought was driving her daughter's aspirations in this regard once again, the normal/abnormal continuum was invoked to explain a turn of events that was to become a normal occurrence up to the time that her daughter met '*the man of her dreams*', an individual to whom she is currently engaged and due to marry in a few years. In relation to her daughter's initial motivation to find a boyfriend, the question of sexual desire was never mentioned; rather, Aileen explained her daughter's behaviour by reference to an urge to embrace a normal identity, and act accordingly. For example, her daughter's first boyfriend, when she was twenty years of age, had an intellectual disability but did not have Down syndrome. According to Aileen, her daughter originally was very happy to be in this relationship. However, she goes on to add that, from her perspective, part of her daughter's positive feelings about having this first experience were because the boyfriend in question '*didn't look as if he had a disability*'. It is interesting to note, that this positing, on the part of Aileen, that adults with Down syndrome in common with most of their non-intellectually disabled contemporaries have criteria that prospective sexual partners must meet is an issue that also came up repeatedly during the interviews with the adults with Down syndrome themselves. When asked to expand on why she believed that it was important for her daughter that a potential or actual boyfriend did not look as if he had an intellectual disability, the mother explained that her daughter would at some level also subscribe to the difference as deficit model when it came to Down syndrome, hence 'she would have been very conscious of the fact that a Down syndrome person looks different to other people'. Consequently, her daughter 'was quite proud of the fact...that she had a boyfriend who was tall, had curly hair, quite handsome...and he didn't have a disability, even though he did...but she didn't see because it wasn't obvious'. Regarding the question of Aileen's contention that her daughter is indeed a sexual being with sexual needs, the next question concerned Aileen's daughter's status as an engaged woman. I asked Aileen if she would characterise this relationship as a 'typical' or 'normal' boyfriend/girlfriend relationship. In response, she explained:

> in the past few years they have gone and spent a couple of nights together in a hotel, be it for New-Year's Eve or birthdays or different occasions...and to be very honest...I have...even though my daughter talks about this relationship, I've no idea whether it's a platonic relationship or whether it has become a sexual relationship.

I then asked whether Aileen's lack of knowledge regarding whether her daughter's relationship was an intimate one due to a reluctance on her daughter's part to discuss such issues, or where their other reasons. In response, she stated:

> She...my daughter wouldn't have a problem talking about anything to me, we discuss everything, but...I kind of feel at this stage in her life that I...I'm leaving it up to her. People have often asked me "why do I not

know the answer to this", but I kind of feel I have treated my daughter in as normal a fashion as is possible, and it's something that...I've held back from asking that question because I've never asked it of my sons, if they volunteer the information to me that's fine...and I have a pretty open relationship with them. So why should I treat my daughter any differently to her brothers? If she wants to tell me it's an intimate relationship...that's fine...she knows she can talk to me about anything... but if she doesn't...I'm not going to ask her...that's her business.

In Claire's opinion, her realization that her son was a sexual being became apparent when he entered the teenage years. The example she offered to illustrate this insight revolved around how her son began to behave when interacting with the female friends of his teenage sisters. The respondent stated that her son would have 'been quite tactile' with his sister's friends, so much so, that not only did he develop 'a crush on one or two of them', but also engaged in 'some inappropriate touching'. In response to the question as to whether she found her son's new found sexual curiosity in any way problematic, Claire answered in the affirmative, stating: 'Yeah I suppose it was'. She went on to explain that while 'part of me had hoped that his condition would mean that would never become an issue', this desire was disabused when Claire 'was told by her GP and by the various experts who make up his support team to expect him to have normal sexual desires'. When asked to detail what her concerns around this were, Claire stated: 'The concern was that he would never be able to find a girlfriend of his own'. When probed, she explained that the root of her concern was due to 'the fact that he has Down syndrome'. According to Claire, this intellectual impairment 'makes a huge difference to how other people, other normal people view you'. Hence, she went on to explain:

> I was afraid that because he had Down syndrome nobody would want him as their boyfriend...and again maybe it's a horrible thing to say but so far all of my fears have been borne out, nobody does want him as their boyfriend, or at the very least nobody he wants as a girlfriend, nobody he finds sexually attractive wants him as their boyfriend.

When Jennifer was asked whether she conceived of her son as a sexual being—as somebody with the same sexual needs as his non-intellectually disabled contemporaries—she answered:

> Yes of course I think of him as a sexual being with all the normal sexual needs of normal men his own age.... that's what makes the fact that he hasn't been in a sexual relationship or never had a girlfriend so sad.

To make explicit in what I thought Jennifer was saying, I then asked whether this meant she wanted her son to have a sexual life via the medium of an intimate relationship. In response, she stated this was indeed the case: 'I want him to have a girlfriend, I want him to experience what it's like to have sex with another human being'. However, in common with Claire, Jennifer also expressed doubts—due to the same factors—as to whether her own, and her son's aspirations in this respect will ever be realized. When I asked her why she held this view, she once again invoked her perception of her son's criterion as to possible girlfriends/sexual partners—which from Jennifer's experience of her son essentially rules out women with Down syndrome from such a category.

When Eimer was asked whether she considered her thirty-three-year-old son to have the same sexual needs as those of his non-intellectually disabled contemporaries, she replied: 'Yeah I do believe that yeah'. I then asked her, given that's the case, whether she was concerned by the fact that he is currently single—and as far as she knows, still a virgin. To this, she responded: 'Yeah...yeah...I think it's very sad'. After leaving a longer pause than usual, I explained that I was still not really sure as to where she stood on the issue and asked for more clarification. In response, Eimer stated: 'Well I probably don't think about it on a daily basis...it's something that I would like him to have but I don't think I would think about it every day'.

Theme 3: Analysis

In relation to whether the respondents viewed their adult sons and daughters as sexual beings, we can categorise the mothers' responses, to a certain extent at least, as an instance of Foucault's resistance to power. Thus, we see, in contradistinction to the dominant discourse, which portrays adults with Down syndrome as essentially asexual beings, there was recognition on the part of all the respondents that their adult sons and daughters have sexual needs. If, as Foucault maintains, discourse has both linguistic and material components (1977, 1978), then based on the accounts proffered by the parents, we can conceptualise their insights as partly stemming from the refusal of their charges to adopt the role of 'docile bodies' and stick to the larger societal script written for them. Therefore, based on the experiential knowledge gained from their sons and daughters expressing sexual interest and/or desire to have a boyfriend/girlfriend from the teenage years onwards, the positive attitudes displayed by the respondents regarding their adult children's sexuality can be interpreted as a rejection of a particular regime of truth as an ideology rather than an as an authoritative body of truth claims. Conversely, the parental consensus regarding their wish for their adult sons and daughters with Down syndrome to find a boyfriend/girlfriend after certain conditions are met can be conceptualised as an instance of Foucault's productive conception of power in action. In this context, the power/knowledge nexus has produced the heteronormative discourse that states that boyfriend/girlfriend relationships are an integral part of what it means to live a worthwhile normal life, and that good parents should rightly be concerned if their sons and daughters do not form such connections.

Theme 4: The privileging of 'loving' boyfriend/girlfriend relationships over sexual expression for its own sake: The gender bias in action

When Rebecca was asked how important it is that her daughter ever experiences what it is like to embark on a sexual relationship, she replied: 'I suppose at the moment it's not that important as she's still living with us and she seems to be reasonably happy'; however, Rebecca went on to add that 'thinking long-term, I suppose I would like her to meet somebody'. The rationale behind this desire is that Rebecca does not 'like the notion of her being alone when we are no longer around or too old to take care of her'. When probed as to whether such a relationship was conceived by her to be solely an antidote to her daughter's loneliness, or whether her wishes were also borne out of a belief that her daughter had sexual needs a boyfriend could meet, Rebecca clarified that her concern is more to do with her daughter 'having someone to love…you know…meeting a special friend rather than the sexual thing'. In relation to the issue of Rebecca believing her daughter to have 'normal' sexual needs, she replied 'that's a difficult one'. For example, while stating that 'according to the stuff I've read I realise my' daughter has 'normal sexual needs', she went on to qualify that her 'priority would be' for her daughter 'having someone to love…and someone who loves her'. When asked whether she felt that the 'the sex thing was important' for her daughter, Rebecca admitted that she didn't 'know how to answer that'. However, in an attempt to clarify further, she went on to add that 'yes in an ideal world it is', and how 'in an ideal world' the respondent would like her daughter 'to experience what it's like to have sex with someone…to have her sexual needs met if you like', but repeated her stipulation that any such sexual activity would have to be the by-product of a loving relationship. When asked whether she actively thought about her daughter's sexuality, Rebecca replied that she tried not to. However, she went on to explain that her self-discipline in this area was far from perfect and admitted that 'there are times when you can't not think about it'; but when such thoughts occurred, they coalesced around what Rebecca described as the 'joy it would bring to her in having a boyfriend she is in love with rather than a focus on someone to meet her sexual needs'. To ensure there was no ambiguity as to where Rebecca stood on this issue, the next question posed was whether she believed her daughter had sexual needs, and if yes, was it important to Rebecca that they should be met. In reply, she stated:

> Well like I said, I suppose in principle she does, that's what I've read, that's what her GP has told me, so yes she has. But on the other hand, I think there is something in this notion that women, normal women or women with Downs don't have the same sexual needs as men. That's possibly a little politically incorrect but from my own experience, and from talking to my female friends that seems to be something we all agree on.

When further clarification was sought, Rebecca replied by stating:

> I think what I'm trying to say is that while women have 'sexual needs' we tend to see sex as something extra...that the relationship is the most important thing...in other words from the female perspective love is what's most important...that unlike for men sex for women is not like scratching an itch...it's something we can do without...especially as we get older...and I don't think that's the case for men.

To leave no doubt as to what Rebecca was trying to convey, the final question attempted to paraphrase what she had been saying by taking the following formulation: 'Okay so when you think about your daughter's sexual needs, you don't see them as being as strong as that of a man's—that if they have to be met, it needs to be in the context of a loving relationship'? To this Rebecca essentially agreed with the position I attributed to her, replying:

> Yeah basically that's what I'm saying, so when I think about it I usually say "yes it would be nice for her to experience what sex is like" but if it doesn't happen then what she will miss out on is not that important, not as important if she was a man, for example.

In response to the question whether she hoped her son would find a girl-friend, Sofia answered in the affirmative, stating that she wants her son to experience what a boyfriend/girlfriend relationship feels like. When then asked whether she held this desire for her son because she sees him as some-one with sexual needs: that is, the sexual needs of a non-intellectually disabled thirty-year-old man or is it something more, she replied: 'I do see him as someone with normal sexual needs so that's definitely a factor, but on top of that I would also like him to find that special someone, someone who he loves and who loves him back'.

Theme 4: Analysis

While all the respondents, again in their own different ways, agreed that they wanted their respective sons and daughters, to as Jennifer puts it, 'experience what it's like to have sex with another human being', this did not mean however, they prescribed to the 'casual view' of sexual interaction. According to Benatar, the 'casual view' concept of sexuality is one which sees sexual expression primarily as a means to pleasure, which from a moral perspective is "like any other pleasure and may be enjoyed subject only to the usual sorts of moral constraints" (2013:397). Benatar poses an important question that serves to ground this conception of loveless sexual expression that has sexual gratification as its sole object, as just another form of life that raises no moral dilemmas. He asks if "having meals with a string of strangers or mere acquaintances is not condemnable as 'causal gastronomy', 'eating around', or 'culinary promiscuity'", then why is it the case that having sexual relations with whomever one chooses is condemned (ibid.)? Nonetheless, the consensus position on the part of the parents was that while their adult children had sexual needs, such needs should not be met in an emotional vacuum. Instead, they argued that sexual relations and a loving relationship are two sides of the same coin, and it was this that they wanted most for their sons and daughters. This stance was expressed with particular vehemence when it came to the issue of facilitated sex (initially at any rate, as we will see below) where the absence of love, or even some lesser form of emotional reciprocity, was compounded by the fact that the putative sexual partner would be a 'stranger'.

As a heuristic guide, we can employ Soble's typology (2013), which makes the distinction between metaphysical sexual 'optimists' and metaphysical sexual 'pessimists', to contend that all the parents can be categorised as sexual 'pessimists'. Soble states that

> the particular metaphysics of sex a person holds, either for rational or emotional reasons, will influence his or her subsequent judgements about the value and role of sexuality in the virtuous or good life and about which sexual activities are morally wrong and which are morally permissible.
>
> (2013:3)

He goes on to define a metaphysical sexual 'pessimist' as someone who believes that "sexuality is morally permissible and prudentially wise only within lifelong, monogamous, heterosexual marriage" (2013:5). From a Foucauldian perspective, it is not coincidental to discover that while all the parents interviewed expressed the belief that their sons and daughters had normal sexual needs, they wanted such needs to be met in the context of a loving boyfriend/girlfriend relationship. If one engages in a genealogy or a 'history of the present' regarding competing Irish discourses on what constitute legitimate and illegitimate forms of sexual expression, it becomes apparent that the myth that Ireland has escaped its Catholic legacy and undergone a permissive liberal 'epistemic shift' where issues of sexuality are concerned is just that. These conclusions also vindicate this book's concentration on the issue of genital sex over and above other forms of sexual expression to explore the autonomy/paternalism debate where the issue of sexual expression for adults with Down syndrome is concerned. As already explained, such debates essentially revolve around answering two questions. Firstly, what is it that differentiates 'autonomous' adults from children and 'vulnerable' adults (who are deemed to lack autonomy), and secondly, are there practices that the former can freely engage in but the latter—for paternalistic reasons—cannot (Conly, 2013)?

According to Inglis,

> over the last fifty years we have moved in Ireland from a Catholic culture of self-abnegation in which sexual pleasure and desire were repressed, to a culture of consumption and self-indulgence in which the fulfilment of pleasures and desires is emphasized.

(2005:11)

However, as this book amply demonstrates, when one accurately maps the discourses that circulate in contemporary Ireland, it is clear that the emphasis on the fulfilment of sexual desires and pleasures applies to certain groups in Irish society rather than Irish society as a whole. In effect, when it comes to the workings of the Irish socio-political economy, there are different normalising discourses propagating different standards of normal sexual expression that are addressed to different sections of Irish society. Such exclusionary practices are nowhere more evident when it comes to adults with intellectual disabilities like Down syndrome expressing their sexuality. When it comes to the sexual needs of members of this population, it is clearly not the case that the dominant Irish discourse is one which emphasises the fulfilment of sexual pleasures and desires. To validate this claim, one only has to look at current Irish law, which legally prohibits a large percentage of adults with an intellectual disability from even embarking on a sexual relationship. To recap, the relevant legislation is to be found in Section 5 of the Criminal Law (Sexual offences) Act of 1993. The Act states that it is a criminal offence for an individual with a mental impairment who is not living independently to engage in sexual relations unless they are married (Johnson et al., 2010).

In addition, regarding the mothers' use of the cognitive ability/autonomy discourse and the frequent analogy they made to the effect that when it comes to cognitive abilities their adult sons and daughters with Down syndrome are in many relevant respects just like children, it is crucial to be cognisant of the fact that the respondents are also subjected to a wider Irish prohibitory discourse around the rights of 'children' to express their sexuality. The scare quotes around the word 'children' are used to problematize the range of people who are subsumed under this umbrella term. As already referenced throughout this chapter, based on the explicit statements made by the respondents when the adult with Down syndrome/child analogy is made, the comparison is not referring to the average 'normal' non-intellectually disabled teenager. Rather, the point being made by the mothers is that when it comes to cognitive capacity and the ability to govern oneself, they believe that their adult sons and daughters with Down syndrome are, and will remain, in many important respects like pre-pubescent children. With this distinction in mind, we can examine in greater detail the normalizing discourses that state that non-intellectually disabled teenagers under the age of 17 do not possess the requisite cognitive skills that would equip them with the rights—both legal and moral—to determine their own sexuality.

One very relevant manifestation of the cognitive ability/autonomy discourse in action can be found in current Irish legislation regarding the age of consent (which is 17) and the crime of statutory rape (Irish Statute Book, 2006). In order to identify and examine the wider societal discourses regarding legitimate and illegitimate forms of sexual expression that the cohort of mothers are being subjected to as to why sexual expression for certain populations remains a dangerous discourse, the following section will focus briefly on the issue of statutory rape.

For most of its history, the law around statutory rape has enjoyed a reified status as a totem-like signifier symbolising the Irish people's commitment to a restrictive Catholic sexual moral code (Bacik, 2004). However, in 2006 its *raison d'être* was briefly destabilised from within the legal field itself when the Supreme Court in the C.C. v Ireland case unanimously declared unconstitutional the same law under which any man is automatically guilty of a crime if he has sex with a girl under 15. The legal judgement followed a case brought before the courts by an adult male who was facing four charges of the statutory rape of a fifteen-year-old girl when as a seventeen-year-old he admitted having consensual intercourse with the girl (his girlfriend at the time), whom he claimed had told him she was 16. The terminology in question is interesting, as the category 'man' was being applied to a seventeen-year-old child/teenager/man. The inconsistent and contradictory labelling clearly begs the question as to the logic behind the situations where the child/teenager-man/woman distinction is willingly collapsed and where the binary is strictly policed. Prior to the Supreme Court's decision, if a male child/teenager/adult was convicted of having sexual intercourse with a female child/teenager/young woman under 15, even if it was consensual, he could face up to life imprisonment under the 1935 legislation and would as a matter of course also be placed on the Sex Offenders Register.

Apropos of some of the mothers drawing on their discursive repertoires to make a distinction between male/female sexuality and corresponding sexual needs, this gender bias based on essentialist notions of sexual difference and sexual desire is also officially marked in current Irish legislation: If the girl/teenager/young woman had been older than the boy/teenager/young man, no offence would have been committed. Following the Supreme Court's decision and the moral panic that followed, the Irish Parliament passed the 2006 Criminal Law Sexual Offences Act. In trying to contextualise the true nature of the negative discourses around sexual expression, it is apparent that the interview responses are caught up in an important legal change that reproduces gender bias in even stronger form insofar as the act now excludes females under 17 from any criminal liability. Thus Section 5 of the Act states "A female child under the age of seventeen years shall not be guilty of an offence under this Act by reason only of her engaging in an act of sexual intercourse" (Irish Statute Book, 2006). Consequently, as things currently stand, Irish law regulating the expression of teenage sexuality states that for a male of any age to engage in a sexual act with a child/teenager under 15 is an offence punishable by a prison sentence of up to a life term, while for a male of any age to engage in a sexual act with a child/teenager between 15 and 17 is punishable by up to five years in jail, or ten years where the accused was a person in authority. Because of the gender bias when it comes to heterosexual sex, if both parties are under the age of consent it is the boy\teenager\young man who commits the offence, and not the girl\teenager\young woman (www.citizensinformation.ie, 2011). Obviously, implicit in such legislation is the reification of a particularly archaic and wholly normative gender stereotype that reproduces the notion that Irish female teenagers under the age of consent are less rational, less intelligent, and less sexual than their male counterparts. Consequently, their choices around the area of sexual expression are choices in name only. Allen explicates the obvious result of deploying this particular gender order taxonomy of 'human kinds' to classify female teenagers below a certain age as de-sexualised legal subjects when she states "without recognition of desire and pleasure as legitimate female experiences, young women are cast within heteronormative discourses of sexuality as the passive recipients of male sexual desire" (2012:458).

However, this legal discourse is not the only one that propagates the dominant Irish regime of truth that states that sexual expression is a dangerous activity for those who fall on the wrong side of the cognitive ability/ autonomy continuum. For example, the long-promised Children's Rights referendum designed to explicitly enshrine children's rights into the Irish Constitution was passed in November 2012. Uniquely, in the long history of Irish referenda it received unanimous cross-party political support with both government and opposition parties actively campaigning for a yes vote. The Prime Minister Enda Kenny hailed the result as an "historic day" for the children of Ireland as the victory constitutes "the first time the constitution of this Republic will recognise them as citizens in their own right" (O'Leary, 2012). Needless to say, this new status as citizens did not allow Irish teenagers under a certain age to take ownership of their own sexuality, as the legislation regarding the age of consent and statutory rape remains in place.

To make it explicit, what can be inferred from the cross-party political support that the new legislation received is the failure to give Irish teenagers under the age of 17 rights to sexually interact with their peers is not due to liberal Ireland losing a discursive battle with its conservative counterpart. Rather, there was no ideological conflict because the current Irish regime of truth, which links cognitive ability with sexual self-determination, transcends left-right differences. Moreover, this convergence of views regarding the dangers of sexual expression for some groups was not limited to the political field alone; it also determined the missing debate within the public sphere as a whole. Consequently, it seems to be the case that for Irish conservatives and liberals alike if the issue of sexuality and teenagers is mentioned at all, its form and content is one that reproduces the dominant negative discourse that propagates the view that teenagers under a certain age should not be allowed to have sex with each other and that the law should reflect this fact and continue to punish anyone—as long as they are male—who breaks it.

When we refer back to Soble's (2013) distinction between sexual pessimists and sexual optimists and apply this to the issue of Irish teenagers under the age of 17 not having the right to control their sexuality, one logical conclusion to draw is that there are no sexual optimists. In effect, the cognitive ability/autonomy discourse around the dangers inherent in sexual expression holds sway amongst both secular liberals and theists alike. Consequently, given the normalising forces exerted by such discourses on the parental regimes of care adopted by parents of non-intellectually disabled teenagers, it is of little surprise to discover that they also inform the practices deployed by the respondents in their role as reluctant jailors of adults with Down syndrome.

However, at this stage, it is important to note that while caring for one's children is a constitutive component of what it means to be a good mother, the good mother subject position does not enjoy a univocal definition. Rather, like all subject positions that are ideologically constructed, there are different notions of what being a good mother entails depending on whether one is a liberal good mother, a conservative good mother, and so on. This added complication can help explain what some may see as a possible contradiction in this analysis. This refers to my conjecture that while legal discourses can be posited as an influence informing the nature of their parental regime of care when it concerns their daughters and their views on female sexuality, such a contention is at odds with one of the empirical findings this book has collected. The relevant findings are that most the mothers claimed that they were not aware of the discriminatory legislation described above and, consequently, it did not inform the nature of their parental regime of care. In addition, however, the consensus view on their part was that they would knowingly violate such laws if that was the only factor standing in the way of their stated aspiration that their respective sons or daughters find a boyfriend/girlfriend. However, any apparent contradiction is just that. This is because, as stated previously, the mothers in question self-identify as secular liberal 'good mothers', a subject position that assents to the proposition that once certain conditions are met, a sexual life is an important component of a good life. This principled position also extends to the quality of life their adult sons and daughters should be allowed to live. Consequently, one result of the perennial conflict between the law and people's moral convictions (outlined in Chapter 2) is that not all legislation enjoys an equal legitimacy in the eyes of a state's citizenry. This is a state of affairs that has obvious, and different, behavioural consequences depending on the ideological camp one identifies with. Thus, although I am arguing that the logic of the secular liberal position is one that should view consensual sexual interaction as just another form of life that raises no unique moral dilemmas, this is not a view actually held by many Irish secular liberals (as previously demonstrated in relation to the legal discrepancies between underage male and female teenagers). Rather, many (and I include most the mothers I interviewed in this grouping) who would align themselves with this ideological classification continue to subscribe to the discourse that propagates the notion of female sexuality as different to male sexuality, hence the need to maintain different formal and informal rules regulating the sexual expression of both genders.

This conclusion that ideology matters when it comes to influencing the nature of a given parental regime of care is also a key factor informing my conclusion that an appeal to formal legal rights, such as those contained within the CRPD, is not the panacea it may seem to many of its advocates in overcoming obstacles to adults with intellectual disabilities such as Down syndrome from entering a sexual relationship (Richards et al., 2012). This is especially the case when the only barrier nominally preventing them from doing so is that of a parental prohibition that is parents occupying the role of conservative good mothers/fathers. The argument that legal rights equals increased sexual autonomy is based on the empirical fact that "disabled people experience sexual repression, possess little or no sexual autonomy, and tolerate institutional and legal restrictions on their intimate contact" (Siebers, 2008:136). The conclusion drawn states that if we are "to liberate disabled sexuality and give to disabled people a sexual culture of their own, their status as a sexual minority requires the protection of citizenship rights similar to those being claimed by other sexual minorities" (Siebers, 2008:154).

Clearly this rights-based approach is of crucial importance when it comes to facilitating the sexual autonomy of adults with intellectual disability who are living under the aegis of some form of state-funded institutional accommodation that prohibits intellectually disabled adults embarking on sexual relationships (Foley, 2014). However, when it comes to the state intervening in family relations, things are immensely more complicated. To ground this deduction, let us look at the following example. What happens in a situation involving two adults with Down syndrome, X and Y, who want to have a sexual relationship with each other and are living in their respective parent's houses? The parents of X, respecting their child's decision in this regard, raise no objections. The parents of Y, however, both for paternalistic and/or religious reasons, are opposed to their adult child becoming involved in a sexual relationship and subsequently prevent Y from exercising their right to control their own sexuality. Using the CRPD as its blueprint, is it legally incumbent on the state to intervene in the situation? Can it impose legal sanctions on the parents in question? Conversely, is it entitled under domestic and/or international law to remove the adult with Down syndrome from the parental home in question, citing some form of humanitarian intervention to justify their actions in the same way it would legally be permitted to do if Y was being subject to 'abuse' as conventionally defined? If the answers to these questions are no, what is the real legal status of the rights enshrined in Article 12 of the CRPD, which states "that persons with disabilities have the right to recognition everywhere as persons before the law"; "that persons with disabilities enjoy legal capacity on an equal basis with others in all aspects of life", and Article 23 which states: "State parties shall take effective and appropriate measures to eliminate discrimination against persons with disabilities in all matters relating to marriage, family, parenthood and relationships, on an equal basis with others" (CRPD, 2006).

In effect, the question needs to be asked whether it is possible to draw up specific legislation to the effect that it is a criminal offence for a parent to block the sexual expression of their adult son or daughter with Down syndrome. If not, why not? And if not, what practical effect can the convention have in rectifying the all too real scenarios set out previously? Alternatively, if the answer to the previous questions is yes, then what? For example, how feasible is it to imagine an adult with Down syndrome being removed from the parental home on the sole basis that their parents are denying them the right to express their sexuality? Putting to one side the crucial issue as to who would alert the legal authorities in the first place and concentrating on the burden of proof question, we can ask what would be the necessary and sufficient conditions that need to be met for this breach to be deemed a crime? Would the word of the adult with Down syndrome be enough? In addition, if criminal proceedings were instigated at time t1, what happens if at time t2, the adult with Down syndrome changes their mind and withdraws their 'charges' on being informed that their parents would be punished, or that they may have to leave the family home? Would the prosecution go ahead anyway? Could the adult with Down syndrome be forcibly removed from the parental home despite their change of mind? The fact that one could formulate an almost infinite array of such questions illustrates the potentially insurmountable problems facing a given state if the rights in question attained legally enforceable status.

Given the indeterminate language the CRPD employs and the centrality of the role that judicial interpretation plays in determining whether the rights protected within a given article have indeed been violated, we can embellish the above thought experiment to expose further the limitations of the CRPD—or indeed anybody of formal legal rights—when it comes to empowering adults with Down syndrome to have the decisive say in whether they will have sex with another person or remain celibate. For the sake of the argument, let us imagine that the legal texts in question are drained of all ambiguity and all the relevant experts agree as to what legal capacity entails and the necessary and sufficient conditions that must be met before one is deemed to possess it. In addition, there exists an infallible method to determine whether someone with Down syndrome has the cognitive capacity to consent to entering a sexual relationship—a test that both X and Y pass. Furthermore, thanks to hypothetical advances in neuroscience, technology exists that can establish whether someone is in love, whether these feelings are reciprocated, and whether either of the parties will ever cause the other any form of emotional or physical harm. After completing these tests, it is proved that X and Y are in love, and that entering a sexual relationship with one another will never cause either of them a moment of emotional or any other kind of harm. In addition, if X and Y happen to be a heterosexual couple, we can control for the fear of pregnancy on the part of the parents by making both parties incapable of having children. In summary, the 'best interest' test has been passed. Yet the parents of Y still insist that they will not 'allow' their adult son or daughter who is living in the family home to have sexual relationships with anyone. Without repeating the specific questions asked previously, what practical steps do the CRPD and/or domestic Irish legislation allow one to take to rectify this situation in such a way as to override the decisions of the parents and in turn facilitate the fundamental right of Y to control their sexuality?

Returning to Quinn's (2009) analogy of legal capacity as a protective shield—as outlined further in the literature review chapter—one is left to wonder if it really is as impervious to third-party intervention as implied. To extend the metaphor somewhat, if legal capacity is a shield and the CRPD as a whole can be likened to a powerful suit of body armour, perhaps the Achilles heel which renders them both redundant in safeguarding the sexual rights of some adults with Down syndrome living in the parental home is precisely the parental prohibition on their sons or daughters actually exercising such rights.

Ultimately, for the legal rights that have implications for sexual citizenship contained in the CRPD to have any real effect on the lives of adults with Down syndrome, it is not enough that they simply exist in legal form. Rather, as long as sexual relations are weighed down with a symbolic significance they do not intrinsically possess, from a secular liberal perspective at least (Singer, 2005), 'then in many instances, the issue of sexual expression for adults with Down syndrome will remain a dangerous discourse'. This is one where emotionally charged attitudes are deemed to carry a greater epistemological status than more carefully measured claims (Rubin, 1984). Consequently, unless there is a change in attitudes from the ground up on the part of those who nominally identify as secular liberals, one must be sceptical as to the possibility of some adults with Down syndrome living in the parental home ever realizing their human rights to control their own sexuality, regardless of what the law says. In legal terminology, we are left with the paradox that for many adults with Down syndrome living in the parental home to exercise their legal right to have a sexual life, they will be dependent on the proxy decisions made by their parents. The absurdity of such a situation—from a legal rather than a moral perspective—is made manifest by Young and Quibell when they state that

> if responsibility for the enforcement of these rights is accorded to those other than the intellectually disabled—for example, advocates, parents

and carers—they cease to be individual rights as intended and, indeed beg the question of their status as rights at all.

(2000:753)

Interviews with adults with Down syndrome

Theme 1: The desire to move out of the parental home

In relation to the question as to whether they either wanted to or envisioned staying in the parental home for ever, all the adults with Down syndrome expressed a desire to have a house or an apartment of their own. For example, Stephen (Mary's son), when asked whether he thinks he will live with his parents forever, looked shocked at the very suggestion. His verbal response to the question was 'no', he has no intention of living with his parents for the rest of his life. When asked why not he stated: 'Because I'm an adult and adults don't live with their parents for ever'. I then inquired whether there was anything Stephen didn't like about living at home. His immediate response was a physical one. This took the form of a rolling of the eyes and a shrugging of the shoulders in an exasperated "where do I begin" fashion. When he finally spoke, he went on to say that one of the main drawbacks of living at home with his parents was that they were 'very nosy'. When I inquired further what he meant by this, Stephen stated: 'well...my mam and dad are always asking me what I'm doing and telling me what to do'. In reply to the same set of questions Paul (Sofia's son) also explained, citing a similar normal pattern of living type criteria, that he had no intention of living with his parents forever. To this end, he expanded on points expressed by Stephen and stated that he actively wanted to have his own house and that the only thing (in his mind) preventing him from realising this dream was a lack of financial means. As to what he would do if this dream came true, he replied that a house of his own would allow him to 'get married and have loads of children'. When specifically asked if, apart from his feeling that he is too old to be still living with his parents, there was anything else he disliked about this arrangement, Paul, again in common with Stephen, invoked the restrictions that accompany the paternalistic regime of care he is subject to and the fact that, for example, his parents wont 'let me go to the pub on my own when I want to'. Sarah (Rebecca's daughter) held a similar view, stating that while in many respects she enjoyed living with her parents, ultimately, she was also very anxious to get her own home. In her own words, Sarah explained that the main rationale driving this goal is the desire 'to get my own space'. In common with all the respondents, Sarah believes that this literal and metaphorical room of her own would provide her with the increased freedom she craves, thereby preventing her parents 'from being so bossy with me'. When Isobel (Angela's daughter) was asked whether there was anything that she did not like about living at home with her parents, she replied 'yeah...loads of stuff'. When asked if she could give a specific example, Isobel stated: 'my mam is always saying "Isobel where are you going"...and then she tells me to ring her all the time'. David (Claire's son), meanwhile, captured succinctly the pros and cons of living with one's parents shared by all the respondents when he stated: 'Well....I love my Mam and Dad but sometimes....eh.... but they're always bossing me about so I'd like to have my own house'. In addition, some of the participants also explicitly mentioned a connection between having their own accommodation and either furthering a current boyfriend/girlfriend relationship or forming one. For example, Catherine (Aileen's daughter) explained that one of the primary reasons behind her desire to have her own house was that it would provide her with a place where she, and her hoped-for future husband (she is currently engaged) and children could live. Similarly, Mark (Eimer's son) explained that one of his main reasons for wanting his own house or apartment was a desire to find and live with a future girlfriend. In addition, he then went on to list another motivating factor shaping his aspiration to move out of the parental home, namely: 'I want to decide things for myself and sometimes my Mam and Dad don't let me'.

Theme 2: The desire to have more control over how their leisure time is spent

According to Patrick (Katy's son), the bulk of his leisure time is divided between going bowling and going to the movies, with the latter a more infrequent event than the former, which takes place at least two times a week. When asked who he went bowling with, he replied: 'With my friends'. In response to the follow-up question as to whether he had many friends, he replied in the affirmative, stating that he had 'loads of friends', among whom 'some are boys and some of them are girls'. As to whether some of these friends include some of those he works with, Patrick clarified that no, none of his friends included people he worked with. Rather, referring to the social facilities organised by the disability service provider he is affiliated with, he stated: 'They're my friends from the club'.

Bowling as a leisure activity is something that unites all the respondents, with each of them engaging in this practice at least once a week. In every case, the bowling is arranged by the relevant disability service, with at least two professionals from the service accompanying the adults in question to monitor proceedings. Some interesting insights regarding a possible discrepancy between how the leisure time of the adults is spent, and how they behave if they were allowed more autonomy in this area were gleaned when the question as to what the respondents do when the bowling is finished was asked. For example, Daniel (Susan's son) explained that while he sometimes asked his friends to go to the pub with him after the bowling was finished, such a trip has yet to be actualised as he, in common with the individuals in question, is always collected from the bowling and then driven home by one or both of their parents. The practice, which sees the parents meeting their adult sons and daughters after the bowling is finished to ensure they get home safely, is another common theme uniting all the respondents' experiences. However, this aspect of the parental regime of care was one which all the respondents found problematic. Thus, Mark, in explaining his wholly representative desire to be allowed, at least sometimes, to make his own way home, stating that his stance stemmed from his insistence that 'I'm not a baby anymore' was essentially echoing a claim made by all the respondents.

For fear of causing upset, I did not ask the question as to whether any of the respondents had non-intellectually disabled friends. However, when I consulted with their mothers on a later date, they confirmed that they do not—not 'real friends' at any rate. This phenomenon is one that has been replicated time and time again in the literature. For example, Emerson & McVilly (2004), in their research project that examined the friendship networks of more than 1,500 intellectually disabled adults found that friendship activities were not only infrequent but when they did take place occurred mainly with another intellectually disabled person.

On the other hand, the comments made by the respondents regarding the extent of their social networks contradicts a theme in the existing literature, which finds that it is very often the case that the friendship networks of intellectually disabled people are typically quite small, with the preponderance of the 'friends' in question consisting of family members and the professional healthcare workers they interact with—usually on a weekly basis (Forrester-Jones et al., 2006). The accounts provided by the adults with Down syndrome I spoke to regarding the existence of a paternalistic regime of care—whether deployed by parents and/or healthcare professionals—when socialising with others at a given moment of time is one that is constantly replicated in the literature. In common with my sample, it seems to be generally the case that when intellectually disabled people—whose cognitive impairment is such that it raises autonomy/paternalism dilemmas—are socialising outside of their home—be that the parental home or some sort of supported living arrangement—such outings are usually controlled and monitored by some non-intellectually disabled third party (Lafferty et al., 2013).

Theme 3: The role played by the mother as reluctant jailor

To gain an insight as to the role, if any, played by the mothers as what I have termed 'reluctant jailors', putting obstacles, for the best of paternalistic reasons, in the way of their adult son's and daughter's leading a more age-appropriate social life, the question was posed whether the respondents ever went to the pub with their friends. Matthew (Jennifer's son) explained that he has never gone to the pub with his friends. When then asked why not, he stated: 'My mam won't let me'. When asked why his mother would not let him, he responded: 'She says it's too dangerous'. A similar response was proffered by Stephen when asked the same questions. Thus, after clarifying that he would love to go the pub with his friends, he also explained that this happens very rarely as 'My mam and dad won't me to go so I don't'. When asked why his parents would not let him, he stated: 'They don't want me to go out on my own at night-time'. When I asked Mark, following his earlier statement that his parents did not allow him to go to the pub at night on his own or with his friends, why he thought this was the case, he replied: 'They think it's dangerous for me'. When I then asked what he thought his parents meant when they said it was too dangerous, he explained that his parents were afraid he might get drunk and/or be taken advantage of by somebody. Except for Catherine, this embargo on unsupervised socialising, particularly where pubs are concerned, is one common to most of the adults with Down syndrome I spoke to.

To investigate further the reluctant jailor theme, particularly around the area of sexual expression, I asked the respondents who are or have been in a boyfriend/girlfriend relationship whether their significant other was ever allowed to stay the night with them in their parents' house. Thus, after Stephen talked about how he liked kissing the girlfriends he has had, I asked whether any of these girlfriends ever slept in the same bed as him at night. He replied no to this question. When I then asked him why not, he stated: 'My Mam and dad said no'. In response to the follow-up question as to why his parents felt this way, Stephen replied: 'They said that I had to wait until I got my own house'. After clarifying that Stephen had often visited his girlfriends' houses—all of whom also lived with their parents—I asked whether he was ever allowed to sleep in the same bed as them. He responded: 'No, I wasn't allowed'. In response to my next question, he explained that it was the parents in question who did not allow him and his girlfriend to sleep together. When Catherine—who has, when holidaying together, slept in the same hotel bed as her current boyfriend—was asked whether she and her boyfriend ever slept in the same bed as her boyfriend when visiting either of their parents' houses, she replied no. When asked 'why not', she stated: 'My mam won't let us'. When asked why her mother would not let them sleep together in her house, Catherine, mimicking her mother's voice, stated: 'She says "you're not sleeping with your boyfriend in my house; you have to wait till you have your own house to do that"'. At this stage, it is interesting to note that elsewhere in the interview Catherine revealed, when talking about a different issue, that her younger non-intellectually disabled brother and his girlfriend currently share a bedroom in the same parental house. I then asked Catherine whether she ever asked, when spending time with her boyfriend in his parents' house, if she could stay the night. To this, she responded no. When I then asked 'why not', she stated: 'Cause I don't know if they will say no or yeah'. In response to the question as to whether she had ever asked her boyfriend to ask his parents if she could stay overnight, she replied: 'Only once'. When I asked what happened on that occasion, Catherine stated: 'They said "no, Catherine you have to go home"'.

When trying to contextualise such findings, one must be ever mindful of the sad fact that there is a paucity of academic literature that actually seeks the perspectives of adults with Down syndrome on the issues this book is concerned with. However, in a relatively rare study (Mill et al., 2009) seeking the views of intellectually disabled adults living in the parental home in regards to their levels of satisfaction with the levels of independence they enjoyed, the findings somewhat contradict my own. Unlike my own sample of adults with Down syndrome, all of whom expressed the desire to be allowed more control over their social/sexual lives, in the Mill et al. (2009) study, more than half the respondents, the majority of whom were not involved in sexual relationships, stated that they were satisfied with the degrees of independence they were allowed to exercise within their parents' existing paternalistic regime of care.

Theme 4: The desire to have a boyfriend/girlfriend

The desire to have a boyfriend or girlfriend was shared by all the adults with Down syndrome who are not currently, or who have never been in an intimate relationship. For example, Daniel, when asked whether he currently has a girlfriend, hesitantly replied: 'No, I'm single'. When then asked whether he has ever had a girlfriend, he responded that yes, he had two girlfriends when he was younger. In response to how he had met these girlfriends, the respondent replied: 'Well they were my sister's friends....and I asked them to be my girlfriend'. When Isobel, who is not currently in a relationship, was asked whether she would like a boyfriend, she replied 'yeah, I want to have a boyfriend', adding that one of the main reasons driving this desire was, in the respondents own words 'cause I like boys'. To the question what it was that she liked about boys, Isobel went on to explain, that amongst numerous other things, she particularly liked kissing and being kissed by them. A similar reply was offered by Daniel who, when asked to explain why he wanted a girlfriend, simply stated: 'Because I love girls'.

As already extensively documented throughout this book, unlike non-intellectually disabled adults who control their own social and sexual lives, adults with Down syndrome living in the parental home are liable to be much more circumscribed when it comes to making those kinds of choices for themselves. The limited research that has been carried out examining the situation in Ireland largely replicates such findings (Hamilton, 2009; Foley, 2013).

Conversely, the desire to have a boyfriend/girlfriend is also a common one in the literature on relationships and sexuality concerning people with intellectual disabilities (Cuskelly and Bryde, 2004: Löfgren-Mårtenson, 2004). For instance, in another Irish study which sought the views of members of the various populations subsumed under this umbrella term—although as far as can be established, none of the participants had Down syndrome— Kelly et al. (2009) report that "the desire to be involved in an intimate relationship emerged as a very strong theme in the data" (2009:31). However, unlike the findings this project has produced—which correspond to most of the extant literature—where most respondents have never been in a sexual relationship, the Kelly et al study found that the opposite to be the case. Thus, they state:

> In the women's group, most of the women either currently were in, or had previously had some form of relationship experience. In the men's group, three men were currently in some form of romantic relationship, two had never been in a relationship before and the other three men said they had a special friend (Ibid.).

Theme 5: What one does in a boyfriend/girlfriend relationship

In response to the question, and related probes, as to what the respondents do or would do in their roles as boyfriends/girlfriends, a range of similar replies were provided. For example, when Stephen was asked the kinds of behaviours he engaged in with his girlfriends, he replied, while smiling broadly, that he 'would kiss them'. In response to the question whether he liked kissing the individuals in question, he replied 'yeah'—a response that was accompanied by a dramatic shrug indicating that he believed this question was an immensely stupid one. Stephen employed similar physical gestures when asked as to why he liked kissing his girlfriends. However, he also verbally answered the question, stating that he liked kissing them 'because they were beautiful and I wanted to kiss them'. Mark, who has never been in a relationship, but who has on various occasions unsuccessfully asked friends of his non-intellectually disabled sister to be his girlfriend, answered the 'what he would do as their boyfriend if any of these girls had said yes' question, by describing how amongst other things, he 'would have kissed them'. When probed to explain why he would have kissed them, he stated: 'Because they're gorgeous…. they're very sexy' (when saying this, he puts his hands to his chest, mimicking a woman's breasts).

As with the autonomy/paternalism debate as it relates to a restrictive paternalistic regime of care generally, the same proviso needs to be acknowledged in relation to the specific aspect of the autonomy/paternalism this book is investigating. Namely, that researchers have generally tended to ignore the views of people with intellectual disabilities themselves and instead examined this aspect of their lives from the third-party perspective, such as those of formal and informal carers, consequently relevant data is hard to find (Stalker, 2012).

Regarding the empirical studies that have been carried out that do seek the voices of people with intellectual disabilities, the consensus reached by the respective authors is that members of this population are still being treated in a paternalistic fashion by both parents—if they are still living in the parental home—and formal carers alike. In effect, when it comes to the issue of who has the right to control their own sexuality, intellectually disabled adults are still not afforded the same sexual and relationship autonomy as their non-disabled peers (Healy et al., 2009; Bernert, 2011).

Theme 6: The desire to be normal—the abject in action

Although empirical research (Deal, 2003) has demonstrated what I already knew based on my experiential knowledge, namely that the disparate populations who are subsumed under the "intellectual disability" umbrella form in/out groups based on who has what impairment. It was still a shock of sorts—at least to me—that a crucial theme to emerge from the interviews with the population of adults with Down syndrome was that a population with a shared impairment, in common with their non-intellectually disabled contemporaries, also have certain criteria as to what forms of embodiment are considered 'sexy/attractive/desirable' and or 'ugly/undesirable'. Criteria moreover, which in many instances identified the unique facial characteristics that is constitutive of the Down syndrome classification as the main physical 'culprit' that differentiates who becomes an object of sexual desire and who does not. For example, Daniel in response to the question whether there was somebody he currently wanted to be his girlfriend, stated: 'Yeah, I think I like one of the girls in work'. According to his mother, the girl in question is an individual with cerebral palsy. When the respondent was asked whether he had asked this individual to be his girlfriend, he responded: 'Yeah, I did ask her, but she said no'. In response to the question why the respondent thought she had said no, he stated: 'She said she liked me.... but she only liked me as a friend'. When the respondent was asked how he felt when the girl in question said that she did not want to be his girlfriend, he replied: 'A bit sad.... cause I really like her.... but my mam and dad said there was loads of girls in the sea so I shouldn't feel sad anymore'. Conversely, in response to the question whether Matthew had ever asked one of the girls with Down syndrome to be his girlfriend, he replied, with some emphasis, 'no'. When asked to explain why not, Matthew bluntly stated: 'I don't like them'—the phrase 'them' presumably referring to other people with visible disabilities such as Down syndrome. When probed as to why he did not like 'them', he initially shrugged in a 'what can I say' gesture, and repeated his earlier statement, namely: 'I don't like them'. When the question was repeated for the third time, the respondent leaned in closer to me, put his hand to his mouth (making a whisper gesture), and states that the reason he has not asked any of his friends with Down syndrome to be his girlfriend is that he thinks 'They are all very fat'. When then asked why he would not like a girlfriend who was 'fat', he replied (while making a gagging gesture with his mouth): 'I don't like fat people...they're very ugly'. When asked whether he would consider asking a girl with Down syndrome—one who was not 'fat'—to be his girlfriend, the respondent said 'no', as according to his criteria 'they're not sexy'. Asked to explain why he felt this way about girls with Down syndrome, he simply stated 'I don't know'. A very similar response, in both form and content, was given by Daniel when asked as to whether any of his previous girlfriends had Down syndrome. He replied they had not, and that the main reason why this was the case was because Daniel did not 'like girls with Down syndrome'. When then asked to explain whether there was anything in particular he did not like about girls with Down syndrome, he prefaced his initial response by stating that he knew that what he was about to say was 'not very nice', but that one of the main reasons for his judgement that he would not consider a girl with Down syndrome as a potential girlfriend for himself was because he thinks that 'They're fat'. When then asked whether he would consider having a girl with Down syndrome—one who was not 'fat'—as his girlfriend, Daniel reaffirmed that he would not. He went on to add, when probed why not, that he did not 'like their faces'—a clear reference to the distinct facial appearance of people with Down syndrome. In reply to the question of whether he could be more specific in terms of what it is exactly that he did not like about the facial appearance of people with Down syndrome, Daniel stated: 'They look like this'—at this stage the respondent stuck out his tongue and left it hanging for a few seconds). Finally, in response to my question—'and you don't like that?'—Daniel said: 'No….it's horrible…I don't think it's sexy'. These responses were also closely mirrored by those of David. For example, when asked whether he had ever asked a girl with Down syndrome to be his girlfriend, he replied 'no'—this verbal response was accompanied by the respondent sticking out his tongue and making a 'disgusted' facial expression. In reply to the follow-up 'why not?', he said: 'I don't like them'. When asked to further expand on why he 'didn't like them', he stated that 'they're ugly', repeating his earlier comment: 'I don't like them', while adding: 'I want a gorgeous girlfriend'. To establish whether this positioning of women with Down syndrome was a default position on the respondent's part, possibly borne out of a feeling of resentment at not being an object of sexual desire by the women with Down syndrome he has met over the years, the question was asked as to whether anybody with Down syndrome had ever asked him to be their boyfriend. In reply, David confirmed (which in turn was verified by his mother) that such overtures had been made, but that he had rebuffed each of these requests.

Analysis of the findings

Within the Foucauldian framework, power relations are a constituent part of the social world. However, unlike other critical traditions that are characterised by an intellectual pessimism regarding the power of the status quo to reproduce itself indefinitely, Foucault is adamant that "as soon as there's a relation of power there's a possibility of resistance" (1980:13). As their current legal status demonstrates, in contemporary Irish society, the difference that is Down syndrome is discursively constructed as a deficit. People with

Down syndrome are to be pitied as their impairment disqualifies them from partaking in certain kinds of activities most people consider constitutive of a worthwhile life. Rather, their intellectual disability is widely thought to condemn them to a life of childlike dependency. However, when analysing the responses of the adults with Down syndrome, the theme of resistance is one that runs through all the accounts proffered. Such resistance manifests itself primarily in the respondent's refusal to stick to the larger societal script that says an age-appropriate 'normal' life is something that 'people like them' cannot (in the sense that they lack the cognitive capacities to formulate certain beliefs/desires) and should not (for paternalistic reasons) aspire to. For example, all the respondents expressed the desire to move out of the parental home into a place of their own. The main reasons driving this goal was the urge to live a more 'normal', age-appropriate, independent life. These included a consensus amongst the respondents that such an outcome would allow them to 'escape' their current paternalistic parental regime of care. In addition, another chief reason provided referred to a desire on the part of some of the respondents to live with their significant other and/or to find a significant other to live with. In that event, we can conclude that the normalising discourse that constructs adults with Down syndrome as either inherently asexual and/or lacking the requisite cognitive ability to become a respectable self-regulating subject equipped with the wherewithal to express their own sexual desires in an appropriate civilised fashion, was also refuted—both in thought and deed. The paradigmatic instance of such resistance is exemplified by the fact that one of the respondents is breaking current Irish legislation that makes it illegal for adults with an intellectual disability to have sexual relations unless they have 'proved' themselves capable of living an 'independent' life and/or are already married—a desire mirrored by most the other respondents (Johnson et al., 2010). Further examples that illustrate the resistance on the part of the adults with Down syndrome to playing the role of the 'eternal child' include the fact that all the respondents who had not ever been in a boyfriend/girlfriend relationship aspired to be in one.

As demonstrated from their responses, in relation to the issues under investigation, we can see that the respondents are fighting power on two fronts: namely the juridical model of power, which has a determinate source in current legislation, and the more amorphous, diffuse flows of power, which are the effects of the regimes of truth propagated by human sciences such as psychology and psychiatry. However, as the facts regarding what the respondents do and/or want to do—in terms of leading more age-appropriate independent and sexual lives—bear witness, the general societal attempt to deploy various regulatory practices to construct the desired docility and contain the unruly body of these adults with Down syndrome has in many respects failed.

If as Foucault maintains, discourses are practices as well as external and internal structures then, in behavioural terms, it is clear the dominant normalising discourses regarding the kind of life adults with Down syndrome should be satisfied with living have failed in their objective. Despite being subjected to the all-seeing gaze of the panopticon in its societal or generalised-other form, members of this population decline to respond when 'hailed' to occupy the 'Peter Pan' subject position that has been ascribed to them. This refusal to govern themselves 'appropriately', to participate in their own subjection, sees them instead speaking and acting out a counter-discourse (Foucault, 1977, 1980). This is one that putatively positions them as normal adults with the rights to lead a kind of normal life, with all that entails for increased self-determination around the control of their sexuality, and which is taken for granted by their non-intellectually disabled contemporaries.

In referring back to the 'conceptualising disability section' in Chapter 2, it is clear that the adults with Down syndrome, more than likely unbeknownst to themselves, are trying to embody some of the central tenets that make up the philosophy of normalisation/SRV: that is, they want to live the kinds of lives they see their non-intellectually disabled peers and significant others living. As Chapter 2 illustrated, normalisation/SRV, and indeed those adults with disabilities who aspire to lead a more 'normal' life came under criticism from social model advocates. Consequently, at this stage, it is apposite to see if such attacks have the normative power they claim for one to assent to the proposition that the adults with Down syndrome interviewed for this research are somehow being duped to want what they should not want. As we have already seen, the charges are that in order to "to emulate the norm, the disabled individual is required to embrace, indeed to assume, an 'identity' other than one's own" (Campbell, 2009:21) and that that "the assimilationist aspect of normalisation/SRV is at odds with the type of empowerment strategy used by other devalued groups (ethnic minorities, women, people with disabilities, gay) who have instead glorified their differences and openly congregated" (Culham and Nind, 2003:71).

Taking the latter critique first, we can see that the facts of the matter clearly demonstrate it is not actually true that all the previously listed social groups have being empowered solely by such means. Nor is it the case that all them have glorified in their differences. An obvious example would be to point to the fact that many ethnic minorities, particularly those who subscribe to the Islamic faith, cannot—for both fear of social censure and in many European countries, legal restrictions—celebrate their differences in the manner implied (Brock, 2013). In fact, the Cullham and Nind quotation begs the question under scrutiny. In other words, it is not clear who women and gay people are meant to be 'essentially' different from as the unique differences that are said to characterise women and gay people are nowhere enumerated. Hence, we are left with a series of unanswered questions. Namely, what could the allegedly unique differences refer to and how do they manifest themselves in behavioural terms? The same questions obviously need to be asked in relation to people with intellectual disabilities. In behavioural terms, what practices is normalisation/SRV allegedly imposing an embargo on?

Campbell's claims to the effect that disabled people who subscribe to a normalisation agenda are somehow betraying their 'true' identity also need to be examined to reveal their paradoxical nature. The first paradox arises from the fact that one of the driving forces behind the formation of the social model of disability is to challenge the essentialising notion that disabled people have a 'true identity'—one typically defined by reference to their impairment. The second paradox arises from the fact that a central principle of social model thinking is that in all cases, it is the voice of the disabled person that needs to be privileged over all others in any issue affecting them (Goodley, 2011). Yet it seems to be the case that for social model critics of normalisation/SRV, the one subject position that intellectually disabled people are not allowed to aspire to is the so-called 'normal' subject position. Such confusion regarding the invocation of essential characteristics to differentiate/to not differentiate intellectually disabled people from their non-disabled contemporaries begs the question as to what essential characteristics are being referred to, and how it is that normalisation/SRV is intent on changing them.

As should be clear, a key question to ask and attempt to answer when trying to evaluate both the merits of normalisation/SRV and the attacks against them—and by implication the adults with Down syndrome who participated in this project—is how different can anyone be? To function in western contemporary societies, the individual needs to subscribe to social norms. That most people conform in this manner ensures that we do not inhabit a social world that in behavioural terms is radically indeterminate—one in which we are always in doubt as to how our fellow citizens will act (Burkitt, 2008). Therefore, one can argue that the invocation of such normal/alternative inclusion/assimilation binaries is predicated on a false premise: namely that when it comes to questions of social identity, contemporary western societies are more heterogeneous than they really are. At a fundamental level, however, this is largely an illusion. Regarding what most people aspire to, it seems to be the case that we are not as different to each other as some would like to claim. For example, the desires expressed by the adults with Down syndrome to embark on sexual relationships, to love and to be loved, etc. seem to be human universals (Pinker, 2003; Rogers, 2011).

In addition, and equally importantly when it comes to answering the question of how different one can be, is the human predisposition for people to define themselves negatively, a phenomenon that, as we have seen, was also a key data finding—particularly in regards to the sexual criteria employed by many of the adults with Down syndrome. This is the contention that "knowing who's who involves processes of classification and signification that necessarily invoke criteria of similarity and difference", a process that inevitably results in the formation of in/out groups (Jenkins, 2008:23). Such social groupings are held together by an adherence to a shared and prescriptive set of beliefs and practices—in effect, their own particular philosophy of normalisation. However, despite this plenitude of social tribes, the behavioural tower of Babel that is said to follow enjoys only a nominal existence. Hence, despite our attempts to differentiate ourselves from others, the attitudes and practices we cultivate to make ourselves appear intriguingly enigmatic, original, authentic and so on are perfectly intelligible by reference to the cultural codes most adults in contemporary western societies are intimately *au fait* with (Smith, 2006). For example, for the 'leftist' disability academic to embark on their conception of the 'transgressive' road less travelled, the costs are minimal, while the benefits in terms of economic, cultural, and symbolic capital are considerable. This is because in reality, said road does not constitute some form of *terra incognita* for this grouping, but is in fact well-trodden territory. Such academics belong to a class that can afford to engage in symbolic or literal acts of 'resistance' to the status quo without fear of censure or ostracising from fellow travellers, as this form of 'non-conformist' conformist behaviour is a necessary condition of belonging to the social grouping they align themselves with.

In summary, the real debate around normalisation/SRV and the hopes and aspirations expressed by the adults with Down syndrome I interviewed, as with human behaviour generally is not whether there should be restrictions on how different one can be but where the line is drawn and the criteria used to draw it. Consequently, the normal/abnormal binary is not as easy as it once was to call upon if it is to be engaged as a credible analytic tool to make a substantive point regarding identity formation. If used at all in such a manner, surely the criteria used to categorise the distinctions in question should be clearly stated, as should the behaviours being subsumed under such classifications—two conditions which, it must be pointed out, are almost never met in the 'relevant' literature.

To close this section, and to clarify further what exactly is at stake regarding the criticism that normalisation/SRV, unlike the social model of disability, puts the onus on people with intellectual disability adapting to a normalising society rather than society adapting to them, another key question that needs to be answered: To what extent is the adaptation to society that normalisation/SRV is said to be calling for on the part of the adults with Down syndrome different in degree or kind from the kind of 'conformist' behaviour that is required from their non-intellectually disabled contemporaries in order for them to occupy socially valued roles such as that of an academic within the discipline of disability studies? Because this question effectively answers itself, it is not unfair to conclude that such academics are involved in a performative contradiction when it comes to the alleged homogenising tendencies of normalisation/SRV. The rationale behind classifying such a stance as a 'do as I say, not as I do' form of reasoning is because while such academics rail against normalisation/SRV and its 'insistence' on people with disabilities having to conform to societal norms to obtain socially valorised roles, such academics, by definition of their own status, already occupy socially valorised roles and have had to conform to societal norms to get them.

My assent too many of the key principles of normalisation/SRV may seem at odds with the use of a Foucauldian theoretical framework with its implicit critique of the power of normalising discourses to make us who we are. But this is to misunderstand the nature of Foucault's insights regarding the distinction between conventional and unconventional behaviour. Part of what Foucault means when he claims that the subject positions we occupy are a product of the power/knowledge nexus is that so called unconventional and/ or transgressive subject positions are as much the product of normalising discourses as those that are subsumed under the label of conventional or conformist behaviours. In other words, the logic underpinning the construction of such subject positions is identical, and Foucault does not arrange them hierarchically by reference to any normative criterion (Hook, 2007).

When concluding that the cohorts of adults with Down syndrome are exercising resistance, however, the distinction between resisting dominant societal discourses and the specific regime of care they are subject to needs to be made. While resistance to the former can easily be discerned, when one focuses primarily on the respondent's relationship to the parental regime of care, things become much more ambiguous. As I have shown from the analysis of the responses given by the parents of the adults with Down syndrome regarding the regimes of care they subject their sons and daughters to, the world the respondents inhabit particularly within the normalising institution that is the family is one of constant surveillance. From the Foucauldian perspective, the chief insight to bear in mind when analysing the responses provided by the adults with Down syndrome is that this population live their lives in a field of constant visibility. This entails that at all times, either literally or metaphorically, they are subject to the panoptic gaze of the parent. Thus, they have, like the prisoners described in *Discipline and Punish* (1977), internalised this fact and have learned to police themselves accordingly. Because of occupying such a subject position, there are severe constraints on their ability to resist the normalising discourses that are used by their parents to condition and regulate both their thoughts and actions. In effect, the governmental nature of the parental regime of care they are subject to has ensured that their mental outlook *vis-à-vis* how they should conduct themselves closely mirrors the prescriptive guidelines formulated by their parents.

In consequence, the analysis of the adult responses that tells us something about the power dynamics that exist between them and their parents, makes Foucault's contention that the exercise of power induces resistance much harder to assent to. For example, there was typically little if any overt resistance to the parental regimes of care that insisted that the socialising they engaged in had to be in some form or another supervised. Similarly, despite the wish of many of the adults with Down syndrome to make their own way to and from the bowling sessions they attended, the respondents' responses seemed to indicate that, in respect of this and other issues measuring the degree of autonomy they exercised, their parents, or more specifically their mother, 'knows best'. Broadly speaking, when it comes to the area of sexual expression and the issue of boyfriend/girlfriend relationships, the same principle applies. For example, while many of the respondents raised the issue with their parents of their boyfriend/girlfriend 'staying the night with them', when the parent/s vetoed such proposals, there was little overt resistance to such decisions. Hence, as far as can be gathered, such instances of the parental regime of care in action did not lead to arguments between the two parties as it may have done if this same stipulation was imposed on one of their contemporaries without intellectual disability.

The interesting exception to this rule that sees the respondents effectively acting as 'docile bodies' in relation to their parent's expectations and demands is one which is shot through with a dark sense of irony, given the nature of some of the normative claims that define disability studies as an academic subject: Despite the best efforts of some of their mothers, most of the respondents who expressed the view that they did not find other people with Down syndrome sexually attractive refused to accede to their parent's exhortations to give such suitors a chance. This was the case even when it was made clear by the other person with Down syndrome that they wanted one of the respondents as their boyfriend/girlfriend.

While the Foucauldian framework—with its emphasis on notions of exterior governmentality—is limiting in explaining this phenomenon, the expression of disgust on the part of some of the respondents regarding the possibility of embarking on a boyfriend/girlfriend relationship with someone with Down syndrome can be theorised by reference to Julia Kristeva's concept of the abject. From a sociological perspective, such a conclusion may seem counter-intuitive as many may see this state of affairs as simply an effect of internalised oppression. This is the hypothesis that adults with Down syndrome in question have imbibed the 'beauty myth' (Wolf, 1991) and the counter discourses that portray intellectually disabled people as undesirable and act accordingly—a social phenomenon the Foucaulidan framework is eminently able to deal with. However, the difficulty with this logic once again involves the ontological status of people with Down syndrome and where they are aligned on the normal/abnormal continuum. The problem lies in the fact that if the internalised oppression hypothesis fully explains the nature of the sexual criteria one operates within, there would be a difference between the sexual criteria adopted by those who are internally oppressed and those who are not. However, in reality, this difference is difficult to discern. In other words, it is also the case that many non-intellectually disabled people, even those who have escaped from this cave of 'false consciousness', do not find those with Down syndrome to be objects of sexual desire (Millar, 2000; Green, 2008). Consequently, a more fruitful explanation as to why this is can be found by incorporating the role psychic factors play in the 'othering' process. The blueprint in this instance is proffered by Shildrick (2007, 2009), who theorizes that the non-normative disabled body is a source of psychic anxiety for both the non-disabled and the disabled alike—in their attempt to appropriate the 'normal' subject position.

At first sight, given the role that abjection plays in the process of othering—the construction of 'in/out' groups—this proposition may sound slightly paradoxical. The apparent paradox in positing that some people with Down syndrome see other people with Down syndrome as figures of abjection is that the difference/sameness distinction is collapsed, at the physical level at least. The male respondents in question, in categorising women with Down syndrome as 'ugly/not sexy' were pointing primarily to the anomalous form of embodiment, that is the distinct facial appearance of people with Down syndrome—but this physical set of characteristics is one they also share. However, as the analysis of the data has already shown, one of the dominant themes to emerge from the responses provided by the cohort of adults with Down syndrome is their bid to repudiate the abnormal subject position they have had ascribed to them and to reposition themselves as 'normal' people.

Two issues are at play here. Firstly, Kristeva's claim that "the abject has only one quality of the object-that of being opposed to I" (1982:1). Secondly, to remind ourselves that identity construction is a relational process marked by difference. This is the contention that we define ourselves negatively, in both a descriptive and normative sense, by reference to who we are not. It is useful then to conceptualise the instances of abjection displayed by some of the respondents with Down syndrome as an attempt to ward off threats to this attempt to define themselves as normal. In a sense, to police the psychic borders between self and other, the normal and the pathological—the human and the non-human—the oppressed has become the oppressor (Elliott, 2007). However, as the analysis has also shown, in relation to the instances of abjection displayed by some of the respondents with Down syndrome, not everybody subsumed under the intellectual disability umbrella term is abjected. Hence, Catherine, who, when seeing people with Down syndrome on the television would say '*yuck*' and request the programme be switched off, felt extremely proud of the fact that one of her boyfriends, while being intellectually disabled, looked completely normal. Another example of the adults with Down syndrome ranking intellectual impairments hierarchically was the case of respondent Daniel, who while refusing outright to entertain a boyfriend/girlfriend relationship with somebody with Down syndrome as he thinks 'they're very ugly' admitted to having sexual feelings for a colleague at work who had cerebral palsy, but who again looked 'normal' in relation to her facial features.

Utilising the psychoanalytic framework, a logical conclusion to draw from such reports is that, as with their non-intellectually disabled counter-parts, forms of embodiment matter when it comes to the criteria used by some of the respondents to distinguish 'us' from 'them' (Elliott, 1996). Hence, it seems to be the case that in the unconscious minds of the preceding respondents, the anomalous form of embodiment that distinguishes people with Down syndrome from other groups labelled intellectually disabled is one which breeches conventional normative standards of embodiment, and thus must be abjected. We can theorize such responses on the part of the respondents—which take the form of 'You are not of me. You are other, alien'—by returning to Shildrick's metaphor of 'human born monsters' (2003) to denote the 'matter out of place' that is the visibly anomalous body of somebody with Down syndrome. In effect, the processes that inform who becomes a figure of abjection for the normative subject are also at play in relation to the respondents with Down syndrome, who see other people with Down syndrome as 'monster-like', as abject. One can therefore conclude that the explicit nature of the abjection engaged in by some of the respondents can be explained by positing that the material manifestation of the desire to disavow one's vulnerability is in inverse relation to the difficulty in denying self-recognition in/of the abjected other.

Conclusions

The preceding analysis vindicates my decision to apply two distinct the-oretical frameworks to both the conceptual issues raised by the research questions, which can essentially be subsumed as a variation on the age-old autonomy/paternalism debate, as their respective strengths and weaknesses cancel each other out when married together. Consequently, the typology, modelled on the conceptual framework employed by Foucault in *Discipline and Punish* (1977), which conceives of the parent/adult child with Down syn-drome relationship as analogous to that of a reluctant jailor and a contented prisoner respectively, has proved to be a useful heuristic device. However, the fact that the mothers interviewed, in 'saying no' to requests made by their adult sons and daughters with Down syndrome, do at times play the role of the all-powerful sovereign causes a conceptual problem for a whole-sale application of Foucault's productive conception of power when it comes to providing a theoretical explanation regarding how and why the parent/adult child with Down syndrome relationship takes the form it does. As this analysis has shown, when it comes to instances of overt conflict between parent and adult child, such as the parental refusal to accede to their son or daughters request regarding their wish to engage in unsupervised socialis-ing at night time—particularly if this involves visiting a pub—or for their boyfriend/girlfriend be allowed to sleep in their room overnight, it is typi-cally the former who has the final say. Consequently, it seems apparent that when it comes to delineating the kinds of power that underpin such parent/adult child relationships, that power in its negative, coercive formulation plays an equally constitutive role to that of its productive counterpart.

In addition, there are similar limitations in relying solely on the Foucauldian framework when it comes to answering the real-life question of how parents can, and the normative question as to why they 'should' either stop acting as gatekeepers on to their sons and daughters social and sexual life and/or institute a parental regime of care that ensures that their sons and daughters do enjoy a non-celibate sexual life. The limitations in question revolve around Foucault's reluctance to argue why we should retain certain contingent social practices and work to get rid of others. However, this particular Achilles Heel is an inherent facet of the ontological commitments upon which his productive conception of power is based. In other words, and as Dews correctly observes, "if the concept of power is to have any critical political import, there must be *some* principle, force or entity which power 'crushes' or 'subdues', and whose release from this repression is considered desirable" (1997:90). To unpack such criticisms, and by extension the impossibility of appropriating Foucault as a modern-day *Virgil*-like figure, we can turn to Ruse, who captures some of the salient contradictions within Foucault's *oeuvre*. Chief among these is the fact that while on the one hand Foucault suggests that the dictates of the power/knowledge nexus ought to be resisted, he also "resolutely rejects the idea that there is any ground or standpoint from which such a call to resistance could be legitimated" (102). Yet as Fraser rightfully argues, it is only with the introduction of such normative judgements that we can say what is wrong with the power/knowledge nexus and why we ought to oppose it (Fraser, 1989).

An example of the greatest relevance to this book is the belief that the current status quo regarding the repressed sexuality of adults with Down syndrome is a regime that should be overhauled. This conclusion is based on the belief that 'normal' sexual expression with a third party is a good in itself. However, in *The History of Sexuality, Volume One* (1978) Foucault maintains that this concept of sexual liberation is itself a ruse of power since there is no escape from power: Power produces all sexual subjects. Hence, promises of liberation thus do not oppose power but extend its grasp (Foucault, 1978). This proposition is based on Foucault's belief that the self is discursively produced. As a result, and as Philp correctly observes, to resist power "would simply be swapping one discursive identity for another, and there seems no basis for having preferences between discursive identities" (1983:44). In other words, if "each liberation involves creating a new other (unless, of course, there is some true repressed subjectivity) and there cannot be any extradiscursive grounds for assessing the respective claims of subjects and their other", then Foucault has no conceptual basis with which to ground a normative argument as to why a particular instance of power should be resisted (Ibid.). However, while power may be everywhere, we should recognise that not all its manifestations enjoy an equal moral status. Thus, one needs a criterion, which Foucault does not provide, which enables one to arrange the exercise of power hierarchically. In effect, one needs a better answer than that proffered by Foucault to the question: 'so what if this practice is the effect of power? It makes me feel good, so why should I not continue doing it'?

To extend this point, despite their titles, Foucault's work on sexuality has next to nothing to say about the value, or not, of experiencing sexual sensations such as that of an orgasm. Rather, because he is predominantly concerned with trying to understand "how we come to understand sexuality as a fundamental 'truth' of our being" (Jackson and Scott, 2010:19), his productive notion of power is essentially irrelevant to either validating or critiquing one of the key premises—which has nothing to do with essential notions of selfhood or any other synonyms Foucault uses to advance the claims he does regarding the constitutive relations between power and sexuality—informing my normative concern with furthering the sexual well-being of adults with Down syndrome. The premise in question, let us remind ourselves, is that in the same way that it is a physiological fact that all things being equal, most human beings do not find the experience of getting sick a physically pleasurable sensation, all things being equal it also seems to be a physiological fact that most men and women (at some point in their lives) enjoy having their genitals stimulated by a sexual partner of their choosing.

4   Third-rail sexual politics under scrutiny

The question of facilitated sex

Focus group findings

As already alluded to, the primary objective behind holding the focus group was to get the parental perspective on the topic of facilitated sex. Two weeks prior to the focus group, the mothers were provided with a copy of a newspaper article that featured the mother of a son with Down syndrome who was actively looking to avail of the services of a prostitute for her son to facilitate him losing his virginity. The rationale the mother in question gave to justify this statistically unusual endeavour was based on her acknowledgement that while her son in his twenties has sexual needs, she fears, based on her experience, that unless she pursues this option, her son may never experience what it is like to have sex with another human being.

When asked, the consensus view on the part of all the mothers who made up my sample was that none of them had ever considered the use of facilitated sex to ensure that the sexual needs of their adult sons and daughters with Down syndrome were met. In this respect Eimer, who stated 'to be honest, the idea of using a prostitute to ensure that my sons 'sexual needs' were met never crossed my mind', essentially spoke for all of the respondents. Jennifer responded in a similar fashion, claiming that she 'never actually thought about going down that road' and that consequently 'it has never occurred to me to hire a prostitute to make sure that my son loses his virginity or has his sexual needs met'. Angela, in her response, also went on to add in a tone of disgust/disbelief that she found the whole notion of employing a third party to sexually interact with her daughter 'pretty disgusting'. However, Claire, while agreeing that 'like everybody else, this is something I have never given any thought to before' added that she found the article 'a bit of an eye-opener' in that it 'was very interesting in a way'. Moreover, she went on to state 'part of me could identify with the mother's predicament', acknowledging that the reasoning employed to make the argument for facilitated sex 'was all very logical'. However, despite these sentiments, she went on to agree that 'like everybody else I can't see myself availing of that option'.

When it came to providing explanations as to why this possibility had never been considered, the responses provided were more varied. For example, Susan summed up the majority view on the part of the respondents (at least initially) when she stated that facilitated sex constitutes 'a pretty disgusting option to even consider'. However, she than went on to pose an interesting question: Because none of her 'other children ever had to go to a prostitute to lose their virginity or have their sexual needs met', wasn't the recourse to facilitated sex perpetuating the notion that people with Down syndrome were abnormal and consequently had to be treated differently from their non-intellectually disabled contemporaries? In reply, I prefaced my next question by suggesting that given none of us could be sure whether anybody has or will use prostitutes to have their sexual needs met, and given that we were all in agreement that it is harder for adults with Down syndrome to embark on a sexual relationship in comparison to their contemporaries without intellectual disability, was the respondents objection to the use of facilitated sex a principled problem with the use of paying a prostitute/sex worker to have sex or did they also have other concerns with such a practice?

In response, Susan clarified that while she had 'no principled problem with what prostitutes do' stated that her objection was with 'the whole idea of paying someone to have sex with her son'. In effect, Susan's primary problem with availing of the that facilitated sex mechanism would be her complicity in creating 'a situation where there is no love...there's no relationship', just her son sexually interacting 'with a complete stranger'. Such a state of affairs is one that, according to Susan, 'just makes my skin crawl'. Given the importance of the debate within feminism as to the rights and wrongs of prostitution per se, I repeated the question as to whether any of the respondents believed that prostitution is morally wrong in principle. Rebecca responded that like Susan she had no principled problem 'with prostitutes doing what they're doing'. She went on to add that 'while it's not what I consider the ideal job for anybody to do, whether they are a man or a woman, I don't think it's morally wrong'. In response to my question, again directed at all the respondents as to whether any of them would disagree with what Rebecca and Claire have said about the morality of prostitution, the rest of the respondents shook their heads to indicate that they agreed with the positions in question.

Returning to Claire, in response to a final probe that took the form of entertaining a hypothetical scenario where the only option available to her son was to avail of the use of a prostitute or go without experiencing a sexual relationship, she stated she didn't know what she would do if such a scenario explicitly presented itself. However, getting back to the 'real world', she explained that she didn't 'even want to think about it'. This was quickly qualified when the respondent added that if her son 'could make that decision for himself it may be a different story', but from her perspective he could not, hence any such decision would have to be made by herself, which she describes as being 'not a very nice prospect'.

Angela meanwhile adopted a similar 'if only' line of reasoning; however, to support her position, she made an argument based on gender, leading her to state that 'the situation might be different if my daughter was a man'. She continued this line of reasoning by stating that, speaking as 'someone who considers herself a feminist' she believes that because 'men need sex much more than women…for women sex is something you do with someone you either love….or at the very least have very strong feelings for' [then]

> in principle, if my daughter was a man and there was absolutely no other option, then I might entertain the possibility of going down the facilitated sex route, but because she's not…that option will not be one I intend to avail of—ever.

When asked to critically reflect on her views on the issue, Mary initially found it hard to articulate her thoughts, hence her initial answer to this question was 'I don't know…it seems such a drastic option'. When then asked for her specific response to the article, her replies seemed to see her moving away from and then back to her original prohibitory stance. Thus, at one stage she concedes that the article 'may prove food for thought at the very least as the mother in the article did make perfect sense in many ways' [in that] 'her son wants to have sex, she wants her son to have sex but she believes that he may never meet a girlfriend so what other option is there? So rationally yes maybe I should consider it but emotionally I don't think I can'. When asked why she did not think she could entertain the idea emotionally, she replied 'the whole thing just sounds a little disgusting and a little sad'. When pushed further to try and explain in greater detail why she thought like that, she confessed that she 'didn't think she could'; and that essentially her position was rather the effect of 'a gut reaction'. After a moment's silence, however, she made another attempt to ground her objections on a more rational footing. To this end, she referred to a previous respondent's answer, and explained that 'maybe it's to do with what X said' [namely,] 'the whole notion of a stranger touching my son in that way'. She further added that, 'perhaps it's also to do with the role that I'd have to play', leading her to posit that if such a possibility was actualised, that she would end up feeling 'like some kind of pimp as I would have to find out all the relevant informa-tion…make the appointment etc.', leading her to conclude that 'the whole thing just sounds like a nightmare'. At this stage, all the other mothers nod-ded in agreement at this statement. In response, I asked whether they would concur with what Mary said regarding the practicalities involved if any of them ever decided to 'go down the facilitated sex road'. Again, the response was unanimous, with all the participants agreeing with Sofia, who expressed the view that 'yeah that aspect of it is particularly nightmarish'. Katy then picked up Mary's use of the term 'pimp' and stated:

> I agree completely with what Mary just said. I didn't actually think of it in those terms before…but she's right that's what it would come down to. It would be us as parents who that responsibility would fall on. No, I don't

think I could do that…it just feels "yucky". Sorry, not the most rational response I know but I can't help it (everybody laughs) …I think "yucky" actually sums it up though…I don't want to be that kind of Mum.

In trying to further tease out the respondents' views on the issue, I returned to Susan and asked whether, because many 'normal people' avail themselves of the use of prostitutes all the time, she found the notion that parents in her situation had some kind of moral obligation to use such a service if that was the only feasible way of their adult children with Down syndrome losing their virginity and/or having their sexual needs met. In response, Susan stated that she did not 'like the notion of having a moral responsibility to get my son a prostitute', concluding that she did not think she had 'such an obligation even if that was the only option left'. The rationale given to support this position was her view that 'it's not the sex' that she thinks 'is most important', rather 'it's companionship…it's love'. A possible lack of consistency in this stance was then presented to Susan, in that she had previously said that she believed that her son has the same sexual needs as 'normal' men his age and given that these are not being met, was it not the case that availing of facilitated sex is a very easy way of solving this problem? She replied that she stood by what she had said about her son 'having sexual needs', but went on to claim that 'there must be a better way of having them met than using a prostitute'. Susan then stated that while she recognised 'that many normal men his age use prostitutes', and conceded that the use of such a mechanism is 'in a way… a very easy way of solving the problem', she just could not see herself 'going down that particular road'. In her final comments, Susan, specifically addressing the question of a possible charge of inconsistency in her position on this issue, made it clear that she was 'well aware that what I'm saying here may contradicted other things I've said about the whole sex issue', but frankly concluded 'that just can't be helped'.

When it came to Aileen attempting to give a reasoned account of why she takes the stance she does in relation to the issue of facilitated sex, she responded: 'I'm not too sure I can provide you with the perfect logical answer I think you are looking for'. Rather, she stated that

> with all this stuff it comes back to the conflict between what you would do in principle and what you would do in real life. In principle, part of me agrees with the mother in question in that she made it sound all so simple,

Aileen, however, questioned whether 'in real life' she would 'do what she did'. To this end, the answer she provided to her own question was 'I don't think so'. When I than asked Aileen why she didn't think so, she, agreeing with a previous interviewee, stated that 'this whole thing is different for girls'. With this gender distinction in mind, she conceded that 'after reading the article, and if my daughter was a man I might give it greater consideration'. She went

on to preface her further explanation with her views on the gender difference, stating that she was speaking as 'a feminist' who believed it was simply
a fact that 'men have greater sexual needs than women'. Consequently, her
reflexive position on the issue of facilitated sex for adults with Down syndrome was that 'if my daughter was a man and this was the only option we
had which would ensure that he would get to have sex before he died, then
maybe I would try and act on it'. However, from her perspective 'the idea of
a stranger touching X sexually does, to use that word again, seems to me
to be a little disgusting'. Apropos of the nature of the discussions that had
already previously taken place with some of the other respondents, she pre-
empted any further questions on my part by stating that 'like everybody else
I'm aware that my answer may be full of contradictions' as she subscribes
to the belief that her daughter, 'as a woman, also has sexual needs'. Despite
such concerns, however, Aileen implied that regarding the sexuality of her
daughter, any role that she as her mother had to play in its expression, reason and logic were limited in their power to influence her stance on this
issue. Hence her conclusion implied that while she 'can't make' her view on
facilitated sex, as an option for her daughter, at any rate, 'more coherent
than it is' in a logical sense, she did not feel she had to. Hence her summa-
tion that 'I suppose what I'm trying to say is that my initial reaction is more
emotional than intellectual...and my emotions are telling me that the idea of
getting my daughter a prostitute is 'all wrong'.'

Focus group analysis

From the Foucauldian perspective, the opinions expressed by the respondents regarding the issue of facilitated sex threw up many interesting issues.
Firstly, there is the fact that most the mothers (in this instance) stayed true
to their secular liberal self-image regarding the legitimacy of prostitution
itself. That is, the majority agreed with Rebecca's statement that 'while it's
not what I consider the ideal job for anybody to do, whether they are a man
or a woman, I don't think it's morally wrong'. Secondly, there is the fact
that many of the respondents again made use of the gender bifurcation/
sexual needs discourse, and in the process repudiated a central tenet of this
'secular liberal' subject position, to ground their objections to utilising the
facilitated sex mechanism. For example, Angela stated 'in principle, if my
daughter was a man and there was absolutely no other option', she might
entertain the possibility of going down the facilitated sex route, but 'because
she's not...that option will not be one I intend to avail of—ever'. Aileen
agreed with this stance, stating: 'if my daughter was a man and this was the
only option we had which would ensure that he would get to have sex before
he died then maybe I would try and act on it'.

However, given the centrality the 'good mother' subject position has
played in the analysis heretofore, perhaps the most salient finding (from the
Foucauldian framework at least), is that it vindicates the insight identified

earlier that this social role imposes certain discursive constraints on the mothers' views regarding the nature of the moral obligations they believe they have in relation to their adult sons and daughters with Down syndrome. For instance, as already established, the respondents believe they have a moral responsibility to deploy a paternalistic regime of care that imposes strict parameters on the freedom their adult children can exercise in the social and sexual realms. On the other hand, the respondents have no principled problem with their sons and daughters embarking on a sexual relationship—albeit, preferably with someone who also has Down syndrome—and to a greater or lesser extent believe they have a moral obligation to facilitate (which in the main they have tried to do) such a relationship developing if the opportunities present themselves. Nonetheless, according to the respondents, the moral obligations they have towards their adult children only go so far. In other words, it does not extend to the belief that they have a moral obligation to pursue the facilitated sex mechanism. To this end, Susan's contention that she did not 'like the notion of having a moral responsibility to get my son a prostitute' is wholly representative of the position adopted by all the mothers.

However, while offering important insights as to why the respondents' replies take the form they do, at this stage, it is also necessary to depart from a purely Foucauldian analysis of the data as there are two important explanatory gaps it fails to fully explain. These refer once again to the gender bias in relation to the notion of sexual needs, particularly as it pertains to the issue of facilitated sex, and why, despite this belief, the respondents believe that facilitated sex constitutes a 'disgusting limit-case' regarding what they could and should do in their roles as good mothers.

Taking the former first, we can see that while all the mothers acknowledged that their sons and daughters with Down syndrome had sexual needs, they made a gender distinction regarding their nature. As demonstrated previously, this officially sanctioned church/state gender bifurcation/ sexual needs discourse is also an integral component of current Irish legislation, which treats non-intellectually disabled female teenagers as less sexual, or at the very least not as autonomous as their male counterparts when it comes to their capacity to choose when and whom to have sex with (Irish Statute Book, 2006). However, when positing a theoretical explanation as to why the parents in question employ the gender bifurcation/sexual discourse to justify their respective regimes of care, it is necessary to go beyond the insights offered by those aspects of the Foucauldian framework that invoke a causal relationship between a dominant regime of truth and the production of 'docile bodies' (Béatrice, 2002). This conceptual move is necessary as, unlike the cognitive ability/ autonomy discourse, which enjoys a hegemonic-like status as a regime of truth allowing it to regulate the field of Irish sexuality with a vise-like grip, the normalising power exerted by the gender bifurcation/sexual discourse is a more context-dependent affair.

As explained in the discussion around the age of consent and the crime of statutory rape, the context in question concerns the issue of teenage sexual expression. However, once the debate around the 'true nature' of female sexuality has as its sole object of study the sexuality of non-intellectually disabled women over the age of seventeen, it is clear that one cannot simply invoke either Catholicism or patriarchy as possible dominant discourses to explain why the mothers who were interviewed—all of whom described themselves as feminists—expressed a belief that men and women were different when it came to both the nature of their sexual needs and the relevance of utilising the facilitated sex mechanism to meet them. This conclusion is based on two factors. Firstly, there exist feminist discourses that also question the pleasure women experience when engaging in heterosexual intercourse (Greer, 2000; Hite, 2004). In addition, there is the fact that many of the relevant claims made by the mothers regarding the gender distinction in terms of sexual needs/pleasure are based on their own phenomenological experiences of having heterosexual intercourse.

Regarding the nature of female sexual desire, many 'second-wave feminists' have advanced the argument that patriarchy has conditioned women into believing that heterosexual intercourse is the mode of being which constitutes the supreme expression of their sexuality (Dworkin, 1983; Greer, 2000). In response, they have produced a counter-narrative that argues that women do not derive the same levels of physiological satisfaction from heterosexual intercourse than the average man, and hence do not need to engage in it as often, if at all. To illustrate this point, one can invoke Germaine Greer's statement that a woman's sexual "pleasure is not dependent upon the presence of a penis in the vagina" (2000:95). One can also point to the fact that Greer's claim has received considerable support in the empirical studies undertaken, by amongst others, Shere Hite. One of the findings of the Hite Report (2004) was that the majority of women surveyed reported that they have never experienced orgasm through heterosexual intercourse alone.

Clearly the existence of competing discourses vying for supremacy regarding the question of whether there is a gender difference in relation to sexual desire and its various manifestations can partially be explained by reference to the Foucauldian framework. For instance, the respondents' use of the gender bifurcation/sexual needs discourse can be conceptualised as solely the effect of the subject position they align themselves with. However, unlike the other normalising discourses referred to in this and preceding chapters where a convincing argument can be made that the parents have in many respect outsourced their thinking on the nature of their paternalistic regimes of care to the 'regimes of truth' propounded by the human sciences, when it comes to examining the justifications offered by the respondents regarding the gender bifurcation/sexual needs debate, the positing of a similar cause-effect relation is more problematic.

This is because, in both form and content, such explanations are also phenomenological in nature. For example, the contention made by many of the respondents that women do not have the same need as men to engage in sexual relations is based on their own experience of having sex. Due to the rationale behind the interviews and the focus group carried out for this study, it was not deemed necessary to explore the sexual lives of the cohort of mothers. As a result, their conception of what 'having sex' denotes regarding specific sexual practices was not established. Hence, it cannot be demonstrated—in any meaningful sense of the term—that their experience of sex was in every instance an experience of 'bad sex'—one that was, for example devoid of clitoral stimulation and so on. Whatever the case may be, a persuasive argument can still be advanced that the mothers' views on the issue of their daughter's sexual needs enjoys a greater epistemic status and are less vulnerable to a purely discursive interpretation.

This conclusion is based on arranging phenomenological accounts hierarchically. In its social science usage, the term "phenomenology" is frequently characterised as a methodology that privileges first-party reports on a given subject matter (Bryman, 2008). Thus, in the banal sense of the term, all the respondents' views are phenomenological in nature, in that they are based on their own experiences. However, there is an epistemological difference in the quality of the inferences that can be drawn from either first-hand experience—knowledge by acquaintance—or those experiences which are parasitic on the knowledge claims of others—knowledge by description (Ayer, 1956; Russell, 1980). According to this line of reasoning, the respondent who concludes, based on her experience of having sex with her male partner, that the 'pleasure' that ensues from such encounters stems from her feelings for the individual in question rather than an effect of the physiological sensations she experiences is justified because the respondent is directly and immediately acquainted with her physiological sensations. This same degree of acquaintance is, however, not present when the same respondent, based on her experience of reading literature that states that adults with Down syndrome are more liable to be sexually abused than their non-intellectually disabled counterparts, concludes that a certain parental regime of care must be deployed.

In a similar fashion, I want to argue that Kristeva's psychoanalytical framework, in particular her concept of the abject, (Kristeva, 1982) has more explanatory weight than any insights offered by Foucault when it comes to illuminating one of the most relevant themes to emerge from the focus group. Namely, the consensus view on the part of the mothers that facilitated sex was an intrinsically 'disgusting' business. Angela summed up this stance when in response to the question whether she had ever considered the facilitated sex option for her daughter replied 'no I have not… to be honest I think the whole thing is pretty disgusting'. In addition, this psychoanalytical framework can help explain the apparent contradiction in overt parental views regarding a gender distinction when it comes to the issue of sexual needs but which rules out the use of the facilitated sex mechanism to meet them by advancing the theory that something else is going on at the unconscious level. For example, another dominant theme to emerge from the focus group discussion was a tension between the head and the heart or between reason and emotion on the part of the respondents. This was exemplified by the acknowledgement on the part of some of the mothers that, when pushed, they could not provide a rational justification for the positions they adopted. For instance, Claire, while claiming that she found the reasoning employed by the mother in the newspaper article to make the argument for facilitated sex 'all very logical', went on to state that she couldn't see herself 'availing of that option'. In a similar vein, Mary stated that 'rationally yes maybe I should consider it' but concluded that 'emotionally I don't think I can'. According to Mary, one manifestation of this tension between the head and the heart concerned 'the role that I'd have to play'. This was her contention that if she did avail of the facilitated sex mechanism, she would end up feeling 'like some kind of pimp as I would have to find out all the relevant information…make the appointment etc.', leading her to conclude that 'the whole thing just sounds like a nightmare'. The nightmarish qualities of what the 'pimp role' entailed were also invoked as a reason by Katy to explain her ambivalence to utilising the facilitated sex option when she stated:

> I agree completely with what Mary just said…I didn't actually think of it in those terms before…but she's right. That's what it would come down to. It would be us as parents who that responsibility would fall on. No, I don't think I could do that…it just feels "yucky". Sorry, not the most rational response I know but I can't help it (everybody laughs)…I think "yucky" actually sums it up though…I don't want to be that kind of Mum.

With such responses in mind, I want to argue that the views expressed by the respondents on the issue of facilitated sex cannot be wholly explained by a rational assent on their part to the proposition that the use of prostitutes is an expression of a 'perverse' form of sexual interaction, which they, as good mothers cannot incorporate into a new paternalistic regime of care. For example, at a discursive level, as many of the parents acknowledged, the recourse to the use of prostitutes on the part of many non-intellectually disabled adults to have their sexual needs met is a universal phenomenon. A practice moreover—as demonstrated in previous chapters—which from the liberal perspective is deemed to be a perfectly legitimate form of exchange, once certain working conditions are in place to ensure that the prostitute is not abused in any way by their client (Sanders, 2005, 2007; Liddiard, 2014). In other words, from a certain liberal perspective—one which the mothers subscribe to—there is nothing intrinsically objectionable in selling one's body for sex (Nussbaum, 1998). Hence Susan's contention:

> Yes, I recognise that many normal men his age use prostitutes…and in a way perhaps it is 'a very easy way of solving the problem' but I just can't

see me going down that particular road.... maybe if you come back to me in five years and if my son is still without a girlfriend I may think differently but at the moment I can't see either me or my husband giving it any serious thought.

In addition, while Susan stated that even to think about her son having sex with a stranger made '*her skin crawl*', at a discursive level, the practice of casual sex with strangers has long become normalised for certain populations—hence the concept of a one-night stand.

One psychoanalytic reading of this inability of reason to penetrate the parent's psychic defences is to invoke Kristeva's contention that our onto-logical security is dependent on keeping the imaginary borders between self and other clear and distinct via the process of abjection (1982). However, to adopt the 'pimp role' alluded to by some of the mothers would be to collapse the self/other distinction—both literally and metaphorically—in a manner different in kind from any other practice that constitutes their current regime of care. In other words, the current regime of care is one that can be carried out at a distance, again both literally and metaphorically. For instance, while the mothers effectively know where their adult sons and daughters are at all times, and what they are doing, the self/other distinction is in a sense maintained: for example, the existence of two separate people occupying different places in space and time actively doing what they both want to do. Thus, the mother could be at home while their adult son or daughter is out socializing with their 'friends', hence an appearance of 'normality' in that, nominally at least, we have two independent parties going about their individual business. The mother and the adult child with Down syndrome just happen to be engaged in practices that also constitute 'normal' parent and non-intellectually disabled adult children relationships—especially when the non-intellectually disabled adult is also living in the parental home. However, my contention is that for the mother to embrace the 'pimp role' mentioned in the focus group and act accordingly, the level of cognitive dissonance that she would predictably experience would be of greater magnitude than that experienced—if any at all—while deploying their current regime of care.

These conclusions are based on the symbolic meanings such an action would represent for the mother. For example, Shildrick states

the disabled body is deeply disruptive to the social body and to normative selfhood alike, not so much in the guise of the clear and distinct other that can be grasped in its difference, but because it remains undecidable, neither self nor other.

(2005:760)

Utilising Kristeva's insights we can therefore argue that the mothers' reluctance to think the unthinkable—to adopt the 'pimp role' and act as the mediator between their adult child and the professional third party who will have sex with them—is borne from the fear that to do so would disturb both their own identity as a separate autonomous individual and their expressed perception that in many respects they do see their adult sons and daughters as leading quite normal, relatively autonomous lives of their own.

This conclusion is based on the psychoanalytic contention that one consequence of seeking to maintain the illusion of the separation and distinction necessary to the sovereign subject is that all encounters between self and other are potentially risky and must be negotiated within a strict set of normative rules and regulations that construct the parameters of safety and danger (Kristeva, 1982). This then is coupled by the fact that in the western cultural imaginary, not only is the right to sexual expression often denied to people with intellectual disabilities like Down syndrome, but that sexual expression in and of itself is a paradigmatically private act. As a result, "the sexual relation itself, and the operation of desire as that which extends beyond the self to the other, is always a locus of anxiety, a potential point of disturbance to the normativities of everyday life" (Shildrick, 2007:225).

Hence, at the psychic level, the threat to the parents' "clean and proper body" (Kristeva, 1982:71) is twofold. Firstly, the mother is faced with the 'realisation' that the level of 'dependency' that defines her relationship with her son or daughter with Down syndrome is deeper than she had hoped. Secondly, to participate in such acts constitutes a further threat to her self-image as a normal person insofar as her adult children—occupying the metaphorical status of "human born monsters" (Shildrick, 2003:29)—did not come into this world *ex nihilo*. In other words, for the parents to incorporate the use of facilitated sex in their pre-existing paternalistic regimes of care would be to collapse the self-other distinction to such an extent that it would result in an exponential increase in the degree of psychic violence or cognitive dissonance they already experience (at some level) by the very fact of having an adult son or daughter with an intellectual disability like Down syndrome.

5   A modest proposal regarding the normalisation of facilitated sex

Introduction

This use in this chapter of the term 'a modest proposal' is both homage and a play on words. Although its true etymology is undetermined, in the collective consciousness, its intellectual copyright belongs to the arch-satirist Jonathan Swift. In his infamous essay deriding the logic underpinning Britain's laissez-faire policies towards its Irish colony, "*A Modest Proposal for Preventing the Children of the Poor People in Ireland from Being a Burden to Their Parents or Country, and for Making Them Beneficial to Their Public*", Swift ironically proposes, through the use of a *reductio ad absurdum* argument, that the rational solution to the poverty that blighted eighteenth-century Ireland was for Irish parents to sell their children as food for their British masters. In relation to the proposition that liberal-minded parents have a duty of care to do everything within their power to ensure that their adult sons and daughters lead fulfilling sexual lives, the homage to Swift consists of taking the logic of a given ideology seriously. By extension, the play on words is the contention, that unlike Swift's ironic use of the term, when posited as a guaranteed solution to the celibate lives led by many adults with Down syndrome, my modest proposal to normalise the use of facilitated sex is just that: namely, a modest proposal in the most literal terms one can imagine.

As the evidence collected for this book has demonstrated, in their roles as reluctant jailors of their adult sons and daughters with Down syndrome, all the mothers interviewed, when trying to achieve the right balance between empowerment and protection, err on the side of caution. This is particularly the case when it comes to the sexual needs of their intellectually impaired charges. Hence, the fact that the discourse around the use of facilitated sex as a mechanism to meet the sexual needs of adults with Down syndrome remains, in the eyes of the cohort of mothers who participated in this project, the most dangerous discourse of all.

As exemplified in preceding chapters, this primary data is also widely replicated in the relevant literature. Hence, the argument for the normalisation of facilitated sex can be derived from these facts alone. However, because the empirical data I have collected has produced new insights regarding both positive parental attitudes regarding the sexuality of their sons and daughters and more negative sexual criteria used by many of the adults with Down syndrome, much of its content will also be geared to ground my conclusion that facilitated sex can also offer a possible answer to the very particular issues raised by the respondents.

The argument I am advancing is that if the only means available to adults with Down syndrome for realising a non-celibate sexual life is for them to mimic their non-intellectually disabled contemporaries and attempt to play the so-called 'normal' sexual interaction language game, then many of them are doomed to failure from the outset. To illustrate this conclusion, we need to first internalise the fact that the sexual criteria used by some of the adults with Down syndrome I spoke to essentially rules out other people with Down syndrome as prospective sexual partners. It is this fact which explains the frustration expressed by many of the mothers—all of whom agreed that their paternalistic regimes of care did allow for such relationships to develop—that they did not possess the requisite power to make their adult sons and daughters find their contemporaries with Down syndrome sexually attractive and thus worthy boyfriend/girlfriend material. Conversely, the data also replicates what has become a truism of sorts in scholarly circles regarding the research into why we choose the sexual partners we do. This is the proposition that there is a logic of reciprocity that informs the sexual choices made by adults without an intellectual disability, and adults with Down syndrome are considered to lack the requisite forms of capital to compete in this relationship marketplace (Millar, 2000; Green, 2008). Clearly, the use of the facilitated sex mechanism can act as an antidote to such *Catch-22* situations becoming increasingly institutionalised.

As evidenced in Chapter 2, the issue of facilitated sex has become almost normalised—in both theory and practice—where the sexuality of physically disabled people is concerned. However, in relation to the sexuality of adults with an intellectual disability, especially when the impairment in question is that of Down syndrome, it retains its taboo status. This chapter is my attempt to redress the imbalance.

According to Shildrick, "images of sexuality in popular culture—which both construct and reflect a powerful set of social norms—usually either preclude reference to disability or see it in a highly negative fashion" (2007:57). In response, a counter-narrative has emerged to combat the hegemonic power of such discourses. As explicated in earlier chapters, the favoured weapon of choice for those concerned with increasing the sexual quality of life for intellectually disabled people is to invoke the language of human rights to ground their normative claims. So much so that in much of the extant disability literature this book has referenced, the proposition that adults with intellectual disabilities have the same sexual needs and thus should enjoy equal sexual rights as those enjoyed by contemporaries without disability, has become a new, albeit much needed, political platitude.

Justified by its many victories, this strategy has proved its usefulness in combating many of the most egregious forms of discrimination and oppression that many members of this population have heretofore been subjected to as a matter of course. However, as already explained, when it comes to the subject at hand, it is a discourse that is largely redundant. For example, the legal right that makes it illegal to prevent an adult with an intellectual disability from embarking on a sexual relationship is a somewhat effective political instrument when dealing with situations where a parent is actively trying to prevent them from doing so (Foley, 2012). But this state of affairs does not accurately represent the situation regarding the parental regime of care deployed by the mothers who were interviewed for this book.

In addition, while the talk of rights remains a crucial tool for achieving social justice for adults with intellectual disabilities in a general sense, in the context of normalising facilitated sex, it seems misplaced. Amongst the most pertinent objections to equating such sexual citizenship with formal positive rights are the perennial questions raised against such attempts at social engineering. These include the probing inquiry as to why should adults with an intellectual disability be privileged over other marginalised populations who also have problems with embarking on sexual relationships and how much would such a policy 'cost the taxpayer' (Di Nucci, 2011). As we have already seen, alongside such generic political question, there is also the very specific and, in some people's eyes, very controversial question regarding the increased exploitation of those who supply such services. Consequently, such strategies, seemingly based on a mistaken assumption that there exists a causal relationship between formal rights and praxis, needs to be supplemented by a new, less repressive way of thinking.

Ideological critiques in form and content

With this objective in mind, I want to bracket the question of rights (whether real, imminent, or wholly aspirational) and instead concentrate on offering an ideological critique of the current sexual status quo that exists between many parents and their adult sons and daughters with an intellectual disability living in the parental home. Integral to this notion of offering an ideological critique is the premise that in many respects most people's understandings of social and political reality are, at times, distorted, inverted, and false. This state of affairs can best be explained by reference to the proposition that the primary way that power works is by making the "artificial appear natural, and what is contingent and arbitrary, absolute and intrinsically valid" (Poggi, 2001:65).

This phenomenon, which sees the oppressed acting in complicity with the social forces that oppress them, is often explained by reference to the notion of false consciousness. Marx and Engels put this point concisely in their contention that a fundamental mistake people have fallen prey too is to "have constantly made up for themselves false conceptions about themselves, about what they are and what they ought to be" (Marx and Engels, 1970:1). While originating within the Marxist tradition, the concept of false consciousness, albeit in a more diluted form, has been co-opted by other critical traditions that do not subscribe wholeheartedly to a Marxist philosophical anthropology. For example, as demonstrated previously in its attacks on the philosophy of normalisation/SRV, it plays a key role within the social model of disability in its contention that a 'disabling society' can only reproduce itself in so long as people with disabilities remain a 'class-in-itself', as opposed to transforming themselves into a 'class for itself' (Oliver, 2009). It has also become a mainstay of many feminist arguments concerned with illuminating the role played by patriarchy in the formation of the consciousness of gendered subjects to explain why many women participate in the reproduction of a system that is antithetical to their own objective interests (Greer, 2000).

As with all such ideological critiques, my task in this endeavour involves unmasking how dominant ideologies have managed to naturalise the contingent by inducing a sense of false consciousness amongst the mothers I spoke to. In this context, to 'naturalise' refers to the processes that legitimise one arbitrary understanding—typically a common-sense understanding—of social reality while actively delegitimizing alternative interpretations as 'unnatural', 'irrational', 'immoral', and so on. For example, the current status quo is one where a contingent social norm regarding what constitutes legitimate sexual expression for people with intellectual disabilities, and the role, if any, their parents should play in enabling such expression, continues to retain its naturalised status as a taboo that must be obeyed. However, from a critical perspective, the primary problem with trying to understand the social world and one's place in it by reference to a 'common-sense' epistemology is that in reifying the contingent, one not only denies the fact that every social practice has a history but that the utilisation of such a conceptual lens typically negates the possibility of making the future different from the past. In effect, such reification acts as a recipe for both cognitive and behavioural inertia.

Because of such theory/praxis confusion, my contention is that the parents in question have effectively outsourced their thinking regarding the nature of their paternalistic regimes of care to a set of ideologies they would otherwise reflexively disown. Conversely, the primary way the ideological critic achieves their aim is to make manifest the fact that dominant ideologies do not reflect some God-given natural order of things. Instead, the possibility of emancipation, in the sense of a change in consciousness leading to a change in practice, is the result of understanding that such dominant discourses are contingent social constructions that enjoy the legitimacy they do solely because they benefit certain sectors of society at the expense of less powerful others.

As exemplified in the analysis sections, particularly in my refutation of social model theorist's invocation of false consciousness to delegitimise the desires of intellectually disabled people to aspire to the social goods already possessed by such academics, any third-party imputation of this contested concept must be handled with care. To illustrate the rationale for such caution, we can cite one of the many attacks on Lukes's use of such a divisive analytical strategy, to wit, according to Hay, in deploying his third face of power he:

> resurrects the spectre of false consciousness which many had thought exorcised from contemporary social and political theory. The problem with such a formulation is the deeply condescending conception of the social subject as an ideological dupe that it conjures up. Not only is this wretched individual incapable of perceiving her/his true interests, pacified as s/he is by the hallucinogenic effects of bourgeois indoctrination. But rising above the ideological mists is the enlightened academic who from his/her perch in the ivory tower may look down to discern the genuine interests of those not similarly blessed.
>
> (1997:47–48)

Due to such negative emotional connotations, which are constitutive of the use of false consciousness-based arguments, I believe it is important at this stage to expand on a point made in the introductory chapter to this book. That is to say, that in levelling such 'charges', I am not attempting, either explicitly or implicitly, to blame the mothers for the regimes of care they deploy. Nor am I attempting to claim that one form of life is *intrinsically* better than any other. Instead, my argument takes the form of a world-disclosing form of critique with enlightenment as its aim. In other words, my argument, built as it is upon Bacon's dictum that 'knowledge is power', is predicated on the belief that a change in consciousness produced by exposure to new ideas has the potential to liberate those affected "from the chimeras, the ideas, the dogmas, the imaginary beings under the yoke of which they are pining away" (Marx and Engels, 1970:1). However, I am not using the term 'enlightenment' in the patronising and condescending sense referred to by Hay to denote that I am somehow intellectually superior to the respondents. Rather, because power is most effective the less visible it is to one's consciousness its usage denotes the fact that they, like all of us, are sometimes the unwitting victims of ideological forces they are unaware of. Therefore, and as Nussbaum accurately observes, a temporal difficulty in thinking (which involves the ability to imagine a counterfactual social order) and acting in accordance with one's real interests can better be explained by reference to "lifelong socialization and absence of information" as opposed to indiscriminately classifying such individuals as ideological dupes (2000:139). In effect, an ideological critique, or at least this one, is based on the supposition that there exists an information differential, and not a variance in intelligence, separating the critic from those to whom his critique is addressed.

In a very general sense, this aim of enlightening such parents involves presenting them with alternative discursive resources that demonstrate that the prevailing social, moral, and political order should not be taken at face-value. More particularly, the hope is that such consciousness-raising will bring about a realisation on the part of parents—those who featured in this book and those who face similar predicaments—that they have more options when it comes to their stated desire that their adult sons and daughters with Down syndrome get to experience a sexual life than they have heretofore been led to believe. The hope is that whatever decision is finally arrived at, such mothers and fathers will begin to logically re-examine the conventional wisdom as to what constitutes the 'unthinkable', and whether they as parents have the moral responsibility to at least begin to think it. This would involve them reaching the stage where they can, without blush or any feeling of cognitive dissonance, co-opt as their own Shildrick's initial formulation of the problem. Namely, that "the issue of facilitated sex raises the question of how far is it justifiable to exclude certain people from the expression of their sexuality when the situation could be easily alleviated" (2007:57).

As already established, the reluctant jailor metaphor is designed to make explicit that there exists an asymmetrical distribution of power between parent and their adult child with Down syndrome. As we also have seen, from the social model perspective, this configuration of rights and responsibilities is deemed to be illegitimate and thus in need of overhauling. However, my analysis will take a different tack. Namely, it will accept, because intellectual impairments such as Down syndrome are autonomy-limiting conditions, that this hierarchical relationship is inevitable and that the parent does indeed have a moral obligation to play the role of reluctant jailor and deploy a paternalistic regime of care. In this regard, I believe it to be a mistake to indiscriminately conceive of the exercise of power in negative zero-sum terms simply on *a priori* grounds. Rather, when examining relationships of dependency, such as those which pertain between the adults with intellectual disabilities and their parents, one must also acknowledge that the ability of the latter to exercise power over the former can be "productive, transformative, authoritative and compatible with dignity" (Lukes, 2005:109).

With such productive use of power over others in mind, the argument I am making is that liberal-minded parents, by not taking full advantage of the asymmetrical power relations between them and their adult sons and daughters with Down syndrome, are in fact not acting paternalistically enough. To this end, I will apply insights from the so-called three faces of power debate, which is typically ignored within disability studies to subvert conventional understanding of parental responsibility to argue that the duty of care can and should be expanded to include more freedoms for their adult sons and daughters in the sexual realm than they presently enjoy.

To justify this conclusion, I must do two things. Firstly, I must demonstrate that liberal-minded parents are not necessarily as powerless as they believe themselves to be. Secondly, I must establish that in relation to their current beliefs and practices regarding the issue as to what constitutes legitimate and illegitimate forms of sexual expression, they are needlessly (in terms of the autonomy/paternalism issues they are grappling with) exercising forms of power over their adult sons and daughters that they may not be consciously aware of—and thereby stifling their real interests in the process.

With this epistemological framework in place, the rest of this chapter will focus on providing a coherent conceptual argument to answer the following question. Namely, can the paternalistic regime of care documented in this book be reconstructed in such a way to include a new ethical imperative, one that states that liberal-minded parents have a moral obligation to do everything in their power to ensure that their adult sons and daughters have their sexual needs met, even if meeting this objective entails availing of the option of facilitated sex?

On *prima facie* grounds, the answer is clearly no. As explicated in previous chapters, unlike the objective status legal rights enjoy, what constitutes a moral right is, as with judgements in the aesthetic field, always in the proverbial eye of the beholder. Hence, there is no attempt on my part, nor is there any need, to attempt to present a transcendental argument in the manner favoured by many ideology critics such as Jurgen Habermas (1972). That is, there is no suggestion that by utilising an 'ideal speech situation' (or some such conceptual device) one can produce a menu of practices that all rational people are, by their ability to reason objectively, required to assent to. Rather, a key tenet of my analysis is based on repudiating the fiction that there exists some non-circular Archimedean point from which one can construct a set of real interests. Instead, my argument is predicated on the belief that the form such real interests will take are irreducibly subject dependent in the sense that they stem from one's ideological affiliations. In this respect, I align myself with the relativist position, which states that the practices to be subsumed under the real interest's classification are the product of one's explanatory framework. In other words, and as Lukes rightly states, there is no reason to believe that there exists a canonical set of such interests "that will resolve moral conflicts and set the seal on proffered explanations, confirming them as true" (2005:148).

Hence, the recognition that the list of such interests will differ depending on where one locates oneself on the ideological spectrum. This concession to moral relativism is an acknowledgement of the logical power of Hume's previously explored fact/value distinction. It also stems from an awareness that the pretensions to truth contained within the panoply of ideologies battling for normative control over our hearts and minds are all playing incommensurable language games and thus cannot all, if any, be true. For instance, given that one's ideological affiliations will influence how different sexual practices are morally evaluated, it is unrealistic to expect parents who still subscribe to a quasi-spiritual conception of sexual expression to condone their intellectually disabled adult sons and daughters meeting their sexual needs outside the context of a loving relationship. However, because from a secular liberal perspective, sexual desires can legitimately be categorised as a form of real needs, this prohibitory stance no longer applies (Goldman, 1977; Singer, 2005).

To this end, my argument is that secular liberal parents are being ideologically consistent if they agree that, all things being equal, they are meeting the real interests of their intellectually disabled sons and daughters when they do everything within their power to maximise the amount of physical pleasure their adult children experience. This involves a partial refutation of John Stuart's Mill's somewhat obnoxious distinction between so called 'higher and lower pleasures': that is, the privileging of so-called intellectual pleasures over those of a more sensual nature. My attack on this typology is partial in nature because although I want to deconstruct this binary, I also wish to retain Mill's inductive test as to how to arrange different experiences hierarchically. With this strategy in place, I, and hopefully interested parents, can once again reclaim the notion that sexual pleasure is a worthy end-in-itself and not necessarily a means to something else (Crisp, 1997).

By bringing the body back into the equation in this way, the typically punitive biology equals destiny-type claims regarding the inability of many intellectually disabled adults to consent to embarking on a sexual relationship can thus be inverted. With these insights in mind, it quickly becomes apparent that the answer to the question as to whether parents who define themselves as secular liberals have a moral responsibility to do everything within their power to ensure that their sons or daughters with Down syndrome have their sexual needs met is not as self-evident as dominant social norms would have us believe.

The three faces of power debate

The 'three faces of power' phrase was originally coined by Steven Lukes in his enormously influential book, *Power: A Radical View,* first published in 1974 and then later republished with significant additions in 2005. Since its initial emergence, it has effectively taken on a life of its own and has become an omnipresent feature of sociological and philosophical debates regarding the nature of power. The phrase itself was used by Lukes to validate his argument that, in contradistinction to previous formulations, power is exercised in the following three ways.

1   The first or visible face of power refers to decision-making power.
2   The second or hidden face of power refers to non-decision-making power.
3   The third or invisible face of power refers to the role ideological power plays in preference formation.

The first face or 'one-dimensional' view of power refers to the standard liberal conception of power that states that "A has power over B to the extent that he can get B to do something that B would not otherwise do" (Dahl, 1957:202). When we unpack this definition, we see it contains four distinct components that constitute the necessary and sufficient conditions that must be met, to claim that an exercise of power has occurred. Firstly, two or more parties must be in an observable overt zero-sum conflict with each other regarding whose subjective preferences are privileged. Secondly, the respective parties must know they are involved in such a conflict situation. Thirdly, to measure the amount of relative power an individual has, one needs to focus on who gets their way regarding the outcome of a decision-making process. In such a situation, the person with the greater degree of power is the person whose decision prevails. Fourthly, all the respective parties are aware that the reason why one individual's decision trumps all others is not due to them creating a consensus by means of advancing the best argument. Rather, all the parties are cognizant of the fact that the reason why the winner of the decision-making process has won is that he/she can sanction them in a way they cannot sanction him/her. As already established, this "reluctant jailor" form of power is constitutive of the parents pre-existing paternalistic regimes of care. For example, it is the first face of power that underpins the parents' refusal to countenance the oft-expressed desire of their adult sons and daughters to engage in forms of unsupervised socialising.

Per its critics, this first-dimensional view of power lacks the explanatory weight to really comprehend what power is and how it works. Its fatal flaw in this respect concerns its exclusive focus on observable conflict in relation to whether A's decision wins out over B's or vice versa. The second face of power attempts to expand the concept of power and its exercise beyond that of an exclusive focus on what happens in a situation of observable conflict. It argues that to truly grasp how power works, it is necessary to also examine what does not happen in such situations. In other words, and as its name suggests, the second face of power maintains that there are in fact two different forms of power. These are decision-making power and non-decision-making power. By invoking this concept of non-decision-making power, proponents of the second face of power contend that the absence of overt grievances between two or more parties in relation to an issue does not in and of itself mean that power is not been covertly wielded with the result that one of the parties still ends up doing something they would rather not do. They argue that this less visible (but still empirically verifiable in the sense that one can ask the respective parties what they really wanted to do) face of power works by establishing the parameters determining what issues can become the subject of discussion in the first place. Because of such agenda-setting power, the context within which conflict over decisions can occur, are not only effectively controlled from the outset but are also limited to relatively non-controversial issues (Bachrach and Baratz, 1962). To take just one example of the many instances of such power contained within the primary data collected for this book, we can illustrate this process in action by pointing to the fact that while most of the adults with Down syndrome I spoke to expressed the urge to make their own way home from their supervised socialising, they typically ended up been driven home by one or both of their parents. Yet, this arrangement does not typically cause any real-time overt conflict between parent and adult child as the latter has effectively internalised the fact that this is not an issue that can be contested. Because of the parents' ability to limit the scope of decision-making and/or what can be argued about to relatively 'safe' issues in this way, the potential for overt disagreement to break out between them and their intellectually disabled sons and daughters is thus greatly reduced.

Steven Lukes's (2005) third face of power posits a more holistic 'three-dimensional' theory of power to answer a different, but related, question to those addressed by the first two formulations. Namely, how do we explain the fact that people sometimes willingly act in ways that are inimical to their own, or the real interests of those they are responsible for, in the absence of any kind of intentional third-party intervention—whether overt or covert? In his attempt to answer this question, Lukes argues that it is necessary to go beyond the important insights offered by the first two faces of power as they remain beholden to the standard liberal conception of freedom. Because they perceive visible conflict over subjective preferences to be a necessary, albeit not sufficient, condition underpinning the exercise of power, they fall prey to the conceptual trap of defining as 'free' any action where the individual is doing what he or she wants to do. For instance, Lukes believes the second face of power's emphasis on covert or hidden forms of power makes it an improvement on the first. However, he goes on to argue that in its insistence that non-decision-making power only exists when there are recognised grievances that are being denied entry into the decision-making process, it remains inadequate to the task at hand. The problem is that the second face of power fails to address the role power plays in influencing why we want the things we want to begin with. Due to this blind spot, it misses the crucial role played by ideological forces in the creation of such internal constraints. Such mental schemata, which go beyond questions concerning the power a given individual has to exercise his or her will, can in turn shape our preferences in such a way to prevent conflict from arising in the first place.

To address this conceptual gap, Lukes poses the question whether it "is not the supreme exercise of power to avert conflict and grievance by influencing, shaping, and determining the perceptions and preferences of others" (2005:26). Accordingly, he argues that to truly understand the workings of power, one needs to acknowledge the capacity of this third dimension of power to prevent the formation of genuine grievances in such a way that the status quo is naturalised and reproduced accordingly. This brings us to another important insight that differentiates the third face of power from its counterparts. Namely, while the first two faces of power insist on a personal connection, no matter how tenuous, between those involved in a conflict situation, the third face of power is equally adamant that power in the form of ideologies and social norms can induce compliance "by influencing desires and beliefs without being "intelligent and intentional"" (2005:136). In other words, while all three perspectives agree that there is always, ultimately, somebody to blame for exercising power in an exploitative fashion, the third face of power also recognises that there is a hierarchy of guilt regarding such practices, as in many instances, the powerful are not consciously exercising their power.

By shifting the focus away from consciously held grievances, whether expressed or not (in this context, the reference is to both the adult with Down syndrome and his/her parents) and onto the mutually constitutive notions of real interests and false consciousness, Lukes argues that power can also be exercised in the absence of any overt or covert conflict between anyone. To operationalise this dialectical interplay between real interests and false consciousness, Lukes introduces a third variable into the equation—the concept of latent conflict. This form of conflict is said to be latent because those who are subject to power—and indeed, in many cases, those who are unwittingly wielding the power—are currently unaware of what is in their best interests, and consequently remain ignorant that the web of power relations in which they are entangled is actively stifling them. In Lukes own words, a fundamental tenet underpinning the third-face understanding of power involves assenting to the proposition that even with the absence of any conflict over subjective preferences, power is still at work if there exists a "a contradiction between the interests of those exercising power and the real interests of those they exclude", even in cases where the "latter may not express or even be conscious of their interests" (Lukes, 2005:24–25). Conversely, it is this lack of awareness regarding what people who are subject to this third face of power would want and prefer if they were presented with such choices that determine when and where such latent conflict will ever metamorphose into actual conflict.

To illustrate such latent conflict in action, we can invoke the much-cited example of the slave who claims to prefer his life of slavery—the only form of life he has ever known—over that of a life of freedom (Hindess, 1996; Hayward, 2000). From the three-dimensional understanding of power, a contented slave is a contradiction in terms. Accordingly, to explain such behaviours, the concept of false-consciousness is called upon to conclude that the contented slave is only contented because they suffer from false consciousness and are therefore unaware of where their real interests lie. Consequently, their stated preference should not be taken at face value (Barnes, 1998). In such a context, it is necessary to ask if such an individual would still valorise a life of slavery if his owners gave him the opportunity to experience what a life of freedom entails. As with the contented slave, so with the intellectually disabled adult. In such a context, it is necessary to ask if such an individual would still be satisfied with a celibate life if his/her parents gave them the opportunity to experience what a sexual life entails?

In this respect, the analogy between the ignorant but otherwise moral slave-owner (not necessarily a contradiction in terms) and the parent of the adult with Down syndrome is also apposite. As in both cases, the imprimatur of a third party is a prerequisite for any possibility of those they have power over closing the false consciousness/real interests gap.

When applied to trying to understand why the paternalistic regime of care takes the form it does, such insights warrant my conclusion that the first two conceptions of power are blind to a form of power in which the beliefs and desires of the parents are being manipulated by ideological forces they are unaware of (Hayward, 2000). In this sense, it is like the relationship outlined earlier in which the parent can be said to exercise power over their son or daughter with Down syndrome even if their adult child consciously wants to do what their parents want them to do. In this respect, we can conceive of the taboo around the use of facilitated sex for people with Down syndrome as constituting a societal norm that has, for all intents and purposes, taken on a real material existence. This societal norm, which bluntly states that 'good normal parents do not entertain such matters', is preventing many liberal parents from even entertaining a possibility that they are logically committed to at least considering, if their goal is to do everything within their power to ensure that their adult sons and daughters have their sexual needs met.

It is at this stage that it is necessary to refer back to the original conceit with which this analysis began, namely the typology that conceives of such adults as 'prisoners' of sorts. In relation to the issue under scrutiny, the thesis being advanced is that in many fundamental respects, a large percentage of adults with Down syndrome living in the parental home remain 'contented prisoners' (Foley, 2013). In other words, if members of this population are on the hedonic treadmill to the same extent as their non-intellectually disabled counterparts, then it seems to be the case that their sexual energy can be sublimated in a far easier fashion. However, from the third face of power perspective, the notion of a contented prisoner is analogous to that of the happy slave (Lukes, 2005). It is in this sense that we can hypothesise that many adults with Down syndrome are victims of false consciousness in relation to their own sexuality, in the same way that they may for example, be unaware of their need to avail of the services of a speech and language therapist if they want to improve their ability to communicate verbally. However, unlike physically disabled people, who have both the relative freedom and the cognitive capacity to employ a form of means-ends reasoning to act on their sexual desires, many adults with Down syndrome are not only unable to formulate such rational strategies to meet their sexual needs, but in some cases also lack the intellectual capacity to classify such feelings as being sexual in nature at all (Cunningham, 2006). It is this conclusion that brings us to the question of parental responsibility, and their role in ensuring that the 'real' sexual needs of their adult sons and daughters with Down syndrome are realized in the same way that their 'real' speech and language needs are met. From a rational perspective, such real sexual needs should be conceived by secular liberal parents as being analogous in nature, or at the very least, simply different in degree rather than kind (Singer, 2005).

In political theory, the contention that some members of the polity are suffering from a form of false consciousness continues to be a matter of much controversy. The principal sources of such debate concern the coherence of the concept itself; that is, what can it mean to say that rational people do not know their own minds, and that their stated preferences are inimical to their true or real interests? In addition, there is the issue regarding the political consequences that follow if such a concept is deemed to have any explanatory power (Gray, 1991). The answer to this question typically involves giving political authority to an elite section of society to formulate and implement social policies that will force their less enlightened counterparts to embark on a process of rational self-actualisation. From the perspective of those who privilege the negative freedom to live their lives in a manner of their own choosing, the solution to the problem of false consciousness if it is imposed at a state level, is to be led down the road to serfdom—a state of affairs where the cure is invariably worse than the disease (Flathman, 1987).

Whether such dangers are a realistic possibility when applied to society at large is a moot point in that when we come to the issues with which this book is concerned, the society/family analogy does not hold in the same way. Firstly, as documented throughout this book, there is already a pre-existing paternalistic regime of care, the need for which is based on the parent's beliefs, which have both a phenomenological and scientific basis, that their intellectually disabled adult children lack the autonomy to take control of their lives in the ways that are considered normal for their non-intellectually disabled contemporaries. Secondly, another key difference is that there is no comparison in terms of what is at stake regarding the predictable or unpredictable consequences that will ensue if such attempts at social engineering are actualised. For example, instead of a class war, or some such, the worst that can happen if the facilitated sex option is implemented is that the adult with Down syndrome experiences an event they are unwilling and will not be forced to repeat. This privileging of the voice of the intellectually disabled adult in relation to the issue of facilitated sex is what I mean by inverting the typical biology equals destiny type claims regarding the inability of many intellectually disabled to consent to embarking on a sexual relationship. For instance, I have compared the meeting of sexual needs as analogous to the meeting of 'genuine health concerns' that are on-going regardless of whether the respective adult with Down syndrome wants to revisit a given health professional at all and/or on the specified date stipulated. However, unlike such 'genuine health concerns', when it comes to the use of the facilitated sex process, it would be the intellectually disabled adult who would have the final say regarding whether to repeat the behaviour in question. Consequently, if the respective parents accept the premise that "policy x is more in A's real interest than policy y if A, were he to experience the results of both x and y, would choose x as the result he would rather have for himself" (Connolly, 1994:64), it follows that the intellectually disabled adult who has experienced facilitated sex is more suitably equipped with the inductive knowledge, whether embodied or intellectual in nature, to decide for him or herself whether such a sexual life is more compatible with them realising their real interests then a celibate one than those who have not had such experiences.

Conclusion

For a normalisation of facilitated sex to take place, secular liberal parents of intellectually disabled adults need to change the conceptual lens through which they currently view this issue. The numerous obstacles preventing such praxis taking place, while immensely powerful, are not insurmountable. For example, the third face of power has illustrated the fact that the conventional common-sense notion of what constitutes being a good parent did not fall from the sky, nor is it a God-given imperative which must be obeyed. Rather, it is, to paraphrase Nietzsche, an arbitrary subject position, which is 'human all too human'. Consequently, its ability to exert the causal power it currently does is tenuous in the extreme. The social identity it bestows enjoys a nominal ontology. Regardless of the conditioning we have been exposed to, the existentialist insight that existence precedes essence, with the concomitant widening of our horizons in relation to what we can think and how we can act, is there for the taking. The only remaining question to be answered is whether secular liberal minded parents of adults with Down syndrome living in the parental home are willing to pick up the gauntlet and act accordingly, or remain haunted at some level, by the spectre of lost opportunity.

The point has been made throughout this chapter that you do not have to be a Marxist to subscribe to a third-face understanding of power and the attendant concept of real interests. Nevertheless, perhaps a good place to begin summing up is to reference Marx yet again and see if his "workers of the world unite. You have nothing to lose but your chains" rallying cry can be co-opted for the issue at hand. Although the syntax may be less than poetic, if we rework this statement to now read 'liberal parents of adults with Down syndrome unite; you have nothing to lose but an archaic conception of what constitutes legitimate forms of sexual expression', arguably we have all we need to begin a rational conversation as to how to go about ensuring that adults with Down syndrome living in the parental home, who have real sexual needs, do not go through their lives as 'willing' or unwilling celibates.

Clearly the recourse to facilitated sex represents a less than optimal option for many members of both populations. In an ideal world, it would perhaps be preferable not to have to think about utilising such a mechanism. In the real world, however, as the voices of both the mothers and their adult children I have spoken to have amply demonstrated, the intransient nature of the structural obstacles preventing people with Down syndrome from meeting their sexual needs in more conventional ways show no signs of melting into thin air. Consequently, the argument I have advanced here is that it is time for liberal-minded parents in their role as reluctant jailors to stop hiding, both from themselves, and behind the biological impairment that is Down syndrome, to justify the imposition of a largely negative regime of care on their prisoners—be they contented or otherwise. By drawing on the resources provided by the three faces of power debate, it has been made apparent that the answer to the question of who or what is exercising power over whom is a more complex affair than the liberal focus on overt conflict would have us believe.

By invoking the notion of real interests, it has demonstrated that the impairment that is Down syndrome cuts both ways. While on the one hand, it limits the ability to exercise self-governance in the way most non-intellectually disabled adults take for granted, it should also act as a constant reminder to their parents, that 'they' like 'us,' have sexual needs that can and should be met. Clearly, what happens next regarding the possible normalisation of the use of facilitated sex for adults with Down syndrome is up to the parents in question.

6 Conclusions

The primary objective of this book was to investigate the proposition that the parental regime of care that many adults with Down syndrome living in the parental home are subject to is an obstacle to them finding boyfriends/girlfriends and thus embarking on a sexual relationship. As explained in Chapter 1, for a mixture of personal and intellectual reasons, I decided to depart from what seems to be the standard practice when studying issues of disability and put the sole focus on the sexuality of this specific population rather than using the umbrella term of "intellectual disability" in an indiscriminate fashion.

One consequence of having a sister with Down syndrome was that I have spent a lot of my teenage and adult life socialising with people with Down syndrome and their families. Based on these experiences, I observed what I considered to be an anomaly. The anomaly in question, which became the sociological/philosophical puzzle that this project has set out to solve, was that although nearly all the people with Down syndrome that I knew were actively searching for a boyfriend or a girlfriend, very few of them had actually managed to find one. Based on how my sister with Down syndrome was treated in a more paternalistic fashion than me or any of my other siblings—a regime of care that continues to this very day—and which, based on my experience of talking to other people with Down syndrome, their parents and siblings, is in no way unusual, it occurred to me that one of the reasons that could explain the mismatch between the stated desires of many people with Down syndrome to have a boyfriend or girlfriend and their lived realities was due to the paternalistic regime of care they were subject to.

To explore this conjecture, I adopted a relatively unique approach. This involved drawing on two nominally incommensurable theoretical frameworks that I was both familiar with and interested in, namely the Foucauldian and the psychoanalytic. I was influenced by Foucault's work, especially his book *Discipline and Punish* (1977), where he introduces the notion of the all-seeing panopticon. The function of the panopticon is to make the prisoners in question become their own overseers in the sense that they condition themselves to think and act in the way the prison guard expects them to.

This regime of 'care' had a resonance of sorts in how I saw my own sister, and how the parents that I knew treated their adult offspring with Down syndrome. Consequently, utilising Foucault's work, I developed a similar typology to act as a heuristic guide in trying to help understand and explain the nature of the parental regime of care that most of the adults with Down syndrome I knew were subjected to: namely, to conceive of the parents as 'reluctant jailors' and their adult sons and daughters as 'prisoners' of sorts.

Regarding the collection of information needed to answer my research questions, I decided to consult a cohort of both mothers and their adult sons and daughters with Down syndrome. Moreover, I needed to talk to them in a manner that lent itself to the production of 'thick data'; that is, I needed to be able to engage the respondents in a debate of sorts, where in response to a given question I could then probe deeper and ask relevant 'why' questions—hence the use of the semi-structured interview and a focus group for the mothers who took part. While the semi-structured interviews had as their focus issues raised by my initial research questions, the focus group was designed to deal with parental responses to the issue of incorporating facilitated sex into their pre-existing regime of care. This concentration on the question of facilitated sex is unique. As demonstrated within this book, there are very few empirical studies or theoretical investigations into this subject matter in relation to intellectually disabled people generally. In addition, and as far as can be established, apart from my own published work (Foley, 2014), there is no academic literature dealing with the issue of facilitated sex specifically in relation to adults with Down syndrome.

As this book progressed, my initial suspicion that the Foucauldian approach would more easily lend itself to the formulation of theoretically informed empirical research questions when compared to the psychoanalytic approach was vindicated. For example, questions drawn from the Foucauldian approach—which in turn helped to shape the questions I asked the respondents—included the following: How is power distributed between the parents and their adult son or daughter with Down syndrome? Do both parties have power? Do both parties have the power to make the other do something that they would not otherwise do? Is this an asymmetrical relationship in terms of the amount of power each of the parties possess or can it be characterised more accurately by reference to a horizontal circulation of power? If parents are trying to regulate the sexual expression of their son or daughter, do their adult children try and resist such forms of control? If yes, how does such resistance manifest itself?

By its very nature, coupled with my reluctance to ask questions that might be perceived to be offensive be they sexually explicit or not, it proved slightly more difficult to operationalise the psychoanalytic approach. This was especially the case in the conversations with the cohort of mothers regarding my contention that because their sons and daughters with Down syndrome inhabit non-normative bodies, their relationship with them was more ambivalent than they would like to admit. However, as explained in the preceding text, this does not mean one cannot draw logically legitimate inferences based on what the respondents do or do not say, which can then be used to explore the explanatory worth of a given psychoanalytic concept. As the reader already knows, this was the approach that I adopted, an approach moreover that I argued did prove to yield useful insights. The 'slightly more difficult' qualification is, however, also important to note. Thus, in relation to the conversations with the adults with Down syndrome themselves, due to a combination of the questions that were asked and the honest, sometimes 'politically incorrect' answers provided and/or offered voluntarily, the contention that the psychic defence mechanism of 'abjection' played a role in what 'kinds of people' many adults with Down syndrome find sexually attractive did prove to be of much explanatory worth.

With the contention that ideas rather than respondents are the subject matter of social research uppermost in my mind, when conducting both the interviews and the focus group the principled approach I employed was to think of the participants as informants who were passing judgement on the various theoretical assumptions that underpinned my research questions. Again, the 'in principle' qualification here is an important one to note, as given the cognitive limitations of adults with Down syndrome and the controversial subject matter I wanted answers to, a lot of the questions that could have been asked were not. In the case of the adults with Down syndrome, this was for fear that they would not fully comprehend the kind of information I was requesting of them. Regarding the cohort of mothers, my reluctance was borne out of the belief that to ask either sexually explicit questions or questions in relation to whether they sometimes perceived their sons and daughters as figures of abjection would be inappropriate.

In relation to the research questions, I wanted answers to the empirical findings revealed much interesting information, some of it relatively predictable given my extensive experiential knowledge of the issues in question, while other data collected proved equally surprising given the set of assumptions I was working with. In terms of offering a relatively brief summary of the findings, it is best to start with the assumption that the paternalistic parental regime of care was one of the chief factors inhibiting the formation of boyfriend/girlfriend relationships on the part of the adults with Down syndrome. It is clear from the responses provided by the mothers that they do subject their adult sons and daughters with Down syndrome to a paternalistic regime of care that is different in kind than that imposed on their non-intellectually disabled sons and daughters. The rationale the mothers provided to justify such practices was, albeit sometimes formulated in different ways, a variation on the notion that to have the congenital intellectual impairment of Down syndrome is to lack the cognitive capacity to fend for oneself in the sometimes-cruel world we all inhabit. Hence, the mothers believed that because their intellectually disabled charges could not look after themselves in the same manner their non-intellectually disabled siblings could, they therefore had a moral obligation to treat their adult sons and daughters in a paternalistic fashion to prevent them being abused, exploited, or taken advantage of in some way. Consequently, all the mothers agreed that they imposed a social embargo on what their sons and daughters could or could not do, and a curfew determining at what times their sons and daughters could do what their mothers allowed them to.

However, despite the deployment of such regimes of care, it is much more difficult to make a 'causal connection' between the regime of care and the fact that many of the respondents with Down syndrome did not have the boyfriends or girlfriends they sought. There are several reasons underpinning such a conclusion. The first of these is the fact that many of the adults with Down syndrome expressed an urge to socialise with their non-intellectually disabled siblings and not with other people with Down syndrome. From what the data can tell us, the parental regime of care allows for such outings in principle. The problem was more with the willingness of the siblings to agree to 'babysit' their adult brother or sister with Down syndrome. In addition, and as previously explicated, even if all the relevant parties were happy with such an arrangement, for an array of reasons, the pool of possible sexual partners for adults with Down syndrome seems to be limited to other people with Down syndrome. Consequently, one can reasonably infer that while the parental regime of care inadvertently played a part in limiting the amount of late nights, if any, the cohort of adults with Down syndrome I spoke to spent frequenting pubs and clubs with their siblings, its deployment was not for fear that any of the individuals in question would find a potential boyfriend/girlfriend and/or have sex with a stranger.

While this parental embargo on unsupervised socialising also applied to the stated wishes on the part of some of the adults with Down syndrome to, for example, go to the pub after a group bowling session was completed with some of their friends with Down syndrome, this data does not lend itself to a firm conclusion as to why such a restriction was actually imposed. It was undeterminable as to whether this parental veto was borne out of fear on the part of the parents that their sons and daughters would 'get up to no good' in the sexual sense of the term rather than a concern that some non-disabled person would say something derogatory and/or do something physically threatening; or whether it was a pragmatic issue for the parents, in the sense they were worried about worrying what might happen while their sons and daughters were not being supervised and so on. The second fact derived from the data that undermines the parental regime of care/lack of sexual partner's conjecture is that many of the mothers interviewed not only expressed a desire to see their sons and daughters embarking on a boyfriend/girlfriend relationship, but in addition also sometimes encouraged their sons and daughters to give some of the suitors they had already rejected another chance.

Nonetheless, there were also numerous instances where the parental regime of care adopted by the mothers did directly manifest itself in a ban on either their son or daughter possibly having sex. Somewhat paradoxically, this was mainly the case when the adult with Down syndrome did actually have a boyfriend or girlfriend. The sexual prohibition in question refers to the parental stipulation that their son's or daughter's partner when socialising in the parental house had to subsequently go home back to their respective parents. In other words, all the adults with Down syndrome interviewed who had a boyfriend or girlfriend were not allowed to have their partner sleep over, even when they specifically asked their parents if they could. This example of 'sovereign power' in action makes explicit that the relationship between parent and adult child with Down syndrome is at times explicitly a power relationship, and an asymmetrical one at that. This empirical finding in turn calls into question one of the Foucauldian insights assumed for the purposes of this research, namely that while power is ever-present, the form it takes is more 'productive' in nature. Thus, from the Foucauldian perspective, one can conclude that examples of such overt conflict should not be taking place as the adult with Down syndrome should be governing themselves in accordance with what their parents want for them. Conversely, the fact that such overt conflict sometimes takes place between parent and adult son or daughter vindicates another one of Foucault's key claims, namely that where there is power there is resistance. Meanwhile, from the psychoanalytic perspective, it is interesting to note, regarding the 'out of sight out of mind thinking' on the part of some of the mothers discussed in the analysis chapter, that one of the parents who did not allow her daughter to have her boyfriend sleep in the parental home played an active part in arranging trips away for her daughter and her boyfriend—trips that involve staying in hotels and sleeping in the same bed.

Some of the most interesting data regarding the mothers' perception of their adult sons and daughters having sexual needs that should be met came in the focus group specifically set up to talk about the issue of facilitated sex. The main findings that arose from this interaction include the following: None of the respondents had ever considered utilising the mechanism of facilitated sex to have their son or daughter's sexual needs met and, when discussing its merits, most the respondents agreed that it made perfectly logical sense to utilise such a mechanism if they believed there was no other option. However, despite the logic involved, most the respondents implied a conflict between the head and the heart, by stating that they would probably never go down that particular road. The one exception to the consensus view was expressed by a mother in relation to the sexual needs of her son, who at the closing of the focus group, indicated that if she truly believed that her son's current single status was to continue indefinitely, she could see herself considering availing of the facilitated sex option. Apropos of the consensus view, this was most vehemently expressed when the relevant mothers were talking about the possibility of facilitated sex for their daughters. These mothers were adamant that facilitated sex would not be an option for their daughters. The reasons given, although sometimes formulated differently, were predicated on the view that the sexual needs of women were not as strong as those of men, and that consequently, if their daughters' sexual needs were to be met, it had to be in the context of a loving boyfriend/girlfriend relationship. In the minds of the mothers, love trumped the idea of sex as an end in itself every time.

As stated at the outset of this book, by situating this work as a critical exercise in applied theoretical analysis, I felt impelled to construct a normative argument that offers suggestions as to how to solve the 'problem' of the celibate lives led by many adults with Down syndrome who are still living in the parental home. This argument draws on the work of Steven Lukes to argue for a normalisation of facilitated sex as a means to this end. In addition, I argued that facilitated sex should become a component of a new, albeit equally paternalistic regime of care compared to that currently deployed by parents of adults with Down syndrome. Although the evidence collected for this project demonstrates that the specific mothers who were interviewed deploy a paternalistic regime of care, the argument being made regarding the need for a normalisation of facilitated sex is predicated on the belief that such regimes of care are in no way unusual for those adults whose intellectual impairment limits their autonomy.

The essence of the argument I put forward was that liberal-minded parents—and all the mothers I interviewed identified themselves as secular liberals—were involved in an ideological contradiction in not even considering the possibility of facilitated sex for their intellectually disabled charges. This conclusion was based on the contention that from a secular liberal perspective, sexual interaction should not be viewed as different in kind from any other form of social interaction. Hence, to take just one example of the many that could be offered, the 'yuck' reaction displayed by many of the mothers when this issue was originally discussed showed a 'failure' on their part to achieve 'praxis' regarding their stated ideological commitments. In addition, the argument for the use of facilitated sex posited that to utilise such a resource, the parents could solve one concern expressed by them all: Namely, how to ensure their adult sons and daughters get to experience a sexual life on the one hand while ensuring they are not abused/exploited on the other. The final point relating the argument for facilitated sex to the evidence collected during this project concerns the fact that many of the adults with Down syndrome considered other people with Down syndrome as figures of abjection, whose anomalous forms of embodiment ruled them out as possible sexual partners.

The main limitation of this study, as with any small-scale research project, is with the ability to generalise from the findings. In strict methodological terms, one cannot generalise from a sample of ten mothers and their ten adult sons or daughters with Down syndrome living in the parental home to these populations as a whole. Nevertheless, with this qualification in mind, I propose the following four premises:

1   Many parents of adults with Down syndrome living in the parental home subject their adult sons and daughters to a paternalistic regime of care that is different in kind and longer lasting that the regime of care their non-intellectually disabled adult children are subject to.

2   Many parents of adults with Down syndrome living in the parental home are at some level concerned with the fact that their sons and daughters have never had a boyfriend or girlfriend, and by extension are living and may be condemned forever to live celibate lives.
3   Parental views on their adult son or daughter with Down syndrome living in the parental home entering a sexual relationship through the conventional means of finding a boyfriend/girlfriend can be arranged by reference to where they stand on a conservative/liberal ideological continuum.
4   Parental views on the role they should play in actively encouraging their adult sons and daughters with Down syndrome to consider having their sexual needs met by recourse to the use of facilitated sex can be arranged by reference to where they stand on a conservative/liberal ideological spectrum.

If one assents to these premises, one can *logically* argue, based on inference to the most plausible explanation, that the insights gleaned from the respondents can offer some support to a wider generalisation to the effect that many adults with Down syndrome living in the parental home are leading largely celibate lives.

Whether one accepts the preceding conclusions or not, given the paucity of research into this area, it is imperative that more work is carried out to provide interested parties with data as to what the key players, namely the parents of adults with Down syndrome (including the fathers, of course), the adults with Down syndrome themselves, and their siblings, think about the general issue of increased freedom for adults with Down syndrome around the areas of unregulated socialising and the formation of sexual relationships. Hopefully, such conversations will in turn lead to the production of various blueprints, be they social policy or family-led, which coalesce around the objective of providing optimal opportunities for adults with Down syndrome to lead satisfying sexual lives.

In addition, there is an urgent need to overhaul legislation, which, as detailed in preceding chapters, makes it illegal unless certain conditions are met, for adults with an intellectual disability like Down syndrome to embark on a sexual relationship. A final recommendation, of the kind which stays within the confines of conventional disability studies at any rate, is to insist that policies are put in place that will help close any knowledge gap that exists between the relevant professionals and some parents of adults with Down syndrome as to whether adults with Down syndrome have the same sexual needs as their non-disabled contemporaries. With all of these changes in place, one can be cautiously optimistic that the paternalistic parental regime of care that most adults with Down syndrome living in the parental home are subjected to—if one assents to at least one of the four propositions set out previously—may become more flexible over time, taking on a new character in the process, the nature of which would provide adults with Down syndrome with the most optimal chances of finding the boyfriends/girlfriends that so many of them desperately seek.

As this book demonstrates, however, when the issue involves parents who have all the requisite information, arguably social policy can go no further in terms of its prescriptions. If there is a hierarchy of knowledge that can help settle the matter in a definitive, objective manner as to whether parents should privilege one side of the paternalism/autonomy debate when it comes to 'allowing' their sons and daughters more freedom around the areas of unregulated socialising and sexual relationships, it has yet to make itself known. To this end, interested third parties not personally affected by any decisions taken, regardless of their 'expertise', might do well to heed Wittgenstein's wise aphorism; 'whereof one cannot speak, thereof one must be silent,' and act accordingly (1960:250).

This may seem like a suitable note to end on, especially if we once again invoke both the ideological continuum referred to previously and the fact-value distinction that has played such a central role in much of the argumentation that this book has engaged in. However, to leave it there would in a sense also constitute a betrayal of many of the normative claims that have also played an equally central role in the construction of this book. Consequently, it is necessary to offer a final recommendation that facilitated sex is a relatively painless mechanism that liberal-minded parents have at their disposal to ensure that their sons and daughters with Down syndrome experience the joys of a non-celibate life, while at the same time responsibly ensuring that they do not become victims of the omnipresent threat—whether real, overstated, or even imaginary—that goes by the name of 'stranger danger'.

Thus, when we consult the fact-value distinction once again, we see that the inability to logically deduce an 'ought' from an 'is' cuts both ways. While closing down the possibility of finding objective answers to ethical questions—because there are none—it conversely has the potential to open up a new ethical horizon for interested liberal parents to at least think the unthinkable and entertain the use of facilitated sex as a means to meeting the sexual needs of their intellectually disabled sons and daughters. The parents who are willing to embark on this road less travelled can do so safe in the knowledge that not only is this way of thinking more in tune with their own ideological commitments, but that in their willingness to at least scrutinize the ethical *bona fides* of the unthinkable that is facilitated sex, they are at best only violating an ethical taboo rather than an ethical fact.

References

Aguilar, F. (1981). *Landlessness and Hired Labour in Philippine Rice Farms.* Norwich: Geo Books.

Allen, J. (2003). A question of language. In Pryke, M., Rose, G. and Whatmore, S. (Eds), *Using Social Theory: Thinking through Research.* London: Sage, pp. 11–27.

Allen, L. (2012). Pleasure's perils? Critically reflecting on pleasure's inclusion in sexuality education. *Critical Social Policy,* 15: 455–470.

Altermark, N. (2014). The ideology of neuroscience and intellectual disability: Reconstituting the 'disordered' brain. *Disability & Society,* 29 (9): 1460–1472.

Alvesson, M. (2002). *Postmodernism and Social Research.* Buckingham: Open University Press.

Appel, J.M. (2010). Sex rights for the disabled? *Journal of Medical Ethics,* 36: 152–154.

Asselin, M.E. (2003). Insider research: Issues to consider when doing qualitative research in your own setting. *Journal for Nurses in Staff Development,* 19 (2): 99–103. Page 46.

Ayer, A.J. (1956). *The Problem of Knowledge.* London: Cambridge University Press.

Bachrach, P. and Baratz, M.S. (1962). The two faces of power. *American Political Science Review,* 56 (4): 947–952.

Bacik, I. (2004). *Kicking and Screaming.* Dublin: The O'Brien Press Ltd.

Barnes, B. (1988). *The Nature of Power.* Cambridge: Polity Press.

Barnes, C. (1992). Qualitative research: Valuable or irrelevant? *Disability, Handicap & Society,* 7 (2): 115–124.

Barnes, C. (2003). What a difference a decade makes: Reflections on doing 'emancipatory' disability research. *Disability & Society,* 18 (1): 3–17.

Barnes, C. (2012). The social model of disability: Valuable or irrelevant? In Watson, N., Roulstone, A. and Thomas, C. (Eds), *The Routledge Handbook of Disability Studies.* London: Routledge, pp. 12–29.

Bauman, Z. (1982). *Memories of Class.* London: Routledge and Kegan Paul.

Béatrice, H. (2002). *Foucault's Critical Project.* Stanford, MA: Stanford University Press.

Behar, R. (1996). *The Vulnerable Observer: Anthropology that Breaks Your Heart.* Boston, MA: Beacon Press.

Beitz, C.R. (2009). *The Idea of Human Rights.* Oxford: Oxford University Press.

Benatar, D. (2013). Two views of sexual ethics: Promiscuity, paedophilia, and rape. In Power, N., Halwani, R. and Soble, A. (Eds), *The Philosophy of Sex: Contemporary Readings* (6th ed.). New York: Rowman & Littlefield Publishers, pp. 395–408.

Berg, D. and Smith, K. (1988). *The Self in Social Inquiry: Researching Methods.* London: Sage.

Bernert, D. (2011). Sexuality and disability in the lives of women with intellectual disabilities. *Sexuality and Disability*, 29 (2): 129–141.

Bevir, M. (1999). Foucault and critique: Deploying agency against autonomy. *Political Theory*, 27 (1): 65–84.

Bhaskar, R. and Danermark, B. (2006). Metatheory, interdisciplinarity and disability research: A critical realist perspective. *Scandinavian Journal of Disability Research*, 8 (4): 278–297.

Bishop, R. (2007). *The Philosophy of the Social Sciences.* London: Continuum.

Blacher, J. et al. (2007). Supporting families who have children with disabilities. In Carr, A., O' Reily, G., Noonan Walsh, P. and McEvoy, J. (Eds), *The Handbook of Intellectual Disability and Clinical Psychology Practice.* London: Routledge, pp. 303–335.

Blaxter, L. (2001). *How to Research.* Buckingham: Open University Press.

Blum, L.M. (2007). Mother-blame in the Prozac nation: Raising kids with invisible disabilities. *Gender and Society*, 21 (2): 202–226.

Boghossian, P. (2006). *Fear of Knowledge: Against Relativism and Constructivism.* New York: Oxford University Press.

Booth, T. and Booth, W. (2003). In the frame: Photovoice and mothers with learning difficulties. *Disability and Society*, 11 (1): 55–69.

Botros, S. (2006). *Hume, Reason and Morality: A Legacy of Contradiction.* London and New York: Routledge.

Boucher, G. (2012). *Understanding Marxism.* London: Routledge.

Brock, G. (2013). *Cosmopolitanism versus Non-Cosmopolitanism: Critiques, Defences, Reconceptualizations.* Oxford: Oxford University Press.

Brock, S. and Mares, E. (2007). *Realism and Antirealism.* Chesham: Acumen.

Brown, I. and Brown, R.I. (2009). Choice as an aspect of quality of life for people with intellectual disabilities. *Journal of Policy and Practice in Intellectual Disabilities*, 6 (1): 11–18.

Bryman, A. (2008). *Social Research Methods.* Oxford: Oxford University Press.

Burkitt, I. (2008). *Social Selves: Theories of Self and Society.* London: SAGE.

Caffrey, S. (2004). Adult relationships and sexuality. In Walsh, P.N. and Gash, H. (Eds), *Lives and Times: Practice, Policy and People with Disabilities.* Dublin: Rathdown Press, pp. 93–122.

Calhoun, C. (1995). *Critical Social Theory, History and the Challenge of Difference.* Oxford: Blackwell.

Cameron, C. (2014). *Disability Studies: A Student's Guide.* London: SAGE.

Campbell, F. (2008). Exploring internalized ableism using critical race theory. *Disability & Society*, 23 (2): 151–162.

Campbell, F. (2009). *Contours of Ableism: The Production of Disability and Abledness.* Basingstoke: Palgrave Macmillan.

Campbell, F. (2012). Stalking ableism: Using disability to expose 'Abled' narcissism. In Goodley, D., Hughes, B. and Davis, L. (Eds), *Disability and Social Theory: New Developments and Directions.* Basingstoke: Palgrave Macmillan, pp. 212–230.

Canguilhem, G. (1991). *On the Normal and the Pathological.* New York: Zone Books.

Carr, J. (2000). Intellectual and daily living skills of 30-year-olds with Down syndrome: Continuation of a longitudinal study. *Journal of Applied Research in Intellectual Disabilities*, 13: 1–16.

Carr, J. (2008). The everyday life of adults with Down syndrome. *Journal of Applied Research in Intellectual Disabilities*, 21 (5): 389–397.

Chappell, A.L. (1992). Towards a sociological critique of the normalisation principle. *Disability, Handicap and Society*, 7: 35–51.

Chomsky, N. (2007). *On Language*. New York: The New Press.

Chomsky, N. (2009). Noam Chomsky. In Gordon, M. and Wilkinson, C. (Eds), *Conversations on Truth*, London: Continuum, pp. 27–38.

Christman, J. (2009). *The Politics of Persons: Individual Autonomy and Socio Historical Selves*. Cambridge: Cambridge University Press.

Clegg, S.R. (1989). *Frameworks of Power*. London: Sage.

Conly, S. (2013). *Against Autonomy: Justifying Coercive Paternalism*. Cambridge: Cambridge University Press.

Connolly, W.E. (1994). *The Terms of Political Discourse*. Oxford: Blackwell.

Crisp, R. (1997). *Mill on Utilitarianism*. London: Routledge.

Culham, A. and Nind, M. (2003). Deconstructing normalisation: Clearing the way for inclusion. *Journal of Intellectual & Developmental Disability*, 28 (1): 65–78.

Cuskelly, M. and Bryde, R. (2004). Attitudes towards the sexuality of adults with an intellectual disability: Parents, support staff, and a community sample. *Journal of Intellectual and Developmental Disability*, 29: 255–264.

Cuskelly, M. et al. (2006). *Families of Adults with Down Syndrome*. Southsea: Down Syndrome Educational Trust.

Cunningham, C. (2006). *Down Syndrome*. London: Souvenir Press.

Dahl, R. (1957). The concept of power. *Behavioural Science*, 2: 201–215.

Danieli, A. and Woodhams, C. (2005). Emancipatory research methodology and disability: A critique. *International Journal of Social Research Methodology*, 8 (4): 281–296.

Darling, R.B. (1979). *Families against Society: A Study of Reactions to Children with Birth Defects*. London: Sage.

Data Protection Act 1988: Available at www.gov.uk/data-protection/the-data-protection-act (Accessed 15 March 2016).

Davis, L.J. (1995). *Enforcing Normalcy: Disability, Deafness and the Body*. New York: Verso.

Dawson, G. (1994). *Soldier Heroes: British Adventure, Empire and the Imagining of Masculinities*. London: Routledge.

Deal, M. (2003). Disabled people's attitudes toward other impairment groups: A hierarchy of impairments. *Disability & Society*, 18 (7): 897–910.

Deeley, S. (2002). Professional ideology and learning disability: An analysis of internal conflict. *Disability & Society*, 17 (1): 19–33.

Dews, P. (1987). *Logic of Disintegration: Post-Structuralist Thought and the claims of Critical Theory*. London: Verso.

Di Nucci, E. (2011). Sexual rights and disability. *Journal of Medical Ethics*, 37: 158–161.

Docherty, J. and Reid, J. (2009). What's the next stage? Mothers of young adults with Down syndrome explore the path to independence: A qualitative investigation. *Journal of Applied Research in Intellectual Disabilities*, 22 (5): 458–467.

Donner, W. (1991). *The Liberal Self: John Stuart Mill's Moral and Political Philosophy*. Ithaca, NY: Cornell University Press.

Dukes, E. and McGuire, B.E. (2009). Enhancing capacity to make sexuality-related decisions in people with an intellectual disability. *Journal of Intellectual Disability Research*, 53 (8): 727–734.

Dworkin, A. (1983). *Right-Wing Women*. New York: Perigree.

Dworkin, G. (2005). Moral paternalism. *Law and Philosophy*, 24 (3): 305–319.

Earle, S. (2001). Disability, facilitated sex and the role of the nurse. *Journal of Advanced Nursing*, 36 (3): 433–440.

Elliott, A. (1996). *Subject to Ourselves: Social Theory, Psychoanalysis, and Postmodernity*. Cambridge: Polity Press.

Elliott, A. (2007). *Concepts of the Self*. Cambridge: Polity Press.

Elliott, A. (2008). *Contemporary Social Theory*. London: Routledge.

Emerson, E. and McVilly, K. (2004). Friendship activities of adults with intellectual activities in supported accommodation in Northern England. *Journal of Applied Research in Intellectual Disabilities*, 17: 191–197.

Etherington, K. (2004). *Becoming a Reflexive Researcher: Using Our Selves in Research*. London: Jessica Kingsley Publishers.

Evans, D.S., McGuire, B.E., Healy, E. and Carley, S.N. (2009). Sexuality and personal relationships for people with an intellectual disability. Part II: Staff and family carer perspectives. *Journal of Intellectual Disability Research*, 53: 913–921.

Feinberg, J. (1986). *Harm to Self*. Oxford: Oxford University Press.

Filmer, P. (1998). Theory/practice. In Jenks, C. (Ed), *Core Sociological Dichotomies*. London: Sage Publications, pp. 227–245.

Flathman, R. (1987). *The Philosophy and Politics of Freedom*. Chicago, IL: University of Chicago Press.

Flick, U. (1998). *An Introduction to Qualitative Research*. London: Sage.

Flickschuh, K. (2007). *Freedom. Contemporary Liberal Perspectives*. Cambridge: Polity.

Flynn, R.J. and Lemay, R.A. (1999). Normalization and social role valorization at a quarter-century: Evolution, impact, and renewal. In Flynn, R.J and Lemay, R.A. (Eds), *A Quarter-Century of Normalization and Social Role Valorization: Evolution and Impact*. Ottawa, ON: University of Ottawa Press, pp. 3–13.

Foley, S. (2012). The UN convention on the rights of persons with disabilities: A paradigm shift in the sexual empowerment of adults with Down syndrome, or more sound and fury signifying nothing? *Sexuality and Disability*, 30 (4): 381–393.

Foley, S. (2013). "Reluctant Jailors" speak out: Parents of adults with Down syndrome living in the parental home on how they negotiate the tension between empowering and protecting their intellectually disabled sons and daughters. *British Journal of Learning Disabilities*, 41 (4): 304–311.

Foley, S. (2014a). A modest proposal regarding the power of parents to optimize the sexual well-being of their adult sons and daughters with Down syndrome. *Sexuality and Disability*, 32 (3): 383–396.

Foley, S. (2014b). Their families or the disability services will take care of them: The invisible homeless and how Irish government policy is designed not to help them. *Disability & Society*, 29 (4): 556–557.Forrester-Jones, R. et al. (2006). The social networks of people with learning disabilities living in the community twelve years after resettlement from long-stay hospitals. *Journal of Applied Research in Intellectual Disabilities*, 19: 285–295.

Foucault, M. (1977). *Discipline and Punish*. London: Tavistock.

Foucault, M. (1978). *The History of Sexuality: Volume One*. Harmondsworth: Allen lane.

Foucault, M. (1980). *Power/Knowledge*. Brighton: Harvester.

Foucault, M. (1983). Afterword: The subject and power. In Dreyfus, H. and Rabinow, P. (Eds), *Michel Foucault: Beyond Structuralism and Hermeneutics*. Chicago, IL: Chicago University Press, pp. 208–226.

Fraser, N. (1989). *Unruly Practices: Power, Discourse and Gender in Contemporary Social Theory.* Cambridge: Polity.

Freeman, M. (2011). *Human Rights.* Polity Press: Cambridge.

Fyson, R. and Cromby, J. (2013). Human rights and ID in an era of 'choice'. *Journal of Intellectual Disability Research*, 57 (12): 1164–1172.

Fyson, R. and Kitson, D. (2007). Independence or protection: Does it have to be a choice? Reflections on the abuse people with learning disabilities in Cornwall. *Critical Social Policy*, 27: 426–436.

Fyson, R. and Kitson, D. (2010). Human rights and social wrongs: Issues in safeguarding adults with learning disabilities. *Practice: Social Work in Action*, 22: 309–320.

Gagnon, J.H. and Simon, W. (1973). *Sexual Conduct: The Social Sources of Human Sexuality.* Chicago, IL: Aldine.

Gair, S. (2012). Feeling their stories: Contemplating empathy, insider/outsider positionings and enriching qualitative research. *Qualitative Health Research*, 22 (1): 134–143.

Galvin, R. (2006). A genealogy of the disabled identity in relation to work and sexuality. *Disability & Society*, 21 (5): 499–512.

Gates, B. (2007). The nature of learning disabilities. In Gates, B. (Ed), *Learning Disabilities: Toward Inclusion.* London: Elsevier, pp. 3–20.

Genovesi, V.J. (1997). *In Pursuit of Love: Catholic Morality and Human Sexuality.* Dublin: Gill and Macmillan.

Geuss, R. (1981). *The Idea of a Critical Theory.* Cambridge: Cambridge University Press.

Gilbert, T. (2004). Involving people with learning disabilities in research: Issues and possibilities. *Health and Social Care in the Community*, 12 (4): 298–308.

Goffman, E. (1990). *Stigma: Notes on the Management of Spoiled Identity.* London: Penguin.

Goldman, A. (1977). Plain sex. *Philosophy and Public Affairs*, 6 (3): 267–287.

Goodley, D. (2011). *Disability Studies: An Interdisclipinary Introduction.* London: Sage.

Gray, J. (1991). *Freedom.* London: MacMillan.

Gray, C. (2009). Narratives of disability and the movement from deficiency to difference. *Cultural Sociology*, 3 (2):115–132.

Green, A. (2008). Erotic habitus: Toward a sociology of desire. *Theory and Society*, 37 (6): 597–626.

Greene, M. (2014). On the inside looking in: Methodological insights and challenges in conducting qualitative insider research. *The Qualitative Report*, 19: 1–13.

Greer, G. (2000). *The Whole Woman.* London: Anchor.

Griffin, J. (2008). *On Human Rights.* Oxford: Oxford University Press.

Griffin, T. and Balandin, S. (2004). Ethical research involving people with intellectual disabilities. In Emerson, E., Hatton, C., Thompson, T. and Parmenter, T. (Eds), *The International Handbook of Applied Research in Intellectual Disabilities.* Chichester: Wiley, pp. 61–82.

Griffiths, D. (2007). Sexuality and people who have intellectual disabilities. In Brown, I. and Percy, M. (Eds), *A Comprehensive Guide to Intellectual and Developmental Disabilities.* Baltimore: Paul Brooks, pp. 573–584.

Habermas, J. (1972). *Knowledge and Human Interests.* London: Heinemann Educational.

Hacking, I. (1999). *The Social Construction of What?* Cambridge, MA: Harvard University Press.

Hall, S. (1997). The work of representation. In Hall, S. (Ed), *Representation, Cultural Representations and Signifying Practices*. London: Sage/Open University, pp. 13–74.

Hammersley, M. (1993). *Social Research: Philosophy, Politics and Practice*. London: Sage.

Hammersley, M. (2000). *Taking Sides in Social Research: Essays in Partisanship and Bias*. London: Routledge.

Hammersley, M. (2009). Why critical realism fails to justify critical social research. *Methodological Innovations Online*, 4 (2): 1–11.

Hamilton, C. (2009). Now I'd like to sleep with Rachel: Researching sexuality support in a service agency group home. *Disability & Society*, 24 (3): 303–315.

Harding, S. (2009). Standpoint theories: Productively controversial. *Hypatia*, 24 (4), 192–220.

Harpur, P. (2012). From disability to ability: Changing the phrasing of the debate. *Disability & Society*, 27 (3): 325–337.

Harrington, A. (2005). Introduction: What is social theory. In Harrington, A. (Ed), *Modern Social Theory: An Introduction*. Oxford: Oxford University Press, pp. 2–15.

Hay, C. (1997). Divided by a common language: Political theory and the concept of power. *Politics*, 17 (1): 45–52.

Hayward, C. (2000). *De-Facing Power*. Cambridge: Cambridge University Press.

Heywood, A. (2012). *Political Ideologies: An Introduction*. New York: Palgrave Macmillan.

Hicks, S. (2004). *Explaining Postmodernism: Scepticism and Socialism from Rousseau to Foucault*. Oxford: Oxford University Press.

Hindess, B. (1996). *Discourses of Power: From Hobbes to Foucault*. Oxford: Blackwell.

Hite, S. (2004). *The Hite Report: A Nationwide Study of Female Sexuality*. New York: Seven Stories Press.

Hodapp, R. (2002). Parenting children with mental retardation. In Bornstein, M.H. (Ed), *Handbook of Parenting*, Vol. 1. Manwah, NJ: Lawrence Erlbaum, pp. 355–382.

Hogan, D. (2012). *Family Consequences of Children's Disabilities*. New York: The Russell Sage Foundation.

Holland, J. et al. (1998). *The Male in the Head: Young People, Heterosexuality and Power*. London: Tufnell Press.

Hollomotz, A. (2009). Beyond 'vulnerability': An ecological model approach to conceptualizing risk of sexual violence against people with learning difficulties. *British Journal of Social Work*, 39: 99–112.

Hollomotz, A. (2011). *Learning Difficulties and Sexual Vulnerability: A Social Approach*. London: Jessica Kingsley.

Hollomotz, A. (2014). Are we valuing people's choices now? Restrictions to mundane choices made by adults with learning difficulties. *British Journal of Social Work*, 44: 234–251.

Holub, R.C. (1991). *Jürgen Habermas: Critic in the Public Sphere*. London: Routledge.

Homer, S. (2005). *Jacques Lacan*. London: Routledge.

Hook, D. (2007). *Foucault, Psychology and the Analytics of Power*. Basingstoke: Palgrave Macmillan.

Horowitz, G. (1987). The Foucauldian impasse: No sex, no self, no revolution. *Political Theory*, 15 (1): 61–80.

Hughes, B. (2000). Medicine and the aesthetic invalidation of disabled people. *Disability & Society*, 15 (4): 555–568.

Hume, D. (1972). *A Treatise of Human Nature.* London: Fontana.

Humphrey, J.C. (2000). Researching disability politics, or, some problems with the social model in practice. *Disability & Society*, 15 (1): 63–86.

Inclusion Ireland (2009b). Sexual Relationships Factsheet. Inclusion Ireland Website. Available from www.inclusionireland.ie (Accessed 12 September 2015).

Inglis, T. (1997). *Moral Monopoly: The Rise and Fall of the Catholic Church in Modern Ireland.* Dublin: UCD Press.

Inglis, T. (1998). *Lessons in Irish Sexuality.* Dublin: UCD Press.

Inglis, T. (2005). Sexual desire and pleasure. *Éire-Ireland*, 40 (3 & 4): 9–37.

Irish Statute Book. (2006). www.irishstatutebook.ie (Accessed 14 November 2015).

Jackson, S. and Scott, S. (2010). *Theorizing Sexuality.* Berkshire: Open University Press.

Jeffreys, S. (2008). Disability and the male sex right. *Women's Studies International Forum*, 31 (5): 327–335.

Jenkins, R. (2008). *Social Identity.* London: Routledge.

Jenkins, S. (2013). Methodological challenges of conducting 'insider' reflexive research with the miscarriages of justice community. *International Journal of Social Research Methodology*, 16 (5): 373–387.

Johnson, K. (2009). No longer researching about us without us: A researcher's reflection on rights and inclusive research in Ireland. *British Journal of Learning Disabilities*, 37 (4): 250–256.

Johnson, K., Walmsley, J. and Wolfe, M. (2010). *People with Intellectual Disabilities: Towards a Good Life.* Bristol: The Policy Press.

Jost, J.T. (1995). Negative illusions: Conceptual clarification and psychological evidence concerning false consciousness. *Political Psychology*, 16 (2): 397–424.

Kanuha, V. (2000). Being native versus going native: Conducting social work research as an insider. *Social Work*, 45 (5): 439–447.

Kellner, D. (1990). Critical theory and the crisis of social theory. *Sociological Perspectives*, 33 (1): 11–33.

Kelly, G., Crowley, H. and Hamilton, C. (2009). Rights, sexuality and relationships in Ireland: It'd be nice to be kind of trusted. *British Journal of Learning Disabilities*, (37): 308–315.

Keltner, S. (2011). *Kristeva.* Cambridge: Polity.

Kiernan, C. (1999). Participation in research by people with learning disability: Origins and issues. *British Journal of Learning Disabilities*, 29: 43–48.

Kitchin, R. (2000). The researched opinions on research: Disabled people and disability research. *Disability & Society*, 15 (1): 25–47.

Kittay, E.F. (2001). When caring is just and justice is caring: Justice and mental retardation. *Public Culture*, 13 (3): 557–579.

Kramer, J., Hall, A. and Heller, T. (2013). Reciprocity and social capital in sibling relationships of people with disabilities. *Intellectual and Developmental Disabilities*, 51 (6): 482–495.

Kristeva, J. (1982). *Powers of Horror: An Essay on Abjection.* New York: Columbia University Press.

Kukla, A. (2000). *Social Constructivism and the Philosophy of Science.* London: Routledge.

Kvale, S. (1996). *Interviews: An Introduction to Qualitative Research Interviewing.* Thousand Oaks, CA: Sage.

Lafferty, A., McConkey, R. and Taggart, R. (2013). Beyond friendship: The nature and meaning of close personal relationships as perceived by people with learning disabilities. *Disability and Society*, 28 (8): 1074–1088.

Lang, R. (2001). *The development and critique of the social model of disability, Working Paper 3.* Leonard Cheshire Disability and Inclusive Development Centre, University College London www.ucl.ac.uk/lcccr/ (Accessed September 2015).

Letherby, G. (2003). *Feminist Research in Theory and Practice.* Buckingham: Open University Press.

Letherby, G. and Zdrodowski, D. (1995). "Dear researcher": The use of correspondence as a method with feminist qualitative research. *Gender and Society*, 9 (5): 576–593.

Liddiard, K. (2014). I never felt like she was just doing it for the money: Disabled men's intimate (gendered) realities of purchasing sexual pleasure and intimacy. *Sexualities*, 17 (7): 837–855.

Lloyd, T. and Hastings, R. (2009). Parental locus of control and psychological well-being in mothers of children with intellectual disability. *Journal of Intellectual and Developmental Disability*, 34: 104–115.

Löfgren-Mårtenson, L. (2004). May I? About sexuality and love in the new generation with intellectual disabilities. *Sexuality and Disability*, 22: 197–207.

Lombardo, P. (2010). *Three Generations, No Imbeciles.* New York: Johns Hopkins University Press.

Lukes, S. (2005). *Power: A Radical View.* Basingstoke: Palgrave Macmillan.

Mackie, J.L. (1977). *Ethics: Inventing Right and Wrong.* Harmondsworth: Penguin.

Marx, K. and Engels, F. (1846/1970). *The German Ideology.* New York: International Publishers.

May, T. (1996). *Situating Social Theory.* Buckingham: Open University Press.

May, D. and Simpson, M.K. (2003). The parent trap: Marriage, parenthood and adulthood for people with intellectual disabilities. *Critical Social Policy*, 23 (1): 25–43.

McCarthy, M. (1999). *Sexuality and Women with Learning Disabilities.* London: Jessica Kingsley.

McCarthy, M. and Thompson, D. (1997). A prevalence study of sexual abuse of adults with learning disabilities referred for sex education. *Journal of Applied Research in Intellectual Disability*, 10 (2): 105–124.

McDonnell, P. (2007). *Disability and Society: Ideological and Historical Dimensions.* Dublin: Blackhall Publishing.

McLaughlin, J. (2006). Conceptualising intensive caring activities: The changing lives of families with young disabled children. *Sociological Research Online*, 11 (1). www.socresonline.org.uk/11/1/mclaughlin.html.

McRuer, R. and Wilkerson, A. (2003). Cripping the (queer) nation. *GLQ: A Journal of Lesbian and Gay Studies*, 9 (1–2): 1–23.

Mendus, S. (2000). *Feminism and Emotion: Readings in Moral and Political Philosophy.* London: Macmillan Press Ltd.

Mercer, G. (2002). Emancipatory disability research. In Barnes, C., Oliver, M. and Barton, L. (Eds), *Disability Studies Today.* Cambridge: Polity, pp. 228–249.

Merriam, S. et al. (2001). Power and positionality: Negotiating insider/outsider status within and across cultures. *International Journal of Lifelong Education*, 20 (5): 405–416.

Mill, A. et al. (2009). Negotiating autonomy within the family: Experiences of young adults with intellectual disabilities. *British Journal of Learning Disabilities*, 38: 194–200.

Millar, G. (2000). *The Mating Mind*. London: Heinmann.

Millar, P. and Rose, N. (2008). *Governing the Present*. London: Polity Press.

Mills, C.W. (1956). *The Power Elite*. New York: Oxford University Press.

Mills, S. (2008). *Michel Foucault*. London: Routledge.

Monk, R. (1990). *Ludwig Wittgenstein: The Duty of Genius*. London: Free Press.

Morgan, D.L. and Spanish, M.T. (1984). Focus groups: A new tool for qualitative research. *Qualitative Sociology*, 7 (3): 253–270.

Morris, J. (1997). Care or empowerment: A disability rights perspective. *Social Policy & Administration*, 31 (1): 54–60.

Morris, J. (2001). Impairment and disability: Constructing an ethics of care that promotes human rights. *Hypatia*, 16 (4): 1–16.

Murphy, G.H. (2003). Capacity to consent to sexual relationships in adults with learning disabilities. *Journal of Family Planning and Reproductive Health Care*, (29): 148–149.

Murphy, G.H. and O'Callaghan, A. (2004). Capacity of adults with intellectual disabilities to consent to sexual relationships. *Psychological Medicine*, 34: 1347–1357.

Namhi. (2003). *Who Decides and How? People with Intellectual Disabilities—Legal Capacity and Decision-Making*. Dublin: Inclusion Ireland.

National Disability Authority. (2009). *Submission on Capacity and Sexual Relations in the Context of the Mental Capacity Scheme of Bill-April 2009*. Dublin: NDA.

Newton, R. (2004). *The Down Syndrome Handbook*. London: Random House.

Nussbaum, M. (1998). Whether from reason or prejudice: Taking money for bodily services. *Journal of Legal Studies*, 27 (2): 693–724.

Nussbaum, M. (2000). *Women and Human Development: The Capabilities Approach*. Cambridge: Cambridge University Press.

O'Connell-Davidson, J. (2002). The rights and wrongs of prostitution. *Hypatia*, 17 (2): 84–98.

O'Farrell, C. (2005). *Michel Foucault*. London: Sage.

O'Leary, J. (2012). Irish Republic votes in favour of boosting child rights. BBC News Northern Ireland. www.bbc.co.uk/news/uk-northern-ireland-20287674 (Accessed 15 June 2015).

Oliver, M. (1992). Changing the social relations of research production? *Disability & Society*, 7 (2): 101–114.

Oliver, M. (1997). Emancipatory disability research: Realistic goal or impossible dream. In Barnes, C. and Mercer, G. (Eds), *Doing Disability Research*. Leeds: The Disability Press, pp. 15–31.

Oliver, M. (1999). Capitalism, disability and ideology: A materialist critique of the normalization principle. In Flynn, R. and Lemay, R. (Eds), *A Quarter-Century of Normalization and Social Role Valorization: Evolution and Impact*. Ottawa, ON: University of Ottawa Press, pp. 163–173.

Oliver, M. (2009). *Understanding Disability: From Theory to Practice*. Basingstoke: Palgrave Macmillan.

Oliver, M. and Barnes, C. (1998). *Disabled People and Social Policy: From Exclusion to Inclusion*. Harlow: Longman.

174   *References*

Oliver, M. and Barnes, C. (2012). *The New Politics of Disablement*. Basingstoke: Palgrave Macmillan.

O'Neill, A. (1984). Paternalism and partial autonomy. *Journal of Medical Ethics*, 10: 173–178.

Pawson, R. (2000). Methodology. In Taylor, S. (Ed), *Sociology: Issues and Debates*. Basingstoke: Palgrave, pp. 19–49.

Philp, M. (1983). Foucault on power: A problem in radical translation? *Political Theory*, 11 (1): 29–52.

Pinker, S. (2003). *The Blank Slate: The Modern Denial of Human Nature*. New York: Viking.

Poggi, G. (2001). *Forms of Power*. Cambridge: Polity.

Porter, J. and Lacey, P. (2003). *Researching Learning Difficulties*. London: Sage.

Potts, T. and Price, J. (1995). Out of the blood and spirit of our lives: The place of the body in academic feminism. In Morley, L. and Walsh, V. (Eds), *Feminist Academics: Creative Agents for Change*. London: Taylor & Francis.

Prado, C.G. (2005). *Searle and Foucault on Truth*. Cambridge: Cambridge University Press.

Pratt, V. (1993). *The Philosophy of the Social Sciences*. London: Routledge.

Priestley, M. (2003). *Disability: A Life Course Approach*. London: Polity Press.

Pueschel, S.M. (2006). *Adults with Down Syndrome*. Baltimore, MD: Brookes Publishing.

Quinn, G. (2009). Bringing the UN Convention on rights for persons with disabilities to life in Ireland. *British Journal of Learning Disabilities*, 37: 245–249.

Quinn, G. (2010). *Personhood & Legal Capacity: Perspectives on the Paradigm Shift of Article 12 CRPD*. Dublin: Inclusion Ireland Website. Available from www.inclusionireland.ie/capacity (Accessed 12 September 2015).

Race, D., Boxall, K. and Carson, I. (2005). Towards a dialogue for practice: Reconciling social role valorization and the social model of disability. *Disability & Society*, 20 (5): 507–521.

Rainbolt, G. (2006). *The Concept of Rights*. Dordrecht: Springer.

Ramsay, K. (1996). Emotional labour and qualitative research: How I learned not to laugh or cry in the field. In Lyon, E.S. and Busfield, J. (Eds), *Methodological Imaginations*. Basingstoke: Macmillan, pp. 131–146.

Read, J. (2001). *Disability, the Family and Society: Listening to Mothers*. Milton Keynes: Open University Press.

Redley, M. and Weinberg, D. (2007). Learning disability and the limits of liberal citizenship: interactional impediments to political empowerment. *Sociology of Health & Illness*, 29: 767–786.

Reinharz, S. (1997). Who am I? The need for a variety of selves in the field. In Hertz, R. (Ed), *Reflexivity and Voice*. London: Sage Publications, pp. 3–20.

Richards, D. et al. (2012). The right to sexuality and relationships. In Griffith, D., Owen, F. and Watson, S. (Eds), *The Human Rights Agenda for Persons with Intellectual Disabilities*. New York: NADD Press, pp. 103–128.

Robson, C. (2006). *Real World Research*. London: Blackwell Publishing.

Rodgers, J. (1999). Trying to get it right: Undertaking research involving people with learning difficulties. *Disability & Society*, 14 (4): 421–433.

Rogers, C. (2003). The mother/researcher in blurred boundaries of a reflexive research process. *Auto/Biography* XI (1 & 2): 47–54.

Rogers, C. (2009). (S)excerpts from a life told: Sex, gender and learning disability. *Sexualities*, 12 (3): 270–288.

Rogers, C. (2011). Mothering and intellectual disability: Partnership rhetoric? *British Journal of Sociology of Education*, 32 (4): 563–581.

Rogers, C. (2013). Mothering for life? Fractured maternal narratives, care and intellectual disability. In Bouvard, M. (Ed), *Mothers of Adult Children*. New York: Lexington Press, pp. 85–96.

Rose, J. (1986). *Sexuality in the Field of Vision*. London: Verso.

Rose, N. (1989). *Governing the Soul: The Shaping of the Private Self*. London: Routledge.

Rose, N. (1998). *Inventing Our Selves: Psychology, Power and Personhood*. Cambridge: Cambridge University Press.

Rothman, J. (2010). The challenge of disability and access: Reconceptualizing the role of the medical model. *Journal of Social Work in Disability & Rehabilitation*, 9 (2):194–222.

Ruddick, S. (1989). *Maternal Thinking: Towards a Politics of Peace*. New York: Ballantine.

Rubin, G. (1984). Thinking sex. In Vance, S. (Ed), *Pleasure and Danger. Exploring Female Sexuality*. London: Pandora, pp. 267–319.

Russell, B. (1980). *The Problems of Philosophy*. Oxford: Oxford University Press.

Russell, B. (1929). *Marriage and Morals*. London: George Allen & Unwin.

Ryan, S. and Runswick-Cole, K. (2008). Repositioning mothers: Mothers, disabled children and disability studies. *Disability & Society*, 23 (3): 199–210.

Ryan, S. and Runswick-Cole, K. (2009). From advocate to activist? Mapping the experiences of mothers of children on the autism spectrum. *Journal of Applied Research in Intellectual Disabilities*, 22 (1): 43–53.

Ryan, G.W. and Russell Bernard, H. (2003). Techniques to identify themes. *Field Methods*, 15 (1): 85–109.

Ryan, J. and Thomas, F. (1989). *The Politics of Mental Handicap*. Harmondsworth: Penguin.

Saaltink, R., MacKinnon, G., Owen, F. and Tardif-Williams, C. (2012). Protection, participation and protection through participation: Young people with intellectual disabilities and decision making in the family context. *Journal of Intellectual Disability Research*, 56 (11): 1076–1086.

Sanders, T. (2005). *Sex Work: A Risky Business*. London: Willan Publishing.

Sanders, T. (2007). The politics of sexual citizenship: Commercial sex and disability. *Disability & Society*, 22 (5): 439–455.

Sanders, T. and Campbell, R. (2007). Designing out vulnerability, building in respect: Violence, safety and sex work policy. *British Journal of Sociology*, 58 (1): 1–19.

Sarup, M. (2002). *Identity, Culture and the Postmodern World*. Edinburgh: Edinburgh University Press.

Scheerenburger, R.C. (1983). *A History of Mental Retardation*. Baltimore, MD: Paul H. Brookes Publishing.

Schroeder, M. (2010). *Noncognitivism in Ethics*. London: Routledge.

Searle, J. (1996). *The Construction of Social Reality*. London: Penguin.

Selikowitz, M. (2008). *Down Syndrome*. Oxford: Oxford University Press.

Serrant-Green, L. (2002). Black on black: Methodological issues for black researchers working in minority ethnic communities. *Nurse Researcher*, 9 (4): 30–44.

Shakespeare, T. (2000). Disabled sexuality: Toward rights and recognition. *Sexuality and Disability*, 18 (3): 159–166.

Shakespeare, T. (2004). Social models of disability and other life strategies. *Scandinavian Journal of Disability Research*, 6 (1): 8–21.

Shakespeare, T., Gillespie-Sells, K. and Davies, D. (1996). *The Sexual Politics of Disability: Untold Desires*. London: Cassell.

Shakespeare, T. and Watson, N. (2001). The social model of disability: An outdated ideology? *Research in Social Science and Disability*, 2 (2): 9–28.

Shildrick, M. (2003). *Embodying the Monster: Encounters with the Vulnerable Self*. London: Sage Publications.

Shildrick, M. (2007a). Contested pleasures: The socio-political economy of disability and sexuality. *Sexuality Research & Social Policy*, 4 (1): 53–65.

Shildrick, M. (2007b). Dangerous discourses: Anxiety, desire, and disability. *Studies in Gender and Sexuality*, 8 (3): 221–244.

Shildrick, M. (2009). *Dangerous Discourses of Disability, Subjectivity and Sexuality*. Basingstoke: Palgrave Macmillan.

Siebers, T. (2008). *Disability Theory*. Ann Arbor: University of Michigan Press.

Singer, P. (2005). *Practical Ethics*. Cambridge: Cambridge University Press.

Smith, P.B. (2006). *Understanding Social Psychology across Cultures: Living and Working in a Changing World*. London: Sage.

Sneddon, A. (2013). *Autonomy*. London: Bloomsbury.

Soble, A. (2013). The analytical categories of the philosophy of sex. In Power, N., Halwani, R. and Soble, A. (Eds), *The Philosophy of Sex: Contemporary Readings* (6th ed.). New York: Rowman & Littlefield Publishers, pp. 1–24.

Spradley, J.P. (1979). *The Ethnographic Interview*. New York: Holt, Rinehart and Winston.

Stalker, K. (1998). Some ethical and methodological issues in research with people with learning difficulties. *Disability and Society*, 13: 5–19.

Stalker, K. (2012). Theorizing the position of people with learning difficulties within disability studies: Progress and pitfalls. In Watson, N., Roulstone, A. and Thomas, C. (Eds), *The Routledge Handbook of Disability Studies*. London: Routledge, pp. 122–135.

Stone, E. and Priestley, M. (1996). Parasites, pawns and partners: Disability research and the role of non-disabled researchers. *British Journal of Sociology*, 47 (4): 699–716.

Stoneman, Z. (2005). Siblings of children with disabilities: Research themes. *Mental Retardation*, 43 (5), 339–350.

Taylor, C. (2011). Biopower. In Taylor, D. (Ed), *Michel Foucault: Key Concepts*. London: Acumen.

Thomas, C. (2007). *Sociologies of Disability and Illness: Contested Ideas in Disability Studies and Medical Sociology*. Basingstoke: Palgrave Macmillan.

Tremain, S. (2002). On the subject of impairment. In Corker, M. and Shakespeare, T. (Eds), *Disability/Postmodernity: Embodying Disability Theory*. London: Continuum, pp. 32–47.

Tremain, S. (2005). *Foucault and the Government of Disability*. Ann Arbor: University of Michigan Press.

Valenti-Hein, D. and Choinski, C. (2007). Relationships and sexuality in adolescence and young adulthood. In Carr, A., O'Reilly, G., Noonan Walsh, P. and McEvoy, J. (Eds), *The Handbook of Intellectual Disability and Clinical Psychology Practice*. London: Routledge, pp. 729–756.

Vehmas, S. and Makela, P. (2008). A realist account of the ontology of impairment. *Journal of Medical Ethics*, 43: 93–95.

Walmsley, J. (1997). Including people with learning difficulties: Theory and practice. In Barton, L. and Oliver, M. (Eds), *Disability Studies: Past, Present and Future.* Leeds: The Disability Press, pp. 62–77.

Walmsley, J. (2001). Normalisation, emancipatory research and inclusive research in learning disability. *Disability and Society*, 16 (2): 187–205.

Walmsley, J. (2005). Research and emancipation: Prospects and problems. In Grant, G., Goward, P., Richardson, M. and Ramcharan, P. (Eds), *Learning Disability: A Life Cycle Approach to Valuing People.* New York: Open University Press, pp. 724–744.

Walmsley, J. and Johnson, K. (2003). *Inclusive Research with People with Learning Disabilities.* London: Jessica Kingsley Publishers.

Wasserman, D. (2001). Philosophical issues in the definition and social response to disability. In Albrecht, G.L., Seelman, K.D. and Michael Bury, B. (Eds), *Handbook of Disability Studies.* London: Sage, pp. 219–251.

Watson, N. (2012). Researching disablement. In Watson, N., Roulstone, A. and Thomas, C. (Eds), *The Routledge Handbook of Disability Studies.* London: Routledge, pp. 93–106.

Weeks, J. (1985). *Sexuality and Its Discontents: Meaning, Myths & Modern Sexualities.* London: Routledge.

Weitzer, R. (2009). Sociology of sex work. *Annual Review of Sociology*, 35: 213–234.

Wetherell, M. (2001). Introduction. In Wetherell, M., Taylor, S. and Yates, S.J. (Eds), *Discourse Theory and Practice: A Reader.* London: Sage Publications, pp. 1–13.

Wetherell, M. and Potter, J. (1988). Discourse analysis and the identification of interpretive repertoires. In Antaki, C. (Ed), *Analysing Everyday Explanation: A Casebook of Methods.* Newbury Park, CA: Sage, pp. 168–183.

Williams, G. (2001). Theorizing disability. In Albrecht, G.L., Seelman, K.D. and Michael Bury, B. (Eds), *Handbook of Disability Studies.* London: Sage, pp. 123–144.

Willig, C. (2008). *Introducing Qualitative Research in Psychology.* Berkshire: Open University Press.

Wittgenstein, L. (1960). *Tractatus Logico-Philosophicus.* London: Routledge & Kegan Paul.

Wolf, N. (1991). *The Beauty Myth: How Images of Beauty are Used against Women.* London: Vintage.

Wolfensberger, W. (2002). Social role valorization and, or versus empowerment. *Mental Retardation*, 40: 252–258.

Woollett, A. and Nicolson, P. (1998). The social construction of motherhood and fatherhood. In Niven, C.A. and Walker, A. (Eds), *Current Issues in Infancy and Parenthood.* Oxford: Butterworth and Heinemann, pp. 1–13.

Wright, D. (2011). *Downs: The History of a Disability.* Oxford: Oxford University Press.

Yates, S.J. (2004). *Doing Social Science Research.* London: Sage.

Young, D. and Quibell, R. (2000). Why rights are never enough: Rights, intellectual disability and understanding. *Disability & Society*, 15 (5): 747–764.

Index

abject: in action 119–20; concept of 126, 138; having quality of the opposing object 127
abjection 60, 64–65, 69, 126–8
ableism 57
adaptive behaviour 2
adult Down syndrome children 1, 2; ability to have sex with non-intellectually disabled adults 29, 38, 99; adapting to a normalising society 122–5; being malleable 4; celibacy due to their parents 84–98; cognitive limitations 67; to determine their sexuality 106–7; as contented prisoners 128, 153; desire to be normal 119–20; desire to control how they spend their leisure time 114–15; desire to have a boyfriend/girlfriend 6–7, 98–102, 117–18, 157, 159–60; desire to move out of the parental home 113–14; forming friendships with non-disabled people 72–74; having criteria defining sexy/attractiveness 119–20, 143; having distinct facial appearance 4, 100, 119–20, 132; having legal rights for sexual expression 36–38, 110–13, 143–4; inability to stay the night with boyfriend/girlfriend 116–17, 161; interviewing 13–14; not finding other Down syndrome children sexually attractive 85–91, 120, 126, 160; paternalistic regime of care 6, 9, 25–26; resisting 102, 121–2, 125–6, 161; power dynamics with parents 125–6, 128–30, 147; as sexual beings as viewed by parents 98–102; sexual desire of 100–4, 143, 149; viewed as abnormal 66, 72, 74–75; wanting to live like non-intellectually disabled

peers 122; what one does in boyfriend/girlfriend relationship 118–19
age of consent 45, 107
Aguilar, F. 32
Allen, L. 108
Alvesson, M. 69
American Association of Intellectual and Developmental Disabilities 2, 3
Aristotle 44
Asselin, M. E. 32
autism 97
autonomous individual 37
autonomy: desire for more by adult Down syndrome children 114–15; of intellectually disabled adults 38–41, 56, 83–95
autonomy/paternalism debate 1, 2, 4, 28, 36–66, 83, 92, 105

balance between empowering and protecting 72
Barnes, C. 18–19, 52
Bauman, Z. 62
'beauty myth,' 126
Benatar, D. 104
biology's role in cognitive limitations 82
biopower 43, 77
Blacher, J. 70
Blaxter, L. 15–16
bowling as a leisure activity 114
boy committing sexual offence but not the girl when having underage sex 108
boyfriends: adult Down syndrome finding 98–102; behaviours in a boyfriend/girlfriend relationship 118–19; desire for adults with Down syndrome to have 6–7, 98–102, 117–18, 157; /girlfriend relationships instead of sexual expression 103–13;